Virtually all legislative theory is built on the assumption that politicians are first and foremost reelection seekers, and because so few countries have ever limited legislative reelection, this assumption has rarely been questioned. As a result, political science has been ill-equipped to offer insights about legislators in the absence of reelection. *Term Limits and Legislative Representation* aims to provide such insights.

Outside of the United States, four nations limit legislative terms constitutionally: Costa Rica, Mexico, Ecuador, and the Philippines. In the latter two countries, the term limits have not been in place long enough to provide data for analysis. This study therefore tests the central arguments made by both supporters and opponents of such reform by primarily examining the experience of Costa Rica, the only long-term democracy to impose term limits on legislators, and by providing extensive comparisons with legislatures in Venezuela and the United States.

Professor Carey challenges claims made about the effects of term limits on political careers, pork-barrel politics, and the effectiveness of political parties in passing their programs. The evidence calls into question many of the arguments made by term limit supporters in the United States and offers general arguments about how severing the electoral connection affects political behavior.

Virtually all legislative theory is built on the assumption that politicians are first and foremost reelection seekers, and because so few countries have ever limited legislative reelection, this assumption has rarely been questioned. As a result, political science has been ill-equipped to offer insights about legislators in the absence of reelection. *Term Limits and Legislative Representation* provides such insights.

Outside of the United States, four nations limit legislative terms constitutionally: Costa Rica, Mexico, Ecuador, and the Philippines. In the latter two countries, the term limits have not been in place long enough to provide data for analysis. This study therefore tests the central arguments made by both supporters and opponents of such reform by primarily examining the experience of Costa Rica, the only long-term democracy to impose term limits on legislators, and by providing extensive comparisons with legislatures in Venezuela and the United States.

Professor Carey challenges claims made about the effects of term limits on political careers, pork-barrel politics, and the effectiveness of political parties in passing their programs. The evidence calls into question many of the arguments made by term limit supporters in the United States and offers general arguments about how severing the electoral connection affects political behavior.

Term limits and legislative representation

Term limits and legislative representation

JOHN M. CAREY
University of Rochester

CAMBRIDGE
UNIVERSITY PRESS

Published by the Press Syndicate of the University of Cambridge
The Pitt Building, Trumpington Street, Cambridge CB2 1RP
40 West 20th Street, New York, NY 10011–4211, USA
10 Stamford Road, Oakleigh, Melbourne 3166, Australia

First published 1996

Printed in the United States of America

Library of Congress Cataloging-in-Publication Data
Carey, John M.
Term limits and legislative representation / John M. Carey.
p.   cm.
Includes bibliographical references and index.
ISBN 0–521–55233–8 (hardback)
1. United States. Congress – Term of office. 2. Costa Rica.
Asamblea Legislativa – Term of office. 3. Venezuela. Congreso de la
República – Term of office. 4. Representative government and
representation.   I. Title.
JK1130.C37   1996
328.73′073 – dc20   95–44289
                                                              CIP

A catalog record for this book is available from the British Library.

ISBN 0-521-55233-8 Hardback

TO LISA

Contents

List of tables and figures   *page* ix
Preface   xi

Part I   Term limits and comparative politics

1   The electoral disconnection?   3
2   Institutions and electoral reform: Comparing the cases   26

Part II   The Latin American cases

3   Term limits and political careers   71
4   Term limits and particularism   103
5   Term limits and legislative party cohesiveness   136

Part III   Term limits and the United States

6   The last-term problem   159
7   Applying lessons about term limits   183

References   201
Index   213

Tables and figures

Tables

1.1	Term limits on state legislators	*page*	10
1.2	Term limits on U.S. legislators		12
2.1	Seats won in Costa Rican Legislative Assembly		30
2.2	Vote to eliminate term limits, Costa Rican Legislative Assembly, 1961		47
2.3	Seats won, Venezuelan Chamber of Deputies		57
2.4	Seats won, Venezuelan Senate		57
3.1	Terms served in Venezuelan Congress		73
3.2	Terms served in Costa Rican Legislative Assembly		77
3.3	Question: "Do you consider yourself a professional politician?"		83
3.4	Prior political experience of Costa Rican deputies		83
3.5	Prior political experience of Costa Rican deputies (missing data excluded)		84
3.6	Appointed posts, Costa Rican deputies		96
3.7	Appointments during term immediately following Assembly service		100
4.1	Partisan distribution of small pork, Costa Rica		108
4.2	Distribution of PE funds among majority party deputies		109
4.3	Dependence of Costa Rican counties on individual deputies		111
4.4	Impact of PEs on party vote shares in counties		123
4.5	Impact of PEs on electoral gains between elections		123
4.6	Impact of electoral support on PEs received by counties		125
4.7	Effects of deputies' performance in their bailiwicks on appointments		130
5.1	Partisan breakdown of vote on 1984 currency bill		144
5.2	Partisan breakdown of vote on 1988 financial system modernization bill		144

5.3   Partisan breakdown of vote on 1988 renter's bill   145
5.4   Question: "Do you ever vote against your party in the
      Assembly?"   150
5.5   Question: "Would you vote against the party if its
      position conflicted with the communities you
      represent?"   151
5.6   Question: "If you were to vote against the Assembly
      party, what kind of sanctions would you expect?"   152
6.1   Effect of aspirant status on variance between
      NOMINATE scores   169
6.2   Effect of ideological extremism on variance between
      NOMINATE scores   170
6.3   Effect of extremism and aspirant status on shifts toward
      statewide delegations   172
6.4   Movement toward state party delegation NOMINATE
      scores by aspirants   174

Figures

3.1   Professionalization of Venezuelan Congress, by party   74
3.2   Successive reelection to Venezuelan Congress   75
3.3   Professionalization of 1988 Venezuelan Congress   76
3.4   Experience of each cohort to Costa Rican Assembly   78
3.5   Patterns of reelection to Costa Rican Legislative
      Assembly   78
3.6   Reelection rates, Costa Rican Congress, 1920–1944   80
3.7   Estimated appointed posts, former Costa Rican deputies   98
3.8   Estimated appointments, former deputies, according to
      party's fortunes in presidential election   100

Preface

Legislative term limits have been a hot political issue in the early 1990s. This makes them attractive to study, but presents a liability as well. Any account of the status of term limits is likely to be outdated quickly. On May 22, 1995, while this book was being copyedited, the U.S. Supreme Court handed down a decision in the case of *U.S. Term Limits, Inc. v. Thornton* that struck down all term limits imposed by states on their representatives to the U.S. Congress – which is to say that all the limits represented in Table 1.2 of this book have been declared unconstitutional. The Court's decision was based primarily on its understanding of the Qualifications Clauses in the U.S. Constitution (Article I, Sections 2 and 3), and has no bearing on term limits that the states have imposed on their own legislators. Thus, all the limits represented in Table 1.1 stand, and more can be expected in the years ahead.

At any rate, this book is not about accounting for the status of term limits, and its goals are not affected by the Court's decision, with which I happen to agree. The primary purpose of the book is to contribute to our general understanding of legislatures. It is almost axiomatic among political scientists to explain legislative behavior as motivated by the desire for reelection. By analyzing legislative behavior and organization where reelection is prohibited, I hope to shed light on how heavily legislative theory ought to depend on the reelection assumption and to suggest some alternative explanations for legislative behavior that rely on other motivations.

The second purpose of the book is to contribute to the ongoing debate in the United States over legislative term limits as an electoral reform. The *U.S. Term Limits, Inc. v. Thornton* decision was the first major setback reformers have experienced after five years of unmitigated success, and it was certainly not the last round to be fired in the term limits battle. The decision makes clear that the only possible route to imposing term limits on Congress is through a constitutional amendment. In response, reform proponents, including U.S. Term Limits, Inc., and Ross Perot's United We

Stand America, vowed to make support for such an amendment a litmus test among congressional candidates in 1996 and beyond. In addition to substantial money, organization, and popular support, moreover, term limits have a unique advantage on the difficult road to constitutional amendment approval – a receptive constituency in the state legislatures. If Congress ratifies a term limits amendment, legislators in at least 21 states will themselves already be subject to limits as they consider ratifying it. These state legislators should welcome the opportunity to limit congressional terms as well, if not out of commitment to the principle, then perhaps because of the offices that congressional term limits would open up higher on the political food chain. In short, the term limits debate promises to continue apace in the United States over the next few years, and this book directly addresses a number of the claims made by both proponents and opponents of reform. On balance, I find that the arguments made by opponents are borne out better by the evidence I consider. I hope that this evidence will be of some interest to those engaged in what has been a highly speculative debate up to now.

Third, the book argues that both policymakers and political scientists can benefit from dropping the conceptual distinction between U.S. politics and politics "everywhere else." The term limits debate in the United States has been stuck at the level of conjecture because no one has taken seriously the possibility that we might learn something about our own politics from countries that actually have experience with limits. Political science, which has traditionally separated the study of comparative politics from the study of U.S. politics, has contributed to the idea that these are unrelated endeavors. Cross-national comparisons frequently offer information that is unavailable when the scope of inquiry is limited to a single country, and this information should not be ignored, either in policy making or in academic analysis.

This book began as my doctoral dissertation in political science at the University of California, San Diego. I therefore owe the people of California a tremendous debt of gratitude for being collectively generous enough to fund my graduate study with their tax dollars, and collectively angry enough at the politicians who appropriated those dollars to impose term limits on them in 1990, just as I was beginning to cast about for a dissertation topic.

UCSD, meanwhile, proved to be a terrific place to combine the study of comparative and U.S. politics. Arend Lijphart was the ideal adviser and academic mentor. Gary Cox's patience in reading early drafts of this work and his ability to sort out the occasional worthwhile idea from all others was truly remarkable. Paul Drake and Michael Monteón provided prompt and insightful comments on early drafts as well. As both teacher and colleague,

Matthew Shugart has been involved in just about every idea I have written down in the past five years, on term limits or anything else. This is a testament to his stamina and to my high regard for his advice. Despite the stellar counsel I received from all of these sources, I undoubtedly have managed to include some errors and inconsistencies in this book. They are entirely my own doing, of course.

Funding for field research in Costa Rica was provided by the Committee on Iberian and Latin American Studies at UCSD and by a research assistantship for Mathew McCubbins. When I was away from San Diego, Steven Swindle helped me out with research and bureaucratic legwork more times than I care to remember, although I am confident he will see to it that I do not forget.

In Costa Rica, the staff at the Archive of the Legislative Assembly, particularly Leo Nuñez Arias, was tremendously accommodating. The willingness of almost all the deputies of the 93rd Assembly to be interviewed for this project was both remarkable and indispensable. Special thanks are also due to Rafael Villegas Antillón, President of the Supreme Tribunal of Elections, whose knowledge of Costa Rican politics is rivaled only by his hospitality.

In Kasilof, Alaska, Jeff and Geri Ransom provided food, shelter, employment, and a welcome sense of perspective during summers away from academia. They also tolerated my writing parts of this book when I should have been out mending nets. And Cook Inlet Processing, Inc., frequently provided the electricity to power my notebook computer, although they did not know it at the time.

At Cambridge University Press, Alex Holzman provided consistently sound editorial guidance. CUP's anonymous reviewers also offered a number of excellent suggestions that improved the original manuscript.

Several factors were essential in motivating me to finish the book. One was the intellectual environment in the Political Science Department at the University of Rochester, which is a constant source of energy and stimulation. Another was my friend Holly Johnson's sustained astonishment that anyone could remain interested in legislative term limits long enough to write a whole book about them. Thanks, Holly. There was also the assistance that my son, Joe, perpetually offered at the keyboard, which encouraged me to hurry up and push the print button before all my files were inadvertently erased. I am confident that I can expect the same sort of support from my younger son, Sam, on future projects.

The greatest thanks go to my wife, Lisa, whose contributions I cannot possibly describe adequately.

Part I

Term limits and comparative politics

1

The electoral disconnection?

How does eliminating the prospect of reelection affect legislative representation? The question is relevant for two reasons – one topical, the other theoretical. First, it is directly applicable to the current, heated debate in the United States over whether the tenure of legislators at both the state and national level should be constitutionally limited. Reformers have scored sweeping victories, and so far endured remarkably few setbacks, among voters and in the courts, in their efforts to pass legislative term limits. Academics have been significantly less enthusiastic than voters about term limits, but there has been little rigorous analysis of their impact. The second reason for this study's relevance is precisely the lack of both empirical evidence and theoretical firepower in the term limits debate. The problem is that theories of legislative behavior are firmly rooted in the assumption that legislators' primary motivation is reelection. As a result, political science is currently ill-equipped to offer insights about legislators for whom the electoral connection has been severed. This study aims to provide such insights.

Until recently, political scientists have rarely questioned the assumption that reelection incentives drive legislative behavior, largely because tenure is limited in so few legislatures worldwide. In the United States, political scientists and pundits have scrambled since 1990 to predict the impact of the term limit measures adopted in 22 states, directed at both state legislatures and Congress. But none of these limits has taken effect yet.[1] So analyses limited to the U.S. case either have remained purely speculative or have attempted to manipulate data from legislatures without limits in order to yield conclusions about how legislatures would operate under limits.

These efforts have ignored the potential for comparative analysis to shed light on term limits. Outside the United States, four nations limit legislative terms constitutionally: Costa Rica, Mexico, Ecuador, and the Philippines.

---

[1] In the case of members of the U.S. Congress, it remains to be seen whether limits adopted in state-level initiative processes are constitutional. This issue will be decided by June 1995 by the Supreme Court, through a review of the measure adopted in Arkansas.

In the last case, the limits were adopted only in 1986 and first kick in in 1995. So Filipino term limits, like their state-level U.S. counterparts, have not yet been in place long enough to provide data for analysis. Ecuadorian term limits have been in place a little longer, since 1978. The Costa Rican and Mexican constitutions, on the other hand, have imposed legislative term limits for decades. Like Latin American assemblies in general, however, the Costa Rican, Mexican, and Ecuadorian legislatures have attracted relatively little academic attention; and those who have studied them have more often than not failed even to note the unusual prohibitions on reelection. This study focuses largely on the Costa Rican experience with term limits, employing comparative analysis to determine the impact of term limits on legislative representation in that country, and to draw more general conclusions about the impact of severing the electoral connection.

The rest of this chapter proceeds as follows. The first section derives some specific questions about the effects of term limits from the broader literature on electoral incentives, then briefly surveys the current literature on term limits in the United States, arguing the need for a comparative approach. The next section introduces the two cases that are the primary foci of comparative analysis for much of the book – Costa Rica and Venezuela – briefly explaining the methodological rationale, and challenge, in studying these countries. The last section presents an outline of the entire volume, explaining the purpose of each chapter and summarizing the conclusions.

The electoral connection and the current term limits literature

Careers, constituents, and parties

To make the analysis tractable, I focus on three specific phenomena affected by legislative term limits: political careers, legislator-constituent relationships, and party cohesiveness in the legislature. All three themes are deeply embedded in traditional theories that explain legislative behavior as driven by electoral incentives. First, where reelection is not limited, the legislative career is assumed to be the prototypical modern politician's goal. The second and third phenomena embody a trade-off between direct responsiveness by legislators to voters and responsiveness to party leaders, whose directives may at times conflict with immediate voter interests. Electoral incentive theories on the nature of this trade-off uniformly assume that legislative behavior is driven by politicians' personal career interests (Cain, Ferejohn, and Fiorina 1987; Epstein 1967; Mayhew 1974; Rae 1971). The evidence presented throughout this work supports this consensus, but illustrates that term limits can have enormous impact on how this personal ambition manifests itself in legislative behavior.

Electoral incentive theories recognize that there is frequently a tension between the collective electoral interests of a given political party and the individual electoral interests of the politicians who run for office under that party label (Ames 1987; Ames 1992; Cox 1987; Fiorina 1977; Kiewiet and McCubbins 1991; McCubbins and Rosenbluth 1995). Sometimes individual politicians prefer to take positions or actions other than those that would most benefit their party collectively. Furthermore, it is widely acknowledged that specific electoral rules shape the nature of the trade-off between personal and partisan reputations. Political science has established some basic tenets on the extent to which individual politicians can benefit by developing personal reputations distinct from those of their party – for example, that, in open-list systems, personal reputation is more valuable to legislative candidates than in closed-list systems (Ames 1992; Geddes and Ribeiro Neto 1992; Sartori 1976; Taagepera and Shugart 1989; Uslaner 1985). More recently, Carey and Shugart (in press) provide a general model to account for the relative value of personal versus partisan reputation under the broad range of electoral rules according to which legislators around the world are elected.

In all cases, conclusions about political careerism, legislative individualism, and party cohesion are based on two assumptions: first, that reelection is possible, and second, that legislators' primary motivation is to ensure their own reelection. These are necessary components of any theory of legislative behavior based on electoral incentives. It follows, then, that, where reelection is impossible, electoral incentive theories cannot be useful in explaining legislative behavior.[2]

This is the challenge posed to political science by the prospect of term limits. If the electoral connection is severed, then the framework on which traditional legislative theory rests must be reassessed. Moreover, the empirical challenge in studying term limits could be even more daunting than the theoretical challenge. If all legislators have been elected in a system that allows reelection, and the desire for reelection is the primary motivation for their behavior, then where does one look for evidence on how legislators will behave once reelection is prohibited?

The current literature

Although political scientists have shown real inventiveness in evading this obstacle to empirical analysis, most have been forced to address issues only

---

[2] It is not the case that legislative term limits necessarily imply that all legislative reelection is impossible. Term limits can restrict reelection in various ways, and these variations are discussed later. The most extreme form of term limits – one term and no reelection ever – would render irrelevant any electoral motivation for legislators. Less extreme limitations, in turn, dampen electoral motivations without eliminating them entirely.

indirectly tied to the question of how limits will affect legislative behavior. For example, some studies have attempted to predict the impact that term limits will have on state legislatures by estimating how many legislators in past cohorts have remained in office long enough to be forced out eventually under various term limit schemes (Moncreif, Thompson, Haddon, and Hoyer 1992; Opheim 1994). The idea is that the more legislators stick around long enough to be retired by term limits, the greater the impact of limits on legislative performance. Such a conclusion, of course, is premised on the idea that the senior legislators who are forced out behave differently from their more junior counterparts. Other studies have explored this link in the argument directly. Hibbing (1991) uses longitudinal data on U.S. House careers to show that members are more active in sponsoring legislation, and far more effective in securing its passage, as tenure increases. For the U.S. Senate, Ahuja and Moore (1992) find similar, but weaker, effects of professionalism. These studies base their conclusions on empirical evidence, but they approach the question of term limits indirectly, through the twin hypotheses that professionalism affects legislative performance, and that term limits will affect levels of professionalism.

Another popular means of avoiding the empirical obstacle has been to isolate subgroups of legislators who have chosen not to contest their next election, and therefore for whom the reelection incentive is absent. The idea is that the performance of such a subgroup should reflect on how legislators will behave once reelection is prohibited. Along these lines, Herrick, Moore, and Hibbing (1994) conclude that term limits should decrease overall legislative activity (bills sponsored, amendments offered) and attention to constituents (trips to the district, size of staff), as well as depressing attendance at roll call votes, but should also encourage specialization on more focused legislative agenda among U.S. House members. Other studies concur that attendance rates fall off among retiring House members (Lott 1990a; McArthur 1990). Still others explore the congruence between the voting behavior of retiring legislators and their constituents' interests, as estimated from demographic and economic data about the district. Overall, the results indicate that the cross-section of retiring House members are as responsive to their constituents' preferences as are nonretiring members (Dougan and Munger 1989; Lott and Reed 1989), although members facing retirement are somewhat less in tune with district interests than they, personally, had been earlier in their careers (Zupan 1990).

For now, focusing on legislators who forgo reelection voluntarily is the best way of testing hypotheses about term limits against empirical evidence from U.S. legislatures.[3] Nevertheless, there are clearly problems in using

---

[3] Beginning in 1996, when term limits kick in for the California state legislature, and thereafter, we shall begin to have empirical data about limits from a number of U.S. states.

the behavior of those who retire voluntarily, for whatever reason, to draw conclusions about behavior among legislators who would be *forced out* of office under term limits. The most obvious problem is that those who choose not to run for reelection in the absence of term limits are disproportionately likely to be retiring from politics altogether, and so are acting without regard to subsequent political career opportunities (Herrick and Nixon 1994). On the other hand, it is reasonable to expect that those whose legislative tenure is curtailed by term limits will be maneuvering to extend their political careers in other offices; and it is plausible that such maneuvering will affect legislative behavior. Indeed, in Chapter 6, I examine House voting behavior among a *subgroup* of the subgroup of retirers – those who leave the House to run for statewide office – in order to test this hypothesis directly.

So, it is possible to construct worthwhile empirical tests on the effects of term limits in U.S. legislatures. Nevertheless, such work is limited on two important counts. First, it invariably requires conjecture about legislators who might be behaving *as if* they were subjected to term limits when, as yet, no one has been. Second, narrowing the focus to small subgroups of legislators complicates any analyses of how term limits might affect the performance of institutions within legislatures in which all members are involved, like parties or committees.[4]

This is probably why so little has been resolved in the debate over term limits despite intense interest by both political scientists and practitioners, and despite some promising attempts to generate hypotheses about how severing the electoral connection might affect legislative behavior and organization. Malbin and Benjamin (1992) suggest, for example, that term limits might intensify individualism in Congress, as members strive to establish personal reputations outside the districts they represent, and might undermine party cohesiveness, as party leaders would lack sanctions to impose on members who cannot remain in the institution. Taking a directly opposite tack, Glazer and Wattenberg (1991) argue that limits, by disconnecting legislators from the competing demands of their current constituencies, will generate *more* cohesive parties in Congress. Among academics, activists, and journalists, both advocates and opponents of term limits have generated lists of claims and counterclaims. Limits are promised to increase the competitiveness of elections, improve the quality of candidates, decrease the influence of lobbyists, and produce "citizen-legislators" who understand and share the interests of voters better than professional politicians (Mitchell

---

[4] A recent article by Gilmour and Rothstein (1994) offers an intriguing and generalizable model to estimate how term limits should affect partisan balance in legislatures, based on the rates at which limits cause parties to lose incumbent seats and the abilities of the parties that initially gain those seats to retain them. The authors then test the model against U.S. House electoral data to predict Republican gains and Democratic losses under term limits. Gilmour and Rothstein are concerned with the electoral performance of parties, however, and not with how term limits might affect the organization of parties within legislatures.

1991; Petracca 1991; Will 1992), but also to restrict voters' choices, *increase* the influence of lobbyists and staff, and generate inexperienced and impatient legislators (Cohen and Spitzer 1991; Kesler 1992).

In short, almost everyone involved in the term limits debate agrees that the reform should have radical effects on legislative representation. Moreover, the debate consistently returns to the central issues of political careers, the responsiveness of legislators to constituent interests, and the strength of parties in legislatures. But by robbing its central assumption of an electoral incentive, term limits have left legislative theory rudderless. The result has been a wave of hypotheses – many of which are mutually contradictory. Without empirical evidence against which to judge the hypotheses, students of U.S. politics are no closer to answering the question of how term limits will affect legislative representation than they were when the issue first surfaced.

The need for a comparative approach

Here is a prime case in which comparative analysis can be indispensable in the study of U.S. institutions. Comparative analysis is generally ignored by students of U.S. politics for a number of reasons. First, there are straightforward logistical obstacles to studying politics outside the United States, like language barriers in most cases. Second, although it is not always explicitly embraced, there is frequently an underlying faith in the idea of American exceptionalism, that politics in the United States is driven by a fundamentally different kind of motor from politics elsewhere (Hartz 1955). It is also the case that the need for comparative data is less pronounced for Americanists than for those who study politics elsewhere. American federalism furnishes 50 close replicas of U.S. government institutions, complete with countless minor variations on the rules of the political game and the players, meaning that Americanists can often conduct genuinely comparative research without leaving home. Next, basic data on institutions, elections, voters, budgets, legislative voting, popular opinion, and demographics is nowhere so abundant and readily available as in the United States. Finding comparable data abroad can be enormously costly, and perhaps impossible. Finally, even if good data are available elsewhere, generating conclusions from comparative analysis that are applicable in a straightforward way to U.S. politics can be a daunting methodological challenge, as we shall see.

For all these reasons, academic analyses of U.S. politics tend to have an "area studies" feel about them. When superior data from within the United States are available, it might be reasonable not to pursue a comparative approach. This kind of provincialism cannot be defended, however, when the best data available are comparative. This is the case quite clearly in the term limits debate. There is no U.S. experience with legislative term limits (yet). There is one country that has imposed term limits on legislators for an extended period, during which competitive elections have taken place in a two-party system, under a presidential constitution. The most promising avenue to pursue in building a theory of term limits based on empirical evidence, then, is a comparative approach.

The cases

The primary case of interest, because it is currently generating the most questions, is the United States. Therefore, it is appropriate to begin by reviewing the specifics of term limits as they currently stand in this country. Next, I review the candidates for comparison with the United States, first explaining why some potential cases do not serve, and finally establishing the rationale for analysis of Costa Rica and Venezuela.

The prospect of term limits in the United States

Between 1990 and 1994, a total of 22 U.S. states passed term limit measures. In 20 states, limits apply to both state legislators and representatives to the U.S. Congress, whereas in 2 states limits apply only to the latter. The details and the status of these measures, and a term limits provision that will be on the Mississippi state ballot in 1995, are outlined in Tables 1.1 and 1.2, for state and federal legislators, respectively. The second and third columns in each table show the total number of years (not terms) a person may serve in a given chamber before term limits kick in. In many cases, this is a simple integer – 6, 8, or 12. In other cases, the measure allows for a certain number of years over the space of a longer period – for example, 6 of the preceding 12 years. This is represented as 6/12. The column marked "Percentage Support" shows the percentage of valid votes in support of term limit initiatives where limits were adopted through direct democracy. So far, only in Utah have limits been adopted by standard legislative procedures. The column marked "Effective as of" shows the years in which incumbent legislators will first be excluded from ballots. In many cases, there are two different years, the first referring to members of the lower house and the second referring to members of the Senate, where limits are frequently longer. Five states employ what are known as "trigger mechanisms" for term limits on representatives to the U.S. Congress, meaning that their term limit clocks will not begin ticking until (and unless) a specified number of other states also have adopted limits. These triggers are meant to protect states against giving up the advantages of seniority in their congressional delegations unless enough other states do so as well. The column marked "Mecha-

Table 1.1. *Term limits on state legislators*

State	State House	State Senate	Year adopted	Percent support	Effective as of	Mechanism	Break in service
Alaska	NA	NA	NA	NA	NA	NA	NA
Arizona	8	8	1992	74	2000	Limit	2 years
Arkansas	6	8	1992	60	1998 and 2000	Limit	Lifetime
California	6	8	1990	52	1996 and 1998	Limit	Lifetime
Colorado	8	8	1990	71	1998	Limit	4 years
Florida	8	8	1992	77	2000	Ballot	2 years
Idaho	8/15	8/15	1994	59	2002	Ballot	Contingent
Maine	8	8	1993	63	1996	Limit	2 years
Massachusetts	8	8	1994	51	2002	Ballot	2 years
Michigan	6	8	1992	59	1998 and 2000	Limit	Lifetime
Mississippi	8	8	On ballot in 1995		2003	Limit	2 years
Missouri	8	8	1992	74	2000	Limit	Lifetime
Montana	8/16	8/16	1992	67	2000	Ballot	Contingent
Nebraska	8[a]		1994	68	2002	Limit	2 years
Nevada	12	12	1996[b]	70	2008	Limit	Lifetime
North Dakota	NA	NA	NA	NA	NA	NA	NA
Ohio	8	8	1992	68	2000	Limit	4 years
Oklahoma	12[c]		1990	67	2002	Limit	Lifetime
Oregon	6	8[d]	1992	69	1998 and 2000	Limit	Lifetime
South Dakota	8	8	1992	63	2000	Limit	2 years
Utah	12	12	1994	Leg.[e]	2006	Limit	2 years
Washington	6/12	8/14	1992	52	1998 and 2000	Ballot	Contingent
Wyoming	6/12	12/24	1992	77	1998 and 2004	Limit	Contingent

Table 1.1 (*cont.*)

[a] Nebraska's state legislature is unicameral.

[b] Nevada's Constitution requires that amendments be passed by majority votes in two separate referenda. The second referendum on term limits is scheduled for 1996.

[c] The Oklahoma measure allows for a total of 12 years of service in either house of the state legislature, or in both houses combined.

[d] The Oregon measure also stipulates that no person may serve a *total* of more than 12 years in the two chambers combined.

[e] Utah's is the only state legislature to pass term limits, in early 1994. In November 1994, Utah voters rejected an alternative term limits initiative, which included other electoral reforms as well, by 65% of the vote.

Sources: Ferry (1994), Benjamin and Malbin (1992), Miller (1992), Warren and Miller (1992), and Fett and Ponder (1993), Stanley and Niemi (1995).

11

Table 1.2. *Term limits on U.S. legislators*

State	U.S. House	U.S. Senate	Year adopted	Percent support	Effective as of	Mechanism	Break in service
Alaska	6/12	12/24	1994	63	23-state trigger	Ballot	Contingent
Arizona	6	12	1992	74	1998 and 2004	Ballot	H: 2 years / S: 6 years
Arkansas	6	12	1992	60	1998 and 2004	Limit^a	Lifetime
California	6/11	12/17	1992	63	1998 and 2004	Ballot	Contingent
Colorado	6	12	1994	51	2000 and 2006	Limit	4 years
Florida	8	8	1992	77	2000 and 2004	Ballot	2 years
Idaho	6/11	12/23	1994	59	2000 and 2006	Ballot	Contingent
Maine	6/11	12/17	1994	63	2002 and 2008	Ballot	Contingent
Massachusetts	8	12	1994	51	2002 and 2006	Ballot	H: 2 years / S: 6 years
Michigan	6/11	12/23	1992	59	1998 and 2004	Limit	Contingent
Mississippi	6	12	On ballot in 1995	74	21-state trigger	Ballot	4 years
Missouri	8	12	1992	74	24-state trigger	Limit	Lifetime
Montana	6/12	12/24	1992	67	1998 and 2004	Ballot	Contingent
Nebraska	6	12	1994	68	2000 and 2006	Ballot	H: 2 years / S: 6 years
Nevada	6	12	1994^b	70	24-state trigger	Ballot	Lifetime
North Dakota	12^c		1992	55	2004	Ballot	Lifetime
Ohio	8	12	1992	66	2000 and 2004	Limit	4 years
Oklahoma	6	12	1994	67	2000 and 2006	Limit	Lifetime
Oregon	6	12	1992	69	1998 and 2004	Limit	Lifetime
South Dakota	12	12	1992	63	2004	Limit	2 years
Utah	12	12	1994	Leg.^d	24-state trigger	Limit	2 years
Washington	6/12	12/18	1992	52	1998 and 2004^e	Ballot	Contingent
Wyoming	6/12	12/24	1992	77	1998 and 2004	Limit	Contingent

Table 1.2 (*cont.*)

[a] The Arkansas, Oklahoma, and Wyoming measures technically prohibit candidates' names from appearing on the ballot after they have served the prescribed number of terms. However, Oklahoma law does not allow write-in votes to be counted, and in Arkansas and Wyoming candidates must be certified in order to be elected. Consequently, the measures effectively amount to strict term limits.

[b] Nevada's Constitution requires that amendments be passed by majority votes in two separate referenda. The second referendum on term limits is scheduled for 1996.

[c] The North Dakota measure allows for a total of 12 years of service in either house of Congress, or in both houses combined.

[d] Utah's is the only state legislature to pass term limits, in early 1994. In November 1994, Utah voters rejected an alternative term limits initiative, which included other electoral reforms as well, by 65% of the vote.

[e] Washington's measure originally included a 9-state trigger mechanism, meaning it would not impose limits on U.S. House members and Senators until at least 9 other states did so. This hurdle, however, was cleared in the same 1992 election in which the Washington measure passed.

Sources: Ferry (1994), Benjamin and Malbin (1992), Miller (1992), Warren and Miller (1992), and Fett and Ponder (1993), Stanley and Niemi (1995).

nism" distinguishes strict term limits from ballot access restrictions. The former prohibit service in the chamber outright, whereas the latter prevent a candidate's name from being placed on the ballot, but do not prevent the candidate from being elected on write-in votes. The last column specifies how long a break in service the limits require, with respect to the specific legislative chamber. For instance, some measures prohibit service in a chamber (or ballot access) for life. Others require a sitting out period – frequently a mere 2 years to prevent consecutive service, but sometimes longer. Others are contingent, requiring a sitting out period whose length depends on how many years, within a longer period, a person has served in the chamber. For example, if a state prohibits service in the state House for any person who has served 6 of the preceding 12 years, and if a representative has served the last 6 consecutive years, then this amounts to a 6-year break in service requirement. If the representative's prior service was not consecutive, however, the required break may be shorter.

Tables 1.1 and 1.2 show the abundant variations in term limit provisions, both among the states and between limits on state versus federal legislators. Most provisions allow less time for representatives than senators, at both the state and federal level, and U.S. senators are generally afforded the longest periods, due to their 6-year terms. On the other hand, Alaska and North Dakota impose limits on representatives to Congress without limiting state legislative terms at all. In most cases, service in one chamber of a legislature does not prevent a person from serving in the other chamber, but state legislators in Oklahoma and federal representatives from North Dakota are limited to 12 years total, in either chamber or both. Although most states (76%) impose strict term limits on state legislators, most (57%) employ only ballot access restrictions on federal representatives. This is because limits on federal representatives are subject to judicial review by the U.S. Supreme Court, where a central argument of term limit opponents is that state measures are unconstitutional if they add qualifications for election to Congress to those already laid out in the "qualifications clause" (Art. I, Sec. 3) of the U.S. Constitution. By prohibiting access to ballots, but formally allowing election by write-in votes, those who drafted term limit measures hoped to find constitutional cover behind the clause (Art. I, Sec. 4) that allows states to establish the "times, places, and manner" of elections. In most states, the clocks started running on legislators as soon as term limit measures were adopted. In Alaska, Missouri, and Utah, however, limits on federal representatives do not take effect until 24 other states also commit to restricting reelection. Nevada will employ a similar trigger mechanism in imposing term limits, but the whole enterprise is delayed by the requirement that amendments to that state's constitution must be voted on twice, in different statewide elections. Judging from the 70% support for term limits in 1994, Nevada will likely complete the constitutional amendment process in the 1996 elections, but the final adoption of term limits will hinge on the 24-state trigger. The Mississippi provision voted on in 1995 includes a 21-state trigger.[5] Finally, although most limits at both the state and federal level merely require a break in service, many limits (33% at the state level; 26% at the federal) apply for life. And where eventual reelection is allowed, the required breaks in service vary from 2 years to 12.

In short, the variations in the term limit provisions currently on the books in the United States are copious and illustrate the degree to which the term limits movement has used the states as laboratories of electoral reform. It may well be that there are discernable differences in the effects of different types of limits on legislative behavior. For example, Utah's allowance of lengthy service in any legislative office, and a mere 2-year required break in service may have significantly less impact on legislative behavior than Arkansas' stricter limits and lifetime prohibition on subsequent service. Despite differences in the details, however, there is enough common ground to consider term limits as a unified electoral reform in most important ways. All the limits, whether state or federal, are between 6 and 12 years. Whether ballot access restrictions or strict term limits, they will effectively prevent incumbents from being reelected. Unless the state measures are overturned by judicial review, then by the year 2000, 15 states will have begun turning incumbent representatives at both the state and federal level out of office. And even if state-sponsored limits on federal legislators are struck down as unconstitutional, term limits will remain the most important electoral reform on the U.S. political agenda for two reasons. First, term limit supporters are poised to mount a formidable campaign for a constitutional amendment to limit all congressional terms. Second, whatever the fate of term limits at the federal level, limits on state legislators will endure, and their effects will likely trickle *up* to the federal level by increasing the pool of congressional candidates who have been displaced from state legislatures.

In subsequent chapters, I revisit the issues of how term limits have been adopted in the United States and how the details of term limits in the U.S. context might shape their effects. For now, however, we have an adequate description of the prospects for term limits in the United States to turn attention to how to proceed with an empirical, comparative analysis that might shed light on the U.S. case.

---

[5] Clearly, 22 other states have already passed term limit provisions. However, given that 4 of these include trigger provisions higher than Mississippi's, it appears that the intent of Mississippi's provision is for its limits not to kick in until at least 21 other states *impose* limits, rather than when they simply adopt measures.

The cases not included

There are only a handful of cases of legislative term limits worldwide, and most of these are inappropriate for comparison with the United States. It is worthwhile to consider why. Closest to home, legislators in both chambers of Mexico's Congress are prohibited from immediate reelection. Term limits have been in effect since Article 59 of the Mexican Constitution was amended to prohibit successive reelection in 1933. I do not include the Mexican case in this study, however, for a number of reasons. In the first place, Mexico does not provide a case for studying the effects of term limits on legislative representation in a democratic context.[6] Despite a series of reforms in recent years that have allowed opposition parties increasing success in congressional elections, Mexico still falls short of providing a fair competitive electoral arena. And throughout most of the term limits era in Mexico, elections have been thoroughly dominated by the Partido Revolucionario Institucional (PRI), partly because of the party's popular support, but also through a combination of patronage, rule manipulation, and outright fraud (Craig and Cornelius 1995).

Second, from their inception, term limits in Mexico have been a tool of the PRI national leadership to ensure control over the behavior of politicians within their own party and to discourage the founding of opposition parties by dissident politicians with strong local bases of support. By eliminating the prospect of parliamentary careers, and making political careers entirely dependent on national party patronage, PRI leaders encouraged obedience among their own legislators and deterred politicians with strong electoral support from challenging the PRI by founding opposition parties (Weldon 1994). In Mexico, the imposition of term limits was a self-conscious effort by national party bosses to centralize political power. In Costa Rica in contrast, as in the Philippines and the United States, the adoption of term limits was motivated by a popular lack of confidence in incumbent legislators and a desire to curb political careerism. The Mexican pattern of patronage careers replacing assembly careers under term limits is mirrored to some extent in the Costa Rican case (Chapter 3). But Costa Rica, with its modern tradition of fair elections and its competitive party system, is a better case for analysis of the impact of term limits on representation in a democracy.

Legislative terms are limited in the Philippines as well. Under the Constitution of 1986, senators may serve a maximum of two consecutive six-year terms, and House members a maximum of three consecutive three-year

---

[6] By democratic, I am referring to the minimum requirements for procedural democracy, as described by Dahl (1971) and O'Donnell, Schmitter and Whitehead (1986).

terms (Art. VI, Sec. 4,7). These limits were imposed by the Constituent Assembly convened after the overthrow of President Ferdinand Marcos and the election of President Corazon Aquino. Rather than an effort by strong parties to control political careers, Filipino term limits were adopted during a transitional period in which the traditional party system was in flux, and there was overwhelming popular opprobrium toward incumbent politicians, whose careers had been built on electoral fraud. In this regard, the conditions under which term limits were adopted in the Philippines were strikingly similar to those of Costa Rica in 1949, although the Filipino limits are less stringent. The impact of term limits on political careers and legislative behavior in the Philippines cannot yet be assessed, however, because the prohibition on reelection kicks in only in 1995 for House members, and 1998 for senators.

Ecuador imposes term limits identical to those in Costa Rica: legislators in the unicameral assembly serve four-year terms and cannot be elected to successive terms (Art. 57). Ecuador's term limits have been imposed only since the end of military rule and the adoption of the current constitution in 1979, however. Moreover, the extreme fragmentation of Ecuador's party system (Conaghan 1992), and the high volatility of party support levels since 1979 (Coppedge 1994) would complicate any analysis of how formal electoral rules influence political careers and legislative behavior. In short, Ecuador's combination of a short history with term limits and an extremely turbulent electoral environment make it an inappropriate case for comparative analysis with the United States.

This exhausts the list of countries, other than Costa Rica, employing legislative term limits. Of course, term limits for executives are far more common. Most popularly elected presidents are prohibited from reelection (Shugart and Carey 1992), and 76% of U.S. governors face limits of some kind (Stanley and Niemi 1994). Why not rely on the experience with term-limited executives to inform analysis of legislative limits? The reason is that the term limits debate focuses on aspects of legislative behavior that are entirely different, or even absent, among elected executives. The primary phenomena examined in this study are legislative particularism and party cohesiveness. The first has to do with the provision of government largesse to narrow geographical constituencies, even at the expense of the broader polity. Legislators who represent geographically defined districts have incentives to traffic in such particularism; executives generally do not. Likewise, maintaining party cohesiveness presents a difficult collective action problem for groups of copartisan legislators; but it is not relevant to unitary executives. Thus, the common experience of term limits among executives does not promise to shed much light on the most interesting questions about term limits on legislators. With this in mind, I turn to the Costa Rican case.

The cases compared: Costa Rica and Venezuela

Since 1949, Costa Rican legislators (deputies) have been subject to rotation-style term limits, meaning they may not serve consecutive terms in the Legislative Assembly. Assembly terms are four years, and the total number of terms a politician may serve is not limited. But the prohibition on consecutive terms means that no incumbent deputy can run for reelection.[7]

At first blush, Costa Rica would seem to present the opportunity for a simple test of the impact of term limits on political careers, legislator responsiveness to constituents, and party cohesion. The Costa Rican legislature under term limits could be compared with the pre–term limits period; and in addition, Costa Rican legislators under term limits could be compared with legislators in other countries not subject to term limits. Both these approaches will be employed in this study, but it is necessary in this introductory chapter to discuss some of the limitations and challenges presented by such a comparative method.

In the first place, comparison of the Costa Rican legislature before and after term limits is complicated by the lack of information on the Assembly prior to the Civil War of 1948 and the new Constitution of 1949. Histories of Costa Rican politics in the pre–Civil War era focus broadly on policy reforms and the actions of presidents, with little attention given to the internal workings of the legislature or political parties (Aguilar Bulgarelli 1981; Dunkerley 1988; Obregón Loria 1966; Salazar 1981).[8] Rosters of all congresses are available as far back as 1920, so data on parliamentary careers can be reconstructed for the era before term limits (Chapter 3). But the lack of information on the legislature itself makes a thorough comparison of legislative behavior before and after term limits impossible.

Comparison of Costa Rica with countries where reelection is not limited is a more promising approach. Any cross-national comparative analysis, however, presents its own methodological challenges (Geddes 1990a; Geertz 1973; Ragin 1987). In order to identify the effects of legislative term limits, one promising method is to identify a country whose politics are as similar as possible to Costa Rica's, but that lacks term limits, in order to isolate the impact of term limits (Lijphart 1971). Given this study's focus on electoral rules, the first priority must be an identity of electoral systems: closed-list proportional representation in large-magnitude electoral districts. Of course, correspondence on electoral rules is not a sufficient basis on which to assume that legislative behavior in two countries ought to be similar. Other institu-

[7] Constitution of Costa Rica, Art. 107.
[8] One notable exception to this pattern is Fabrice Edouard Lehoucq's (1991b) paper on Costa Rica's history of electoral reforms. Even Lehoucq, however, does not address the adoption of term limits and its effect on the legislature.

tional factors, most notably regime type and the constitutional scope of authority accorded the legislature, are critical factors in defining the job of representatives and determining legislative behavior (Mainwaring 1994; Shugart and Carey 1992; Valenzuela and Wilde 1979). Moreover, beyond the formal rules of politics, historical, economic, geographical, and cultural factors all shape the roles of the legislature and its members. Assemblies have to adopt new forms of internal organization, and new divisions of labor among legislators, as governments expand the scope of their activities in regulating the economy (Cox 1987). In addition, the religious and cultural heritage of a country shapes collective conceptions of political community, the relationship between citizens and public institutions, and the appropriate process of deliberation over policy (Stepan 1978). Fortunately, in the instance of Costa Rica, there is another country that shares remarkable congruence on historical, economic, geographical, cultural, and institutional factors: Venezuela.

Both countries share Spanish colonial heritage, and both gained independence from Spain in the 1820s. Moreover, the countries are demographically similar, as well as relatively homogeneous ethnically and religiously. The two countries have among the smallest indigenous populations in the Americas. Only 1.5% of Venezuela's population consists of Amerinds, and a mere 0.6% of Costa Rica's. These figures contrast sharply with many Latin American countries, like Bolivia (59%), Guatemala (60%), Peru (37%), and even Mexico (12%). The relative sizes of Costa Rica's and Venezuela's indigenous populations are more comparable to those of Argentina (1.5%) and the United States (0.7%).[9] Both countries are also overwhelmingly Roman Catholic. Eighty-six percent of Costa Rica's population professes membership in the Catholic Church, and 92% of Venezuela's.[10]

On levels of economic and social development, Costa Rica and Venezuela rank among the highest of Latin American countries on most indicators. In 1989, Venezuela was first in Latin America in per capita GDP ($3,035 in 1988 $U.S.), whereas Costa Rica ranked eighth ($1,659).[11] But Venezuela's superior level of gross product is partially offset by its more skewed distribution of income. Costa Rica's Gini Coefficient, estimating the degree to which income distribution deviates from equal across all households, is the third lowest among 13 Latin American countries measured. Only in Uruguay and Argentina is household income distributed more evenly. Seven of the 13 countries, on the other hand, have distributions more even than Venezuela.[12]

---

[9] Wilkie and Contreras (1992), Table 657, Part 1: 136.
[10] Ibid., Table 1,100, Part 1: 324–325.
[11] Table 3,463, Part 2: 1335.
[12] In addition to Uruguay, Argentina, and Costa Rica, these include Brazil, Chile, Colombia, and El Salvador. The data on income distribution are from ibid., Table 1,419, Part 1: 410.

The important point to be derived from the data on GDP and income distribution is that basic quality of life indicators are similar for the populations of Costa Rica and Venezuela. As of 1986, the 2 countries ranked second and fifth among 19 Latin American countries in having the lowest infant mortality rates. Only in Cuba is infant mortality lower than in Costa Rica, and Venezuela follows immediately behind Chile and Panama on this indicator.[13] The most comprehensive single indicator of economic and social development is the HEC (Health, Education, and Communications) Index, which estimates the gap in living standards between the United States and any other country, based on measurements of five health components, four education components, and three communications components.[14] The final index score is calculated as the scaled percent decrease necessary to bring the United States to parity with any other country. An index score of zero indicates parity with the United States. Among 20 Latin American countries measured as of 1980, Venezuela and Costa Rica ranked fifth and sixth, with index scores of 49.2 and 49.9, respectively. The average across all countries was 59.7.[15]

The two countries share strong similarities in political histories and institutions as well, beginning with the two longest traditions of uninterrupted civilian rule and competitive elections in Latin America. Moreover, in each case the current regime is the product of a moderate nationalist revolt at midcentury: 1948 in Costa Rica, and 1958 in Venezuela. These revolts were not driven by radical political ideology nor consummated by popular revolution. Rather, they were executed primarily by political activists whose primary conflicts with the existing regimes revolved around exclusion from the political system, and corruption that prevented or undermined democratic processes. In both countries, two centrist parties increasingly dominated the electoral process from the 1960s through the early 1990s. In both countries, the 1960s and 1970s saw expansion of state activity in the economy, with state ownership of critical industries, and extensive regulation of prices and trade. Both countries, however, began implementing policies of deregulation and fiscal austerity in the late 1980s and early 1990s, to reduce the state role in the economy.

---

[13] On deaths per 1,000 live births, the best-ranked five countries were Cuba (13.6), Costa Rica (18.0), Chile (19.1), Panama (23.0), and Venezuela (24.7). These compare favorably with Mexico (47.0), Brazil (63.0), and Bolivia (110.0). Ibid., Table 713, Part 1: 148.

[14] The components are as follows: Health–life expectancy at birth, infant mortality, persons per hospital beds, population per physician, population per dentist; education–literacy rate for population over age 15, percentage of school-age population enrolled, percentage of 13- to 18-year-olds enrolled in secondary school, and college enrollment as a percentage of secondary school enrollment; communications–newspaper circulation per capita, telephones per capita, and motor vehicles per capita. Ibid., Table 800, Part 1: 168.

[15] Ibid., Table 801, Part 1: 169.

With regard to political institutions, three general points are critical: both are presidential regimes, with similar distributions of authority among the branches of government. Both electoral systems generate minimal electoral incentives for legislators to cultivate personal reputations at the expense of party labels (Carey and Shugart in press). Finally, of course, Costa Rica imposes legislative term limits, whereas Venezuela does not. The historical and institutional similarities between Costa Rica and Venezuela are discussed in greater detail in Chapter 2.

The critical point here is that the major indicators of national demographics and economic and social development all underscore strong similarities between the countries, both in absolute terms and in relation to other Latin American countries. In making comparisons between the political institutions of Costa Rica and Venezuela, it will be important to remain cognizant of differences that could be driven by historical, cultural, and economic factors. But the general structural conditions of the two countries, measured by conventional indicators, are strikingly similar.

A central theoretical premise of this work is that given the strong similarities between Costa Rican and Venezuelan politics, differences between career patterns and the behavior of legislators in the two countries can be explained by the existence of term limits in Costa Rica and their absence in Venezuela. Chapters 3–5 elaborate these differences and present explicit arguments as to how term limits can account for them. But the goal of this work is more broad than providing a thorough comparison of the Costa Rican and Venezuelan legislatures. The project is to draw from the study of term limits conclusions about the effects of electoral incentives on legislative representation that are generalizable across all electoral systems. This project is complicated, because the same phenomena (career patterns, constituent–legislator relations, party discipline) that are affected by term limits are also affected by other electoral system variables that motivate legislators either toward individualism or toward party loyalty (Carey and Shugart in press). The task of deriving general conclusions is left until after the empirical work of establishing the effects of term limits in Costa Rica is complete. The concluding chapter of this work addresses at length the extent to which the lessons of Costa Rica are applicable beyond that nation's borders – particularly to the United States. For now, it is important to be aware of the sources of complexity in drawing general conclusions from comparative analysis of a small number of cases.

The chapters that follow

Chapter 2 presents background material on the three cases analyzed in this book: Costa Rica, Venezuela, and the United States. For the Latin American cases, general overviews of political institutions and development are provided, and for the United States a review of the literature on legislative organization. The goal is to establish more firmly the comparability of the cases and to establish more clearly the obstacles to comparative analysis that this work must confront. The chapter provides a brief overview of the Costa Rican Legislative Assembly, its constitutional powers relative to the presidency, committee and caucus structure, and increasing domination over time by two centrist parties. Next, it reviews the historical process by which term limits were adopted, with discussion of political reforms during the 1940s, the Civil War of 1948, and Constituent Assembly of 1949, which established the prohibition on reelection. Then the chapter proceeds to review efforts to abolish term limits in Costa Rica since 1949, illustrating how term limits have been perceived by their opponents, and highlighting the similarities between the debates over term limits in Costa Rica and the United States. Next, the chapter provides a similar, but shorter, overview of Venezuelan institutions – the Constitution, party system, and Congress – and of electoral reform efforts designed to improve their performance, noting that term limits have not been among these proposed reforms. Finally, the chapter offers a review of literature that focuses on the organization of U.S. legislatures, particularly on the importance of committee systems. The centrality of committees is contrasted with their marginality in the Latin American cases, suggesting that differences in career incentives (for which term limits, of course, play a major role) can account for this contrast.

With this framework in place, Part II proceeds with the detailed comparison of the Latin American cases. Chapter 3 presents an analysis of political career paths in Costa Rica and Venezuela. Costa Rica's term limits formally prohibit *immediate* reelection, but allow former deputies to serve again in the Assembly after four years out of office. Thus, the first question is to determine the rate of eventual reelection to the Assembly, comparing this against reelection rates prior to the adoption of term limits, and against Venezuelan reelection rates. Next, alternative career paths are explored. Interviews with Costa Rican deputies provide insights into post-Assembly career paths desirable to deputies. Based on archival research, I provide a database of presidential appointments to key positions in ministries, foreign service, and state-run corporations. These data are combined with Assembly rosters to determine the ability of politicians to secure post-Assembly appointments. Combining all these data, I show that although term limits in Costa Rica have virtually eliminated careers in the Assembly, they have not eliminated political careers based on party appointments. Deputies whose parties win subsequent presidential elections are likely to be able to continue in politics. The data from Venezuela, by contrast, confirm that legislators not subject to term limits are far more likely to build political careers within the legislative branch.

Having illustrated the shape of political career paths in Costa Rica and Venezuela in detail, Chapter 4 begins the analysis of legislative behavior under term limits. The central puzzle here is to explain the time and energy devoted by Costa Rican deputies to providing small favors to individuals or community groups in geographically exclusive bailiwicks. Costa Rican particularism and constituency service represent a challenge to electoral incentive theories of legislative behavior, not only because term limits preclude reelection, but also because Costa Rica's electoral system would prevent legislators from benefiting from their personal reputations even if they could be reelected. Indeed, the failure of Venezuelan legislators to devote similar energy to providing small favors to localities is entirely consistent with electoral incentive theory. The chapter begins by establishing empirically the differences between the behavior of legislators in the two countries. Extensive interviews with Costa Rican deputies, as well as budgetary data, are the primary sources here. Then the chapter proceeds to offer an explanation for how Costa Rican parties structure deputies' career incentives around the provision of particularism, which benefits the parties electorally. Again, interview responses consistently support this explanation. The thesis is also tested against a combination of budgetary, electoral, and political career data, with mixed results. The ambiguity in these data, however, is explained by the uncertainty generated by Costa Rica's *presidential* term limits over who will control deputies' post-Assembly career prospects. In one instance in which the responsiveness of deputies to their party's future presidential candidate can be tested, data on careers clearly demonstrates that those who support the candidate are rewarded with post-Assembly appointments, whereas party mavericks are punished.

A number of conclusions are drawn from Chapter 4. First, personal electoral incentives may be sufficient, but are not necessary, to motivate legislators to engage in particularistic behavior. Parties can also structure legislators' incentives so that they will concentrate on constituent service and pork. Thus, term limits alone cannot necessarily be expected to eliminate behavior that political observers have understood to be purely reelection-oriented. Second, the Venezuelan experience suggests that legislative representation without particularism is not agreeable to constituents. Popular as well as academic appeals for electoral reform in Venezuela have rested on demands that deputies increase responsiveness to community interests; and current reforms attempt to shift Venezuelan legislative behavior accordingly. Third, although Costa Rican parties organize deputies to provide particularism, instability among the leadership of each major party creates uncertainty among deputies over who will control political careers. This uncertainty generates divisions within each party's cohort of deputies, especially late in each Assembly.

The theme of intraparty division versus cohesiveness is pursued more extensively in Chapter 5. The basic theoretical premise tested is that in closed-list electoral systems, party discipline is imposed on legislators by party leaders who control list positions on ballots in future elections. When legislators cannot be reelected, the ability to impose discipline in this way should be hampered. This chapter compares party discipline in Costa Rica with that in Venezuela. In the latter country, the combination of reelection and closed lists generates near airtight discipline in assembly voting, just as the electoral incentive theory would predict. In Costa Rica, on the other hand, voting against one's party leadership and against decisions reached by one's party in caucus is not uncommon. Unfortunately, it is not possible to conduct statistical analyses of roll call votes in these legislatures, because roll calls are almost never invoked in either country – in Venezuela because party-line voting is so regular, and in Costa Rica because the Assembly is relatively small. Nevertheless, discipline in the Costa Rican Assembly is examined through two means: (1) extensive interview data with both party leaders and rank-and-file deputies, and (2) analyses of a number of cases of divisive legislation that involved either rare roll calls or public position taking by maverick legislators. The comparison between cases demonstrates two things. First, control over potential future appointments provides some Costa Rican party leaders significant means of imposing discipline. Second, nevertheless, discipline is still considerably looser in the Costa Rican than in the Venezuelan legislature. Under Costa Rican term limits, both the benefits to a deputy of remaining loyal to party leaders and the sanctions imposed for disloyalty are less impressive and less certain than in Venezuela. As a result, term limits in the Costa Rican context weaken party discipline and cohesiveness.

Part III shifts the focus back to the United States, first testing whether general patterns of behavior detected in the Costa Rican case are consistent with behavior of U.S. legislators not bound by a direct electoral connection, and then attempting to apply broader lessons about term limits to the U.S. case. Chapter 6 uses statistical methods that take advantage of the abundance of voting and career data available on the U.S. House of Representatives. Game-theoretical models predict that when a certain end point is imposed on a principal–agent relationship, agents can be expected to shirk against principals, unless a pension system is devised to maintain incentives for good behavior. Chapter 6 examines the voting behavior of House members who have decided to run for statewide office at the end of their current term. Regression analyses determine that such aspirants alter their voting behavior during their last terms in the House so as to cultivate support in their state parties, even at the expense of their current House districts. The analysis demonstrates that ambitious legislators will cater to those who control future career opportunities. This reinforces the results of the Costa Rican analysis – that in a system with term limits, legislators prohibited from reelection are responsive to those who control postlegislative careers – and suggests that the point is generalizable to the United States as well.

Chapter 7 begins by reviewing and emphasizing the common conclusion derived from the evidence in each of the preceding chapters: legislators generally are responsive to those who control their political futures. This idea may seem so obvious as to be trivial, but its implications are forgotten remarkably frequently in contemporary discussions of term limits. Given this situation, and armed with substantial theoretical and empirical firepower from previous chapters, I evaluate the U.S. debate over term limits. I begin with a historical review of the principle of limiting tenure, from the Federalist versus Antifederalist debates, through the informal systems of rotation in public offices established by 19th-century parties, to the case made by term limits proponents today. The focus is on drawing parallels between historical precedent and contemporary evidence regarding the effects of term limits on legislative representation. Specifically, I discuss the extent to which the conclusions pertaining to political careers, particularism, and party discipline in Costa Rica can be applied in predicting the effects of term limits in the United States.

The most straightforward argument is that term limits do not eliminate political careers and restore the fabled citizen-legislator to modern assemblies. The effort to generalize the conclusions regarding particularism and party discipline requires a methodical reexamination of the connection between electoral incentives and legislative behavior. The general conclusion is that the effects of term limits will vary in different electoral systems. Phenomena such as legislative particularism and party discipline could conceivably either wax or wane as a result of term limits, depending on the nature of the electoral system on which term limits are imposed, and on the sources of postassembly careers under term limits. Chapter 7 concludes by outlining general conditions under which term limits will encourage or discourage particularism and party cohesion, and by extending these conclusions to the U.S. case.

2

Institutions and electoral reform:
Comparing the cases

Before evaluating the impact of term limits on congressional behavior and organization, it is necessary to provide some background to the cases that will be considered in this study. Within that agenda, this chapter has four goals: (1) to provide general overviews of the national political institutions of Costa Rica and Venezuela, focusing especially on the national assemblies and party systems of each country; (2) to illustrate the institutional similarities between the two systems, and in doing so, underscore their appropriateness for comparison; (3) to highlight differences in the agenda for electoral reform in the two countries, with the focus, of course, on the question of reelection for legislators; and (4) to contrast the central issues of legislative organization and electoral reform in the Latin American cases with the United States, examining how term limits might account for differences and patterns of change across the cases.

More specifically, the chapter proceeds as follows. First, I provide a brief description of Costa Rica's Legislative Assembly, its relationship with the executive, and its internal organization. Then I review the political events leading up to the Civil War of 1948 and Constituent Assembly of 1949 that imposed term limits. I then examine the Constituent Assembly itself and the attention given to electoral reform by those who observed it and wrote about it. In the next section, I examine the arguments surrounding a number of subsequent constitutional reform proposals seeking to abolish or modify term limits. The task here is to establish the historical context in which term limits were adopted and to explore the possible intentions of those who established them. I do not claim to have determined conclusively the motivations of these reformers, however; and in fact I understand the Costa Rican constitutional delegates' support of a measure that would block their own parliamentary careers to be a puzzle. How term limits have been perceived by subsequent legislators, on the other hand, is more clear. The records of proposed reforms to allow reelection provide extensive documentation of how politicians perceive the impact of term limits on congressional representation.

The next section turns attention to Venezuela. This is the primary case for comparison with Costa Rica because the Venezuelan system closely resembles Costa Rica's on those electoral rules that structure legislators' incentives, with the notable exception of term limits. Venezuela is included, in effect, to hold constant, as much as possible, other electoral factors that affect legislative behavior and organization, allowing for the effects of term limits to be isolated. A couple of other similarities between the countries also contribute to Venezuela's appropriateness for comparison. First, the countries share a similar constitutional structure. Both are presidential, and the constitutions of both countries give their presidents little legislative authority relative to their legislatures. Second, Venezuela and Costa Rica have two of the longest records in Latin America of sustained civilian rule by governments chosen in competitive elections. Despite the two countries' similarities, however, term limits have been entirely absent from the agenda of electoral reformers in Venezuela.

The last part of the chapter shifts attention to the broader comparative project. First, I underscore the important elements of similarity, and the equally critical differences, in the institutional structures of U.S. and the Latin American cases discussed in this work. The point is to clarify further the prospects for comparison and the difficulties of drawing general conclusions across the cases. Second, I discuss the literature on the organization of the U.S. Congress, particularly as it focuses on the importance of the committee system, contrasting the centrality of committees in the United States with their lesser importance in the Latin American cases. The discussion of committee structure is a critical example of how institutional differences between the U.S. and the Latin American cases must be accounted for in comparative work; and it also generates some hypotheses on what is at stake in the decision to adopt legislative term limits. Third, I provide a brief review of the term limits reform process in the United States up to 1995, comparing this with the manner in which term limits were adopted in Costa Rica.

Costa Rican political institutions

Weak presidencies

Costa Rica has a constitutional tradition of a relatively weak executive. My emphasis here is on the constitutional tradition, because during the 19th and early 20th centuries, Costa Rica was marked by many periods of rule by presidents who seized power extraconstitutionally and governed with scant attention to the legislature (Lehoucq 1993). When they have been respected, however, the formal rules of Costa Rican politics have established executives who were far from dominant. A number of Costa Rica's earliest political charters provided for plural executives. And under the first postindependence pact organizing Costa Rican politics, there was a provision that the residence of the presidency was to be shifted every three months among the four major cities: Cartago, San José, Alajuela, and Heredia (Gutierrez Gutierrez 1984: 28; Seligson 1987). The idea was that the presidency should go to the people, rather than exist as a physically independent power base.

The current Constitution is consistent with this tradition, in providing for an executive with relatively weak constitutional powers, and a correspondingly strong Legislative Assembly (Shugart and Carey 1992). The Costa Rican president does not have any constitutional authority to legislate by decree, and even in cases of national emergency, any presidential motion to suspend constitutional guarantees must be ratified by two-thirds vote in the Legislative Assembly before it can take effect. Perhaps most significantly, however, the president's veto power is void on the national budget law (Art. 125). While on all other legislation, the presidential veto can only be overridden by a two-thirds majority in the Legislative Assembly, the veto cannot be exercised on the annual budget. This means that on most appropriations legislation, the Legislative Assembly is sovereign.

Organization of the assembly

The current Legislative Assembly is also characterized by a set of standing committees with fixed jurisdictions, but with rotating membership. Most legislative work is done in committees charged with policy areas such as justice, budget and appropriations, and foreign affairs. Legislation, whether introduced by the executive or deputies, is reviewed, amended, and voted on in committees. North American political scientists studying the Legislative Assembly have noted the importance of committees in preparing legislation (Baker 1971; Hughes and Mijeski 1973; Mijeski 1977). It is also the case, however, that substantive debate and negotiation over the details of legislation continues during floor proceedings in Costa Rica to a much greater extent than is possible in larger legislatures. Because of its small size, the Legislative Assembly can afford to engage in crafting final legislative outcomes on the floor; the need to delegate authority over this crafting to standing committees or party committees is not as pressing as in legislatures with many hundreds of members.

A couple of further points should be noted with respect to Costa Rican committees. First, committee members generally do not hold the same posts from year to year. And second, committee assignments are made unilaterally by the president of the Assembly. Since the 1960s, the president of the Assembly, likewise, has generally been replaced each year. The president is elected each May in a strict party-line vote,[1] so the actual selection of the president is taken by the majority party caucus. The important point is that Costa Rican deputies do not establish permanent, or quasi-permanent, membership on particular committees, as for example, in the United States. Furthermore, deputies know that the next president of the Assembly will determine their assignment for the next year, but the presidency is determined by the majority party caucus.

If the committees are where much of the procedural legislative work is done, the party caucuses are the most important fora for the presentation of and debate over general policy strategies. Each of the two major parties meets in caucus for one morning each week. It is in these meetings that party positions are communicated from the leadership to rank-and-file deputies, discussed, and generally ratified. If there is to be a strict party position on a vote, the position must be ratified in caucus. The importance of the caucuses, and their ability to impose party discipline on deputies, will be central to much of this volume.

The party system

Despite proportional representation and moderately large district magnitudes[2] (average $M = 8.1$), the Costa Rican system since 1949 has moved steadily toward dominance by two catch-all parties. In the immediate aftermath of the Civil War and Constituent Assembly, the 1949 Assembly elections were dominated by the supporters of president-elect Otilio Ulate in the National Union Party (PUN). The pre–Civil War majority Republicans were in disarray, with many members in exile or at least withdrawn temporarily from politics. By 1953, José Figueres Ferrer, who led the victorious forces in the Civil War, had organized the social democratic National Liberation Party (PLN), which has since been the country's most successful in both presidential and Assembly elections. Also by 1953, some old Republicans reentered the electoral arena. The 1953, 1958, and 1962 elections witnessed the improving fortunes of the Republicans and the corresponding decline of the PUN, at the Assembly level, while the PLN retained a consistent majority or large plurality. By 1966, the PUN and Republicans joined forces to present unified lists in Assembly elections and a single presidential candidate against the PLN. Except for 1974, this alliance has since remained stable, managing presidential victories in 1966 and 1978. By 1982, the coalition united in the new Social Christian Union Party (PUSC), which managed to win the presidency and a slim Assembly majority in 1990. A handful of

---

[1] The one exception to party discipline in these elections is discussed in Chapters 4 and 5.
[2] District of Magnitude (M) refers to the number of representatives elected from a given electoral district.

Table 2.1. Percentage of seats won in Costa Rican Legislative Assembly

President	Year	PUN	PLN	Republicano/ Unificacion/ UNIDAD/ PUSC	Leftist	Other
PUN	1949	71(31)	7(3)^a	15(9)^b	0(0)	6(3)
PLN	1953	26(12)	67(30)	7(3)	0(0)	0(0)
PUN	1958	22(10)	44(20)	24(11)	0(0)	9(4)
PLN	1962	16(9)	51(29)	32(18)	0(0)	2(1)
PUNIF	1966	—	51(29)	46(26)	4(2)	0(0)
PLN	1970	—	56(32)	39(22)	4(2)	2(1)
PLN	1974	—	47(27)	30(17)	4(2)	20(11)
UNIDAD	1978	—	44(25)	47(27)	7(4)	2(1)
PLN	1982	—	58(33)	34(19)	7(4)	2(1)
PLN	1986	—	51(29)	44(25)	4(2)	2(1)
PUSC	1990	—	44(25)	51(29)	2(1)	4(2)

Note: Number of seats is in parentheses.
^{a} In 1949, before the formation of the PLN, the Social Democrats won three Assembly seats.
^{b} This column shows the seats held by the heirs to Rafael Calderon Guardia's Republican Party. Beginning in 1982, this group has been unified in the PUSC. In earlier elections, they have run under labels including the Constitutional Party, Republicans, National Unification, and UNIDAD.

Assembly seats have consistently gone to minor, regional or leftist, parties in Costa Rica. Nevertheless, the parties supporting serious presidential contenders have dominated Assembly elections as well (Table 2.1).

Two aspects of Costa Rica's electoral system have contributed to the tendency toward two-party dominance at both the presidential and Assembly levels. First, the unique quasi-plurality rule used in presidential elections has encouraged the formation of broad coalitions behind fewer candidates than would be the case in a majority runoff system (Shugart and Carey 1992: ch. 10). Second, Costa Rica's concurrent electoral format has contributed to the dominance of Assembly elections by the parties supporting these presidential contenders. As Shugart (1988) has demonstrated, in systems where presidential and Assembly elections are held on the same day, the parties presenting the top two presidential candidates benefit in Assembly elections as well, despite proportional representation. Thus, across all elections since 1949, the average effective number of parties winning seats in the Legislative Assembly has been 2.6 (Shugart and Carey 1992: 220).[3]

In addition, the ideological difference between the dominant parties in Costa Rica is not dramatic. Both the PLN and what is now the PUSC were

[3] The "effective" number of parties is a self-weighted measure of the number of significant parties in the system. See Laakso and Taagepera (1979).

staunchly anticommunist during the Cold War years and committed to a market economy. Even their historical differences over issues like nationalization of the banks are now shrinking, as the PLN shifts toward deregulation. The bottom line is that Costa Rican politics under the 1949 Constitution have generally, and increasingly, been marked by dominance by two catch-all parties.

Costa Rican politics on the road to term limits

Reform under Calderón and Picado

During most of the 1940s, Costa Rica experienced a period of profound social reforms under the administrations of Rafael Angel Calderón Guardia and Teodoro Picado. These policies earned the two administrations the opposition of many of Costa Rica's landowners and employers. In addition, Calderón and Picado faced opposition among intellectuals who supported a series of political reforms to accompany those in social and economic policy. It was this coalition of economic conservatives and political progressives that ultimately ousted the existing regime in 1948 and wrote the Constitution of 1949, prohibiting the immediate reelection of deputies to the Legislative Assembly.

Calderón won the 1940 presidential election, bringing with him to office a group of reformers known as "the forty-year-olds," because they were a new generation of leaders in Costa Rican politics (Aguilar Bulgarelli 1986). Calderón and his Republican Party in Congress passed a sweeping agenda of social and economic legislation, including:

- the establishment of Costa Rica's first progressive income tax;
- the establishment of a Social Security pension system; and
- the creation of the National University (Aguilar Bulgarelli 1986; Salazar 1981).

From 1941 to 1944, the real expenditures of the government almost doubled, and the budget deficit in 1944 was 15 times that in 1941 (Aguilar Bulgarelli 1986).

Calderón's policies drew strong opposition from economic conservatives and the wealthy. These opposition forces charged the government with fraud after the 1942 mid-term congressional elections in which the Republicans lost some ground. Facing this threat, Calderón and the Republicans entered into a coalition government, mediated by San José Bishop Monseñor Victor Manuel Sanabria, with the Communist Party led by Manuel Mora. In coalition with the Communists, the government managed to pass a constitutional reform providing a labor code guaranteeing a minimum wage; an eight-hour workday; the right to unionize; the right to housing, basic safety, and sanitation conditions in the workplace; and priority for Costa Rican workers over foreigners (Salazar 1981).

In 1944, Calderón's hand-picked successor, Teodoro Picado Michalski, defeated the conservative Leon Cortes by almost two to one. The Republican–Communist coalition retained a majority in the Assembly, and the opposition again cried fraud. In a surprising move, however, Picado announced in 1944 his intention to oversee the reform of Costa Rica's electoral laws. The reform law passed by the Assembly in 1946 is notable for a couple of reasons. First, it marked an explicit effort to curtail the ability of incumbent presidents and Assembly majorities to manipulate the electoral process. The 1946 Code established a National Electoral Tribunal (TNE) to supervise elections, appoint local electoral officials, and adjudicate complaints. These authorities had previously been exercised by presidents. The Code also allowed representatives from all parties to participate in poll supervision and vote counting. It eliminated absentee ballots in an effort to curb multiple voting. And the Code reformed Costa Rica's quotient system so as to allow minor parties to gain seats more easily than in the past (Lehoucq 1991b: 10–11). These provisions, which abetted the efforts of opposition politicians and parties at the expense of incumbent majorities, represent a remarkable case of incumbents changing electoral rules in a way that evidently undermined their own career interests. The second notable feature of the 1946 Code was that it was passed by a cross-party coalition. President Picado was opposed on the reform by most of Calderón's followers among the Republican deputies, and by Calderón himself. He depended on Republicans not aligned with Calderón, the four Communist deputies, and the deputies of the main opposition Democratic Party (Lehoucq 1991b: 12).

The support of Democrat and Communist deputies for the bill is not difficult to explain. These parties stood to gain from the new Code's measures to reduce fraud and from the more lenient barriers to entry for small parties. However, the interest of Picado and any Republican deputies in the reform is more puzzling, as their own authority and career prospects were being undermined. Fabrice Edouard Lehoucq, who has undertaken the most thorough analyses of electoral reform in Costa Rica, argues that some majority politicians were willing to support the change, because they perceived the alternative to be destabilization of the entire political system – a potentially worse outcome for incumbent politicians than merely facing honest elections (Lehoucq 1991a, 1991b). Given the consistent charges of electoral fraud throughout the 1940s, this is a reasonable interpretation. At any rate, the 1946 reform by itself was not sufficient to prevent further conflicts over electoral fraud, nor the resulting destabilization of the system in 1948.

Sources of opposition: Conservatives and progressives

Most studies of the period preceding the Costa Rican Civil War of 1948 have understood Calderón's reforms as having alienated the Costa Rican economic elite. Some have argued that the Civil War was a capitalist reaction against the redistributive policies of the Calderón and Picado administrations (Rojas Bolaños 1979; Salazar 1981). Lehoucq (1991a), however, has rejected such class-based theories, arguing that political, rather than economic, differences best explain the crisis. I share Lehoucq's suspicion of strictly class-based theories, given that both sides of the Civil War consisted of coalitions with broadly diverse economic ideologies. It is true that the Calderón/Picado economic reform agenda was divisive and provided the motivation for conservative opposition; nevertheless, the political basis of opposition to the Republican governments from the relatively new Social Democratic movement was at least equally important.

By the mid-1940s, a group of intellectuals had organized the Center for the Study of National Problems (CEPN), based at the University of Costa Rica's Law School. These Social Democrats supported the Calderón/Picado policy agenda, but opposed the government on two counts. First they objected to an alliance with the Communists on any basis. And second, they opposed what they claimed was political foul play by the government. In addition to concurring with allegations of outright electoral fraud, they charged that both the Calderón and Picado administrations were using the newly founded institutions, such as the Social Security administration, to distribute patronage and favors for direct electoral profit (Aguilar Bulgarelli 1986; Dunkerley 1988).

The crisis of 1948

By the 1946 elections, the conservatives behind Leon Cortes, as well as another group led by Otilio Ulate, joined forces with the Social Democrats organized by the CEPN, and a small Acción Democrática Party created in 1945,[4] to form a united opposition in the congressional midterm elections. When the governing coalition took 56% of the national vote to 41% for the opposition, there were the familiar charges of fraud, and once again there was no response. Aguilar Bulgarelli (1986), who generally treats the *calderonistas* sympathetically, acknowledges that there were certainly irregularities in all the elections during the 1940s, but doubts in any case that the virtual outcomes would have differed much. In any case, in 1947 and 1948, protest and scattered violent acts against the government increased. The opposition

---

[4] This was the same year that Acción Democrática first came to power in Venezuela, in an administration that would end 3 years later in a military coup that brought Gen. Perez Jimenez to power for 10 years.

did its best to exploit divisions within the government coalition, supporting strikes to divide the labor movement and making women's suffrage a central campaign plank for 1948 (Salazar 1981).

For the 1948 election, the Social Democrats initially supported Jose Figueres Ferrer for president. Figueres had been exiled in 1942 for speaking out against the government's decision to declare war on Germany. He had spent three years in Mexico and had been active in a group of dissident Central Americans, supported by the Arevalo regime in Guatemala, who plotted to overthrow the Somoza regime in Nicaragua, the Trujillo regime in the Dominican Republic, and the Calderón regime in Costa Rica. In the Pacto del Caribe, this group pledged mutual support to each other's rebellions, with the ultimate goal of establishing a pan-Central American republic (Aguilar Bulgarelli 1986).

Nevertheless, with the election approaching, the Social Democrats opted to coalesce with the main conservative opposition groups behind Ulate and Cortes, eventually agreeing on an Ulate candidacy. On February 8, 1948, Ulate defeated Calderón in his effort to retake the presidency, by 54,931 to 44,438 votes. However, the Republican–Communist coalition retained a majority in the Assembly. Again, there were charges of fraud – on both sides this time. The TNE declared Ulate the winner of the presidential election in February, but on March 1, the new Assembly convened and, at Calderón's request, nullified the presidential election.

A number of attempts were made by members of the TNE, and by Monseñor Sanabria, to effect a compromise solution to the electoral standoff that would be acceptable to both sides (Lehoucq 1991a). But by this time, Figueres had retired to his ranch south of Cartago and was rumored to be assembling an army. When government troops went to investigate the rumor, Figueres attacked them, launching what would be a six-week civil war. With about 600 men, mostly Ulate supporters, Figueres took the towns of San Isidro del General and the port of Limón. By the time he marched on Cartago, there was no resistance; the fighting was over.

The adoption of term limits in Costa Rica

Reform versus retrenchment: The junta and the Constituent Assembly

In May 1948, Figueres assumed the presidency of a junta that governed the country for 18 months, while a Constituent Assembly was elected and rewrote the Constitution. Figueres agreed to oversee the installation of Ulate in the presidency, but a new Legislative Assembly would be elected for the term beginning in 1949. The junta initially ruled the current 1871 Constitution dead, except for the social and individual guarantees, whose current status were largely the product of the Calderón/Picado reforms. The junta's other seminal action was to nationalize Costa Rica's banks – a reform that only now is slowly being dismantled. But on the heels of the junta's early progressive policies came conservative retrenchment, particularly with the election of the Constituent Assembly (Dunkerley 1988).

The Assembly was dominated by Ulate's Partido Unión Nacional (PUN), which held 34 of 45 seats. The Social Democrats (PSD) managed to win only 4 seats, and the remnants of *calderonismo*, reconfigured as the Partido Constitucional (PC), held 6. The *calderonista* weakness may not have accurately represented actual electoral strength in Costa Rica at the time. Calderón himself, along with many Republican and Communist politicians, were in exile. Many Republican supporters, intimidated by the junta's special tribunals to investigate and try members of the fallen regime, withdrew from politics. And Communists were prohibited from participating in electoral politics altogether (interview with Arguedas 1992; Dunkerley 1988; Volio Jimenez 1992). Nevertheless, the important point is that the conservative *ulatistas* were a dominant force as the new Constitution was being written, and they quickly demonstrated their unwillingness to allow the Social Democrat Figueres to dictate the terms on which the new political order would be constructed.

The most important point of difference was over Figueres's move to scrap the 1871 Constitution. Figueres's evident intention, as the bank nationalization and his support for the constitutional social reforms suggest, was to consummate a fundamental change in Costa Rica's political order begun by Calderón in 1940. The PUN constitutional delegates balked, ultimately reversing Figueres's decree and adopting the 1871 charter as the basis for discussion (Asamblea Nacional Constituyente 1951; Dunkerley 1988; Volio Jimenez 1992). But the delegates were not perfectly accommodating to Ulate's wishes either, and decided to weaken the constitutional powers of the presidency as well.[5] These decisions represented less than ideal outcomes for both Figueres and Ulate.

Despite the Social Democrats' numerical weakness in the Constituent Assembly, however, many of the electoral reforms they had initially supported were adopted in the 1949 Constitution with PUN support. Among the most important were:

[5] The key measures here were (1) subjecting presidential emergency power to immediate Assembly approval by two-thirds majority, (2) eliminating the president's veto on the national budget, (3) mandating an eight-year intervening period before an ex-president could serve again, (4) mandating that all conventions and treaties be subject to Assembly approval, (5) explicitly prohibiting the pocket veto and any executive refusal to sign legislation passed over presidential objections, (6) providing for the interpellation and "censure" of cabinet ministers (although censure does not imply sanction, as in parliamentary and president-parliamentary systems). See the earlier discussion of presidential powers.

1. women's suffrage (Art. 93);
2. a new agency, with constitutional status as an independent branch of government (Tribunal Supremo de Elecciones – TSE), to ensure elections free from government influence (Arts. 99–104);
3. public campaign financing for political parties (Art. 96); and
4. the creation of autonomous institutions and a merit-based civil service intended to limit government patronage influence in elections (Titles XIV and XV; Arts. 188–193).

Silence on term limits

The reforms just listed are counted by scholars of Costa Rican political institutions as among the most profound wrought in 1949 (Aguilar Bulgarelli 1986; Muñoz Quesada 1981; Salazar 1981; Ventura Robles 1984); yet remarkably little attention has been given to the electoral reform with which this work is centrally concerned: the prohibition on reelection for members of the Costa Rican Legislative Assembly (Art. 107). So little importance has been attributed to this provision that one scholar was able to write a book modestly entitled *Political Representation*, on the electoral connection between constituents and deputies in the Legislative Assembly, without so much as mentioning the prohibition on reelection (Ventura Robles 1984). Other well-known students of the institution have similarly ignored the importance of term limits (Hernandez Valle 1991; Muñoz Quesada 1981).[6]

Deliberations of the Constituent Assembly

Even more remarkable – and no doubt contributing to the tendency of scholars to ignore the phenomenon – is the fact that the adoption of term limits in Costa Rica sparked so little debate during the Constituent Assembly itself. The format of Assembly elections was debated by the delegates over four days in May and two days in June 1949. The language prohibiting the immediate reelection of deputies was tied from the start with the issue of whether the new Constitution should retain midterm elections in which the Assembly would be renewed by half, as under the 1871 document. The first point, on which all the delegates agreed, was that the no-reelection clause and the midterm clause were separate issues, each critically important in its

---

[6] More recent, and as yet unpublished, work has paid more attention to the effect of Costa Rican term limits on Assembly representation. Volio Guevara (1988) and Casas Zamora and Briceño Fallas (1991) are the best examples. But so far, these works – especially the excellent analysis by Casas Zamora and Briceño Fallas – have not enjoyed circulation outside a small circle of legal and legislative scholars.

own right, and that they should be debated separately so that each could be given proper consideration (May 2 session). This opinion was echoed in *La Prensa Libre* the following day, in Rubén Hernandez Poveda's column, which consistently provided the most thorough journalistic coverage of the Constituent Assembly (Hernandez Poveda 1991).

Despite these noble intentions, the prohibition on reelection was never discussed at any length. Of the four motions originally offered to govern Assembly elections, three explicitly prohibited reelection, differing only on whether there should be midterm elections and how they should be conducted. The fourth made no mention of reelection at all, but its author later made clear that he supported term limits (sessions of May 2 and 5).

When the issue was first raised, PUN delegate Ricardo Esquivel was the only participant even to mention term limits, asserting that "the prohibition on the indefinite reelection of deputies will prevent the establishment in the future of the despicable *"cacique* politics" of the past, for which the 1871 Constitution was largely responsible" (May 2). Those students of the Constituent Assembly who have mentioned term limits at all have affirmed Esquivel's opinion as the rationale for banning immediate reelection (Casas Zamora and Briceño Fallas 1991; Muñoz Quesada 1981; Volio Guevara 1988; interview with Volio Jimenez). All contend that the broad consensus among delegates to prohibit reelection was a reaction to the perceived corruption of the Congress prior to 1948, in which indefinite reelection was allowed. This sentiment was galvanized, of course, by the 1948 Congress's nullification of Ulate's election to the presidency.

Nevertheless, Hernandez Poveda's commentary the day after Esquivel's comments urge that debate on term limits not be framed in the context of past electoral abuses, because with the establishment of the TSE, such abuses should not be possible under the new Constitution. Rather, Hernandez argued that the reelection issue should be considered according to its consistency with democratic theory. Hernandez arrives at the same answer as the constitutional delegates, nonetheless contending that "reelection is contrary to the general principle of democracy, which is the renewal of values, of ideas, and of deeds; democracy is the right of all to participate in public life" (Hernandez Poveda 1991).

A couple of other potential justifications for term limits are also notable only because of their absence from the Constituent Assembly's debate. First, one might have expected adherents of term limits for legislators to point to the existing prohibition on immediate presidential reelection as justification for their position. If term limits are good for presidents, the logic might be, then they are fitting for legislators as well. Second, Mexico had amended its Constitution in 1933 to prohibit the reelection of legislators (Weldon

1994).[7] This precedent, set fairly recently by a prominent neighboring country, might well have been considered relevant for Costa Rica, either in support or opposition to term limits. Yet neither the presidential precedent nor the Mexican precedent surfaces anywhere in the records of the Constituent Assembly nor in accounts of the period.

Once all parties had affirmed the importance of a serious debate over term limits, the question was promptly put aside, never to be raised again. The session of May 3 was devoted mainly to the question of midterm elections. And on May 4, while all debate continued to center on midterm elections, 40 of 45 delegates voted in favor of prohibiting the immediate reelection of *deputies*. Among those who opposed term limits were at least three of the PC delegates. But among the PUN and PSD partisans who had been on the winning side in the Civil War, there was almost uniform agreement (Volio Jimenez 1992). Hernandez Poveda (1991) expressed his approval for the result the next day.

Interestingly, in the same session, PC delegate Celso Gamboa Rodriguez offered a motion to prohibit the immediate election of constitutional delegates to the Legislative Assembly in the elections scheduled for 1949. The motion was attacked by a host of PUN delegates, each of whom prefaced his comments with a defensive denial that any personal interest determined his position. Gamboa's motion was eventually rejected by voice vote, although some PUN delegates supported it (May 4 session). Gamboa himself evidently took the Assembly's decision to heart and went on to win election in 1949 to serve San Jose province as a deputy for the PC.

The debate over midterms continued on May 5, then was put aside, and continued on June 22 and 23. The case for eliminating midterms was that such elections had consistently been manipulated by the government, were too expensive, and disrupted social tranquillity, such that the nation was constantly in the midst of political campaigns. Those who supported midterms dismissed the argument regarding fraud, expressing confidence in the newly founded TSE. They held that midterms served as the only opportunity for citizens to ratify or check the agenda of an administration. Social Democrat Rodrigo Facio Brenes dismissed the "social tranquillity" argument, observing that "politics is the price of democracy" (June 22). And he anticipated a finding not elaborated by North American political science until more than 40 years later, pointing out that midterm elections protect

---

[7] This study does not devote much attention to the Mexican case, because elections in Mexico were not competitive by any stretch of the imagination, until perhaps the late 1980s, and then only in limited cases. Without electoral competition, and with political careers in all institutions so clearly structured by a single party, the Mexican case does not promise to shed much light on the term limits debate currently underway in the United States. Nevertheless, in the Costa Rican context of the 1940s, the Mexican decision to prohibit legislative reelection may well have been both relevant and prominent.

the ability of minority parties to win representation, because in concurrent elections popular attention is focused on the presidential race and the parties of the top presidential contenders (see Shugart 1988).[8]

In the end, midterm elections were rejected, in large part because they failed to gain much support among delegates of the then-dominant PUN. Party leaders sensed a landslide in 1949 and saw no reason to subject the expected mandate to a plebiscite two years hence. But a further rationale was added by PUN delegate Fernando Vargas Fernandez, to the effect that to allow for midterm elections would be to cancel the effect of the prohibition on immediate reelection that had already been adopted. Vargas suggested that ex-deputies would then be able to run again a mere two years after leaving office, which would "practically amount to reelection" (June 23). He goes on to cite broad popular support for term limits, and so concludes that their effect should not be compromised by retaining midterm elections. Vargas Fernandez's comment marked the only discussion of the term limits issue for the duration of the Constituent Assembly – and his premise was that the principle of term limits was a given and that the effect must be protected.

The adoption of term limits: Conclusions

Although it is generally dangerous to base conclusions on a scarcity of data, the virtual absence of debate over prohibiting immediate reelection supports the premise that there existed in 1948 an overwhelming popular consensus in favor of term limits. The primary reason for this consensus was evidently a blanket rejection of the pre-1948 electoral system, which included unlimited reelection, on the part of the PUN and PSD delegates and their supporters. Still, the decision of the Constituent Assembly is extraordinary in that it seems to contradict one of the most hallowed axioms of political scientists: that politicians will never choose rules that will undermine their own career prospects (Geddes 1990b; Mayhew 1974).

Some observers of Costa Rican politics have suggested that the link between personal career interests and reelection may not have been straightforward. Carlos Arguedas suggests that with so many of Costa Rica's career politicians in exile or hiding, many of those who served as delegates to the Constituent Assembly were literally thrust into politics for a one-time stint.

---

[8] Facio's argument drew the rebuttal that midterm elections in which the Legislative Assembly would be renewed by halves should hurt minority parties, because with only half as many seats at stake, district magnitude would effectively be halved as well. Reduced magnitude reduces the proportionality of proportional representation (PR) systems, to the disadvantage of small parties. Both sides of this debate make valid points and demonstrate an admirable degree of sophistication with regard to electoral laws.

The Assembly was their first experience with elected office and the last they would seek, so they genuinely had no political aspirations. Arguedas (1992) describes the public spiritedness of such delegates as "political virginity."

While virginity might characterize some of the constitutional delegates, Arguedas's assessment is at least incomplete. Twenty-nine percent of the delegates served subsequently in the Legislative Assembly as deputies, and 18% had served in Congress previous to the Constituent Assembly. Thus, 40% of the delegates served as deputies apart from their service as delegates.[9] In addition, at least 15% served subsequent to the Constituent Assembly, either as party officers or in posts appointed by the president. In the end, at least 50% of the constitutional delegates held at least one national political office or party office apart from their role of delegate. How many others sought posts unsuccessfully is impossible to determine.

The point is that it is unrealistic to characterize the delegates as devoid of political aspirations. Some may genuinely have been without ambition, but most clearly were not. Moreover, among the PSD – and particularly among those who had begun their political activism through the CEPN – opposition to reelection was based on the belief that term limits ensured more opportunities to open up political careers to young challengers. These PSD members were themselves young, and most had never held elected office. Term limits, by guaranteeing turnover in the legislature, promised greater access – even if only for a limited time – to the Assembly (Volio Jimenez 1992). Thus, the official PSD party position in favor of term limits was linked to the career interests of its members.

Of course, the electoral interests of parties and the career interests of their elected representatives are often directly contradictory, and when such a conflict exists, incumbent politicians tend to sacrifice partisan goals for individual security (Cain 1984). Finally, the Constituent Assembly's decision to allow its members to run for the Legislative Assembly in 1949 is evidence that career interests were being carefully weighed, and that a majority was willing to sanction the reelection of delegates as deputies.

Ultimately, the basis of the Constituent Assembly's decision to ratify term limits cannot be stated conclusively. Assertions of a public consensus to prohibit reelection cannot be gauged without polling data. Party organizations may have supported term limits, but they were likely to meet resistance to this position among delegates to the Constituent Assembly, who expected to be among the first to serve as deputies. Some delegates may indeed have had no political aspirations, and simply favored term limits on principle. But the subsequent career data demonstrates that many of the delegates were

---

[9] Four of those who had served previously also served subsequently. Thus, the total of those who served apart from the Constituent Assembly is not simply the sum of those who served before and after.

politically ambitious, so "political virginity" cannot by itself explain the overwhelming support for term limits among delegates.

Three things, at least, are remarkable about the adoption of term limits by the Constituent Assembly of 1949. First, and most simply, is that the prohibition was passed at all, given that in the most mechanistic way term limits ran contrary to the interests of those who adopted them. Empirically, this result is clearly extraordinary, given the scarcity of term limits on legislators worldwide. Second was the fact that the adoption of such a radical reform followed with virtually no debate or opposition at the time. Third, from the perspective of North American political science in the 1990s, the logic that Costa Ricans relied on in embracing term limits is remarkably familiar. The themes of an electoral system that has been corrupted by incumbents, of opening the system to new ideas and new leaders, and of the need for representatives who have no career aspirations in politics – the fabled citizen-legislator – are among the most familiar sounded by proponents of term limits in the United States in the early 1990s.

Term limits and reform in Costa Rica

The best way to learn how Costa Rican politicians themselves perceive the effects of term limits on political representation is to examine the many efforts made since 1949 to abolish them. The records of such proposals, the arguments made by their proponents and opponents in committee, and their ultimate fate when voted on are all preserved in the Archive of the Legislative Assembly. The patterns of argument, and of the broader reform proposals of which reelection schemes are a part, all provide ample grounds to study how term limits are understood within a system that has employed them for over 40 years.

Any student of constitutional reform must keep two qualifications in mind when considering these records. First, the statements of politicians on the record cannot necessarily be taken at face value. As the fates of these reforms demonstrate, political ambition and personal career interests drove much of the support and opposition generated by reform proposals. Yet those who debated and voted on the reforms scarcely mention these concerns. Second, archival materials on the reform of term limits in Costa Rica overwhelmingly present the case for doing away with the prohibition on reelection and provide much less material in support of the post-1949 status quo. The reason is simple enough: any reform, by definition, attacks the status quo. Those who advocated reforms sought to make their cases in the proposals, in the committees, and on the floor, as the reforms were being considered. Supporters of the status quo reacted when threatened, or ignored the reformers altogether when possible. As a result, the voice that was entirely missing from Costa Rican political debate in 1949 – that which opposes term limits – is quite clear in reform efforts. The case for term limits, on the other hand, still needs to be pieced together largely from the structure and fate of the reforms presented.

Rotation-style term limits: The effect on reelection rates

Costa Rican term limits are not blanket prohibitions against all reelection of deputies to the Legislative Assembly; they prohibit immediate reelection. Former deputies can be reelected once a four-year period has passed. Nevertheless, since 1949, the vast majority of those who have served in the Assembly have not been reelected, primarily because of term limits.

The data since 1949 are most clear. Of all those who have been elected as deputies to the Legislative Assembly since that year, 87% were not reelected, 11% were reelected one time, and only 2% were reelected twice. No one has served more than three terms in the Legislative Assembly under the Constitution of 1949. From this, it is clear that a career in the Legislative Assembly itself is not a reasonable expectation for an aspiring Costa Rican politician.

Of course, the effects of the 1949 term limits on assembly careers can only be assessed in comparison with reelection rates prior to 1949. Here, it is slightly harder to evaluate the data. I have examined rosters of each Congress elected from 1920 to 1946, including 326 different deputies. Over this time, those elected to Congress served only one term in about 60% of cases, two terms in about 23%, three terms in about 12%, four terms in about 4%, and in two cases, five terms.[10] Compared with reelection rates in the 80–90% range, such as those in the post-WWII U.S. House, this reelection rate is not inordinately high. On the other hand, with four-year terms, 40% of those who could secure election at all could look forward to at least eight years in Congress. And in the 1940s prior to the Civil War, the probability of serving more than two terms was on the rise as well.

A subsequent chapter will explore in detail the reelection rates and career paths of Costa Rican deputies before and after 1949. For now, the bottom line is that the imposition of term limits cut the prospects for any reelection for deputies to one-third their previous level and virtually eliminated the possibility of serving more than two terms. Since 1949, as a result of rotation-style term limits, it has not been realistic for a Costa Rican politician to think of building a career in the Legislative Assembly alone.

Since term limits were adopted in Costa Rica, there have been eight proposals to reform Article 107 of the Constitution to allow for immediate

[10] More precise data, and graphic displays of patterns of reelection rates, are presented in Chapter 3.

reelection of deputies. Of these eight, only one was limited strictly to ending term limits. The others have included combinations of a host of other electoral reforms, including reinstating midterm elections, prohibiting reelection for ex-presidents, extending the terms of presidents and deputies, expanding the size of the Legislative Assembly, or reducing district magnitude – even to single-member districts. Because other items have been on the agenda, the ultimate failure of these efforts to allow reelection cannot be wholly attributed in every case to support for term limits. On the other hand, in some cases, elements of the reform package were passed, while term limits themselves have remained impervious to attack. The reasons for this are spelled out next.

How reformers have seen term limits

A number of themes surface consistently in arguments to repeal Costa Rican term limits. Prohibiting immediate reelection is portrayed as an accident of history without theoretical foundation, as inhibiting the accumulation of legislative experience, as undermining legislative productivity in both the first and last years of each Legislative Assembly, as deterring talented individuals from serving in the Assembly, and as undermining the responsibility of deputies to their constituents. I address each of these issues in turn.

Historical accident. Reform proposals have invariably attributed the adoption of term limits in Costa Rica as the product of a unique historical circumstance, rather than recognizing any general justification on democratic principle for prohibiting the reelection of legislators. Like historians of the period, reformers have pointed to the abuses of the electoral process in the 1940s, culminating in the annulment of the 1948 presidential election, as the only basis of the decision to adopt term limits. Once the threat of such abuses is removed, so too is the justification for prohibiting reelection. In 1960, would-be reformers wrote, "The fact that in other times cacique politics endangered democratic stability should not be considered a threat to our public life today, because of the advances of recent years in our civic institutions and the ability of our political parties to choose candidates for deputy through internal partisan assemblies" (ALCR, Expediente #A-15-E-2154).[11] Similar references to the extraordinary conditions of 1949, hostility

---

[11] Assembly debates on constitutional reforms and on legislation are referred to by their file (*expediente,* in Spanish) number in the Archive of the Legislative Assembly (e.g., A-15-E-2154). Subsequently, citations to files from the Legislative Assembly will be referred as "ALCR Exp." followed by the file number. In the References section of this book, the files are listed under "[ALCR] Asamblea Legislativa de Costa Rica, Constitutional and Electoral Reform Proposals."

toward the *caciques* who perpetuated their tenures in Congress through fraud, and the lack of theoretical basis for term limits were included in reform proposals in 1971 (ALCR, Exp. A-25-E-5803), in 1980 (ALCR, Exp. 8484, original proposal), and by Dr. Ruben Hernandez Valle, in hearings before the Special Committee studying reform in November 1987 (ALCR, Exp. 10,541).

Legislative experience. An even more consistent theme of reformers is the need for a parliamentary career, to allow deputies to gain legislative experience. Here, Costa Rican reformers generally sound a theme common to much of the literature on the U.S. Congress – that policy making has become increasingly complex in the second half of the 20th century, and that the job of legislator correspondingly requires more specialization and expertise.[12] Costa Rican opponents of term limits generally suggest that the increased size of the Costa Rican state has correspondingly increased the need for expertise among legislators, while at the same time, the actual legislative expertise of those who serve as deputies has been hamstrung by term limits. The majority committee report on a 1964 proposal to allow reelection states:

Today, the job of deputy has become highly specialized. The current organization of the Assembly tends to stimulate activity by legislators on specific issues, such that the obstacle to reelection causes the country to lose valuable experience accumulated in legislative work. It is precisely at the moment when the deputy has gained a thorough understanding of the country's problems, and his own jurisdiction and capacities, that he is compelled to abandon his post according to the current constitutional provision. (ALCR, Exp. A-18-E-4131, November 6 hearing)

The same criticism is leveled in every reform proposal, and indeed, by every academic author who has addressed the issue of term limits at all (Casas Zamora, Volio Guevara, Muñoz Quesada). The 1964 proposal, in addition, draws an interesting parallel between service in the Legislative Assembly and the Civil Service, contending that since a merit-based Civil Service was instituted by the 1949 Constitution, longer tenure among employees had improved the performance of the state bureaucracy. The same principle would apply to the Legislative Assembly, if deputies were allowed careers in the institution (ALCR, Exp. A-18-E-4131, original proposal).

---

[12] The "increasingly complex world" argument is made so frequently, and asserted with such self-assuredness, that actually substantiating it is usually regarded by its adherents as unnecessary. In the U.S. case, increasing complexity is credited with necessitating a more elaborate committee system in Congress and increased division of labor among representatives (Polsby 1968). However, there is no shortage of other, more compelling theories for the development of the modern U.S. congressional committee system (Cox and McCubbins 1993; Fiorina 1977; Krehbiel 1992; Mayhew 1974; Rohde 1991).

Learning curves and job searches. In addition to the general arguments about experience and expertise, opponents of term limits contend that because the entire cohort of deputies is turned out of the Assembly each term, and because fewer than 15% of their replacements generally have served previously, the first year of each Assembly is lost to organizing the Assembly, as well as learning the policy issues and the legislative process (ALCR, Exp. A-15-E-2154 1960; A-25-E-5803 1971; 10,541 1987; 11,407 1991). Where 87% of deputies have no legislative experience, this criticism of term limits in the Costa Rican context is not surprising. And for students of term limits in the U.S. context, it should not appear troubling. Where only a fraction of the assembly is turned out of office each term, there likely will never be such a dearth of experienced legislators.

More relevant, and provocative, for the U.S. context, however, is the argument that legislative performance, as well as the incentives of individual deputies, are compromised during the last year in each four-year assembly term, because deputies are preoccupied with securing postassembly employment. The Special Committee report in favor of a 1980 proposal to do away with term limits states:

> The current situation is that deputies attend to their duties relatively well during the first three years of their terms, and then ignore their legislative work in order to look for a position to replace their current post in the Assembly; in every Assembly, the fourth year is that in which the institution functions with the greatest difficulty. (ALCR, Exp. 8484, minority report)

The failure of deputies to work on behalf of their constituents as the end of their term approaches is a manifestation of the last-term problem, which has interested game theorists, economists, and political scientists alike (Becker and Stigler 1974; Lott 1987; Ordeshook 1986; Zupan 1990). The crux of the problem is to ensure accountability and responsiveness of agents to their principals – a challenge that grows when the principal–agent relationship is soon to end.[13] Costa Rican reformers see the solution in simply allowing reelection, because "a parliamentary career will make the deputies see the need for staying in touch with their constituents and tending to the job with which they have been entrusted" (ALCR, Exp. 8484, committee report; see also ALCR, Exp. 10,541, original proposal). Costa Rican opponents of term limits here sound much like James Madison (Hamilton, Jay, and Madison 1961), as he affirms the need for frequent elections for citizens to control their elected representatives.

---

[13] In a later chapter, I find evidence that members of the U.S. House of Representatives who leave their seats to run for statewide office alter their voting patterns on floor roll call votes, shifting ideologically toward the position of their state party cohort.

Discouraging talent. A final complaint lodged against Costa Rican term limits by those who would abolish them is that term limits inhibit talented people from serving in the Legislative Assembly. Testifying before an Assembly committee studying term limits reform, Hernandez Valle asked, "Why is it that many capable people are unwilling to dedicate themselves to [the job of deputy]? Because they know that if they have to abandon it in four years, when they return to their old career they'll find themselves economically ruined" (ALCR, Exp. 10,541, committee report). According to Hernandez Valle, the ideal of a citizen-legislator, who does not depend on politics for a career, deters good people from entering politics at all. But this objection raises the further question of whether term limits in Costa Rica imply the absence of political careers. It is certainly true that term limits have made Assembly careers virtually impossible in Costa Rica. But in a later chapter, I show that the possibility of a career built on political appointments remains a possibility for ex-deputies.

Term limits pose the question of whether legislators whose careers in their current institution are over, but whose political careers are not over, make significant changes in the principals to whom they are responsive. It is precisely this phenomenon that Miguel Angel Rodriguez Echeverría describes when he contends that Costa Rican deputies, especially toward the end of the assembly term, cannot speak on behalf of their constituents because of their dependence on their parties for their career prospects (ALCR, Exp. 10,541, committee hearings). Rodriguez's statement is equally true in any closed-list system, like Venezuela's, for example, in which party leaders control ballot access. But Rodriguez favors the creation of single-member districts for half the seats in the Assembly, in order to strengthen the link between legislators and constituents. His concern is that even single-member districts would not strengthen this bond in the presence of term limits. The evidence presented in Chapters 4 and 5 supports Rodriguez's conclusions.

The fate of term limit reform efforts

To abolish term limits in Costa Rica would require a constitutional amendment, which in turn requires a two-thirds vote in the Legislative Assembly in two consecutive ordinary sessions (two years in a row) (Art. 195). This requirement of extraordinary majority, coupled with Costa Rica's competitive electoral environment, has meant that term limit reforms would require the support of a multiparty coalition. And indeed, reform has not been the domain of any particular party or bloc. Moreover the fate of term limit reforms has evidently hung on the manner in which they affect the career prospects of those who would vote on them. I examine each of these points in turn.

Table 2.2. *Vote to eliminate term limits, Costa Rican*
Legislative Assembly, November 11, 1961

Party	Yes	No
PLN	10	8
PUN	5	5
PR (Partido Republicano)	2	6
Independent	0	3
Total	17	22

Patterns of partisan support. Of the eight proposed reforms to eliminate term limits in Costa Rica, only two have been voted on in plenary session of the Legislative Assembly – and only one of those by roll call vote. Thus, it is not an entirely straightforward process to measure the levels and sources of support for reform. Nevertheless, by examining cosponsorships of reform proposals and committee reports, it is possible to draw some conclusions about partisan support for term limits.

First, the reform agenda has belonged to no one party alone, and has generally cut directly across partisan lines. The first proposed reform was subject to roll call vote. The partisan split is listed in Table 2.2. There is no pattern of partisan support here at all. On some subsequent proposals, cosponsorship was apparently partisan, but the records of debate among deputies in committee and in plenary session, and the reform proposals themselves, contain little reference to partisan positions on the question of term limits.

The 1964 reform was cosponsored by 9 PLN, 2 Partido Republicans (PR), and 1 PUN deputies and enjoyed unanimous support among the 5 members – from all three parties – of the Special Committee reporting on it. But it was withdrawn from the floor agenda in 1965 for lack of support. Similarly, a 1971 proposal was cosponsored by 25 of 32 PLN deputies, by 12 of 22 Partido de Unificación (PUNIF) deputies, and by both UAC (Unión Agrícola Cartaginés) deputies. The 39 cosponsors were more than enough to amend the Constitution, but for reasons discussed later, this cross-party support disappeared. The reform was rejected on the floor of the Assembly, but without a roll call vote. Proposals in 1966, 1974, and 1991 likewise have been cosponsored by coalitions of deputies – so far without having sustained sufficient cross-partisan support to have an impact. Likewise, a purely PLN proposal (all 25 deputies cosponsoring) from 1980, and a PUSC proposal (11 of 25 cosponsoring) from 1986 have languished in committee and remain pending before the Assembly.

The point is that term limits reform has not been an issue that divides

Costa Rican parties from each other; but neither has it been an issue capable of mobilizing and sustaining broad support among deputies. The latter point, like the initial adoption of term limits, presents a puzzle. Repealing limits would appear to be in the career interests of incumbent deputies. If reform is not a partisan issue, then why have term limits not been abolished?

Grandfather clauses and self-interested deputies. Incumbent Costa Rican deputies have faced a dilemma in not wanting to appear to be legislating on their own behalf, but simultaneously not wanting to shoot their careers in the collective foot. Reform proposals that disadvantage incumbents have uniformly failed to gain widespread support. Other proposals that would advantage incumbents have generated initial enthusiasm among deputies, then been attacked as self-interested, and when amended in response to these criticisms, have been abandoned for lack of support.[14]

The key factors influencing levels of support for term limit reforms are the eligibility of incumbent deputies for reelection and public skepticism about the motives of those who support reform. Faced with criticisms against those who would reform the system to their own advantage, those intent on abolishing term limits have at times included a grandfather clause in their reforms, which would exempt incumbent deputies – those who would pass the reforms – from eligibility for immediate reelection. To adopt this clause, however, would pose a double obstacle for deputies who seek careers in the Legislative Assembly. The first obstacle is that the prohibition on their own immediate reelection would remain in place. Second, if deputies aspire to run for reelection four years hence, they would be challenging the first cohort of incumbents who were, in fact, eligible for reelection.

Not surprisingly, deputies have proved unwilling to confer such an advantage on those who would prove to be future political competitors. In order to deflect criticisms about reformer self-interest, both the 1964 and 1966 reforms included grandfather clauses exempting incumbents from eligibility for reelection (ALCR, Exp. A-18-E-4131; ALCR, Exp. A-29-E-6304; Arguedas 1992). In both cases, the proposal to eliminate term limits did not survive committee review and never reached a vote in plenary session.

---

[14] The three most recent reforms, introduced in 1980, 1987, and 1991, had neither failed nor succeeded in the Legislative Assembly as of 1992 – each was still pending. Each also proposed a dual system for electing deputies, by which part of the Assembly would be elected by PR from nationwide lists, while the rest would be elected in either single-member districts, two-member districts, or by PR in provinces, as they currently are. In each case, the proposed reform would increase the size of the Assembly. In the first two cases – the 1980 and 1987 reforms – none of the current provincial seats would remain after the Assembly was restructured, and there is no mention of prohibiting incumbents from running for the newly created seats. Nor in the 1991 reform is there any prohibition on incumbents being reelected immediately, either to the remaining provincial seats or to the new nationwide seats.

Debate over the career interests of deputies and public backlash against self-serving reforms was most explicit in 1971. The 1971 proposal was introduced by Deputy Edwin Muñoz (PLN), who explicitly stated his pledge not to accept reelection in 1974 if it passed (ALCR, Exp. A-25-E-5803, original proposal). The reform as initially proposed, however, would not have legally prohibited incumbents from immediate reelection. Not surprisingly, initial support was more widespread than for any of the other proposals to do away with term limits: 40 of 57 deputies initially cosponsored the bill – surpassing the two-thirds majority necessary for constitutional amendment.

The plan was immediately attacked, both in the press and within the Assembly, as self-serving. In a floor debate on November 28, 1972, Deputy Fernandez Morales offers a remarkably frank explanation for the fate of term limit reforms, both past and present:

A number of times since 1949, deputies have tried to amend the Constitution to create a parliamentary career, abolishing the prohibition on reelection for deputies. Other reform proposals have met hostile responses because they have suggested allowing reelection for deputies, but beginning with the following Assembly; that is, preventing the incumbent deputies from benefiting from the reform. I think that for this reason, the reforms have been rejected.

Nevertheless, Fernandez Morales goes on to argue, "I do not believe that anyone should legislate on his own behalf, nor that the beneficiaries of such a reform should be the incumbent deputies. If a reform is presented that excludes incumbent deputies from eligibility for reelection, I shall gladly vote for it" (ALCR, Exp. A-25-E-5803).

Under attack as self-serving, the proposal remained in committee for almost two years. By May 1973, however, even a positive vote by the current Legislative Assembly could not have enacted the reform soon enough that incumbent deputies could have benefited. Constitutional amendments must be passed in two successive years, and by the time a year passed, a new Legislative Assembly would have been elected. As with the earlier, grand-fathered proposals, to pass the reform at that point could only have benefited the next cohort of deputies, whom the current incumbents would have to challenge to gain subsequent reelection. Deputy Lacle Castro, apparently misreading the problems now confronting the reform, understood the principal difficulty to be how to explain to the public that reform was for the good of the country:

I am aware that the Legislative Assembly is subject to permanent attacks on the part of certain public opinion leaders. And although this reform, if approved, would not benefit incumbent deputies, because it would have to be approved by the next legislature, I have the feeling that if we approve the reform without a clear enough explanation to the country that incumbents do not stand to gain, there are those who will attack the Assembly as scandalous. (ALCR, Exp. A-25-E-5803, session of May 23, 1973)

Lacle urged deputies to take pains to make it clear that their support for the reform could not possibly be based on self-interest. But the point was moot. Now that the reform would help only future deputies, and likely hurt incumbents, support withered. On June 25, the proposal that was initially cosponsored by 70% of the Assembly was rejected on the floor in a voice vote.

None of the other reforms offered has provided as explicit a debate over deputy career interests as that of 1971, but there are some points worth noting. The 1960 proposal initially included a standard grandfather clause postponing eligibility for immediate reelection until the next cohort (ALCR, Exp. A-15-E-2154, original proposal). But in committee, this provision was quietly amended, so that neither would the subsequent cohort (to be elected for the 1962–1966 period) be eligible for immediate reelection. Eligibility would begin with those elected in 1966. But this cohort could include the very incumbents voting on the reform! This clever twist gained the 1960 proposal some support, but not enough to carry the floor vote, in which it was rejected, 17 to 22 (ALCR, Exp. A-15-E-2154, session of November 11, 1961).

Finally, the 1974 reform proposal, while not spurring any serious debate in the Assembly, provides stark evidence of the degree to which the pursuit of individual career interests can drive the reform process. The 1974 plan, which would have divided the country into 57 single-member districts while also eliminating term limits, was written by Deputy Juan Guillermo Brenes Castillo, of the Unión Agrícola Cartaginés (UAC). The UAC has been the most successful provincial- (as opposed to national-) level party in Costa Rica since the Civil War. Its support base, concentrated in a few of Cartago Province's counties, has provided the UAC with one seat in four of five assemblies since 1974, and the UAC deputies in turn have worked single-mindedly to secure public works projects for their counties, and to provide constituent services.[15] The UAC's particularistic brand of politics is better suited to cultivating support in a system that rewards deputies for cultivating strong personal reputations (Chapter 1) than in Costa Rica's closed-list system. Moreover, Brenes Castillo has held strong personal control over the party since its inception, serving as its sole deputy twice, while his nephew served in an interim Assembly. In short, Brenes Castillo would benefit by decreasing district magnitude (M) in Costa Rica's system, and so increasing the value of his personal reputation among constituents. Not surprisingly,

---

[15] The UAC's peculiar brand of localistic politics within a PR system is discussed further in Chapter 4. For now, the point is that UAC deputies have acted as completely nonideological vote traders, with the exclusive goal of securing pork for their client support base.

then, his first significant act on being elected in 1974 was to initiate a term limit reform designed to secure this.

Initially, his proposal attracted some PLN and Socialist support (ALCR, Exp. A-30-E-6566). After its introduction, however, two of the original PLN signatories petitioned the president of the Assembly to remove their names as cosponsors, claiming that Brenes Castillo had requested and secured their support for a reform solely to abolish term limits, but had not allowed them time to read in its entirety the document he ultimately submitted. They had not known they were cosponsoring a proposal for single-member districts and had no intention of supporting Brenes Castillo's ploy (ALCR, Exp. A-30-E-6566, October 29, 1975). The two deputies' names were withdrawn from the proposal, which subsequently was tabled without ever being assigned to committee.

Term limit reform efforts: Conclusions

The efforts to eliminate term limits in Costa Rica do not help much to resolve the puzzle of why the provision was adopted in the first place. But they do provide a side to the debate that was entirely absent in 1949: criticisms of term limits. Once again, the arguments mirror many of those currently being offered in the United States by those opposed to term limits. Costa Rican critics argue that the prohibition on immediate reelection was a drastic measure, aimed at a symptom of what was wrong with the Costa Rican Congress until 1948, not the cause. These critics contend that term limits perpetuate a lack of legislative experience that makes the Legislative Assembly slow to act and less productive than it might be. The critics suggest that the performance of Costa Rican deputies is compromised, especially as their terms draw to a close, by their search for post-Assembly employment. And the critics argue that by making a parliamentary career impossible, term limits deter talented persons from entering politics.

These criticisms have been leveled by those who would reform the Costa Rican Constitution to eliminate term limits. By and large, their charges have not been answered directly by opponents of reform. Moreover, reform and opposition to reform have not been the domains of any party in particular. Rather, the factor that has most consistently shaped the fate of reform efforts has been the career interests of those who would vote on the reforms: the deputies to the Legislative Assembly.

Venezuela

The overview of Venezuelan political institutions and electoral reforms parallels that of Costa Rica, and the focus is on two points. The first is to underscore the similarities between Costa Rica and Venezuela. The second is to highlight the absence of term limits from the Venezuelan reform agenda.

Party power versus presidential power

A number of studies of Venezuelan politics characterize the presidency as a particularly strong office (Kelley 1973, 1986; Levine 1973). In particular, scholars frequently note the dominance of the presidency over Congress in Venezuela (Vanderdijs and Torres 1981). Yet the foundation of this alleged dominance is more frequently asserted than explained. David Myers states that "the president has complete authority within the national executive, which receives an upper hand in dealings with congress" (1973: 42). He goes on to list the command of the military, control over the bureaucracy, and the appointment of governors, as critical presidential powers in this regard.[16] It is not clear how any of these authorities offer presidents advantages over Congress in legislating.

Those who attribute great legislative strength to the Venezuelan presidency frequently fail to distinguish the constitutional authorities vested in the office from the influence of party leaders over legislators in Venezuela. In fact, the constitutional authority of the Venezuelan president over legislation is relatively limited. Presidential vetoes can delay passage of legislation for up to 14 days, but can be overridden by a simple majority in each house of Congress – the same majority that passed the legislation initially (Constitution of Venezuela, Art. 173). The Constitution does not give the presidency clear authority to legislate by decree, as is found in some other presidential systems, as in Brazil and Colombia (Power 1995).[17] Congress may choose to delegate such authority, but only by majority vote; and of course the lack of an effective veto means such decree authority can be taken away through the same process by which it is given (Carey and Shugart 1995). In short, the Venezuelan president's constitutional authority over legislation is even more constrained than the relatively weak Costa Rican

---

[16] Myers also points to the president's authority to suspend civil liberties in times of emergency. However, he fails to note that this authority cannot be exercised without majority support in Congress. Moreover, it is not clear how much this authority has to do with executive dominance in the field of legislation. In addition, although Venezuelan presidents appointed state governors at the time Myers wrote, since 1988 governors have been chosen by popular vote.

[17] Although legislative decree authority is not clearly bestowed on the president in the Constitution, and generally must be delegated by Congress, presidents have at times exercised emergency powers in manners that appear to be unconstitutional and contrary to congressional preferences. In some cases, Congress has overturned such presidential actions. In at least one recent case involving a suspension of property rights by President Caldera in 1994, however, the president has ruled by decree over congressional opposition (Crisp 1995).

president, who at least retains substantial veto authority over nonbudgetary legislation.

This is not to say that all Venezuelan presidents are politically ineffectual. However, their influence is derived as much from their position as national party leaders as from the formal powers of the presidency. The link between party power and presidential power, best elaborated in Coppedge's (1994) excellent work, is twofold. In the first place, presidents are the most visible representatives of their party in Congress, whose performance is identified with, and judged in light of, presidential performance. More directly, however, presidents' influence over policy derives from their position on the national executive committee of their party. Executive committee power, in turn, hinges on the ability to control recruitment, nominations, and list positions of candidates for political office, not only at the national level, but down to the state and municipal levels as well. It is important to note that the position of presidents on their party's national executive committee is an empirical regularity, not an inherent characteristic of the office.[18] Thus, a good deal of what has conventionally been perceived as presidential power is the product of the extreme centralization of authority within Venezuelan parties (Coppedge 1994).

Because the power of party leaders is so important, Venezuelan presidents whose parties hold majorities in Congress have been far more effective than those who face opposition majorities. Majority presidents have enjoyed consistent congressional support for their legislative proposals. Three Venezuelan presidents have enjoyed majority partisan support in both chambers of Congress. In all three cases, Congress has delegated to these presidents the authority to legislate on economic policy by decree: to Betancourt in 1961, Perez in 1974, and Luscinchi in 1984.[19] Moreover, minority presidents have faced intransigent opposition to their proposed legislative programs in Congress (Martz 1980). Coppedge notes that the majority congressional opposition to the first Caldera government not only legislated over the

---

[18] The exception that proves the rule here was the election of Rafael Caldera to the presidency in 1993. Caldera, who had served previously as president (1969–1974) under the Comité de Organización Política Electoral Independiente (COPEI) banner, ran outside the two traditional parties in 1993. Moreover, stormy relations between Caldera and the Congress in the first year of his term support the proposed connection between legislative compliance and presidential dominance of the national executive committee of a major party.

[19] Until 1993, no minority president had been given this authority by Congress (Gabaldón and Oberto 1985). Moreover, the nonpartisan, caretaker president, Ramón Velazquez, could be seen as having majority support, given that he was the consensus choice of both the Acción Democrática (AD) and COPEI to replace impeached President Carlos Andres Perez. Under this interpretation, the only four presidents to have bicameral majority support received delegated decree authority. The only exception to this pattern, then, would be the delegation of decree authority to President Caldera in 1994. Crisp (1995) explains this anomaly by the extreme fragmentation of the congressional party system in the wake of the 1993 electoral realignment in Venezuela.

president's ineffectual veto, but removed the president's powers of judicial appointment as well, giving them to a special panel dominated by opposition parties (Coppedge 1989; see also Blank 1980; Kelley 1977). In the end, congressional majorities in Venezuela have an unrestrained ability to legislate.

The electoral system

Beginning during a three-year experiment with electoral democracy in the 1940s, Venezuela's congressional elections have been conducted by proportional representation in statewide districts (Brewer-Carías 1989). The system in place through 1988, established by the Suffrage Act of 1959, has provided for representation in the Congress that closely approximated proportionality to the nationwide congressional vote. The large magnitude of Venezuala's electoral districts contributes to this result. But the critical factor is that after seats are allocated in each state, nationwide seats are allocated to each party that wins at least 0.55% of the nationwide vote, to compensate for deviations from proportionality generated at the state level (Taagepera and Shugart 1989).

Venezuela's system provides for somewhat greater proportionality to the nationwide vote than Costa Rica's, but the similarities between the systems are more striking than the differences. Like Costa Rica, shortly after the instauration of the current regime, Venezuela established a national electoral commission, the Supreme Electoral Council (CSE), to appoint local electoral officials, distribute ballots, oversee polling, count votes, and arbitrate disputes over electoral practices. The most important similarity between the systems, however, is that both countries use closed, blocked lists to elect legislators. Voters choose among party lists, slates of candidates selected by the parties. Voters cannot add names to the lists, nor can they alter the list position of the candidates. Thus, the probability of candidates winning seats in the Venezuelan assembly is determined primarily by their list position, which in turn is determined wholly by national party leaders. In both countries, party leaders exercise strict control over access to ballots, votes are pooled across entire parties, and voters indicate a single preference for a political party in legislative elections. Moreover, the mean district magnitude (M) in each country is about the same – 8.1 in Costa Rica and 8.7 in Venezuela.

The centralization of authority in the national party leadership in drawing up party lists has been noted by virtually every scholar of Venezuelan electoral politics. The 1959 Suffrage Act has a section entitled "Nominations," but that section does not actually stipulate any procedures governing how nominations or lists are to be made (Wells 1980: 43). The result is that the parties can establish their own rules for list formation without legal constraints; and in fact the national party committees of all major parties reserve the prerogative of ordering all lists (Brewer-Carías 1989; Rachadell 1991). The result of this system is extraordinarily strong party discipline in Congress (Coppedge 1994).

Organization of the Congress

Studies of Venezuelan politics, like those of virtually all Latin American systems, have paid remarkably little attention to the internal organization of Congress. The unifying theme throughout this literature is acknowledgment of the remarkable strength of the national party leadership, and the corresponding lack of independence on the part of individual legislators (Brewer-Carías 1989; Coppedge 1994; COPRE 1990a, 1990b; Rachadell 1991). The basis of discipline is the party's centralized control over drawing up ballot lists, not only for the national Congress, but also for the state legislatures. Politicians at any level who value the prospect of a future in the party have no option but to obey the directives of the central leadership, or their careers will be terminated (Myers 1973 and 1986). The implication of this for voting in Congress itself is that parties reliably vote as unified blocs. Individual legislators almost never cast votes in dissent of the rest of their caucus. One manifestation of this is that roll call votes are almost never needed, despite the size of the institution (Gabaldón and Oberto 1985). Coppedge's (1994) account of congressional floor proceedings is as follows:

The normal procedure in the Congress is for the Speaker to have a bill read; debate is opened, at which time one designated spokesman for each party states his party's position on the bill; the Speaker then closes debate with the ritual statement, "Deputies who are in favor of approving [this bill], please indicate it with the customary sign"; and without counting votes, often without even looking up, he brings down his gavel and announces, "Approved." There is no need to count votes, because everyone knows that the votes would reflect exactly the relative sizes of the party delegations present. (p. 24)

In addition to the consensus on strong party discipline and the resources available to party leaders, however, scholars have noted the relative lack of resources available to other elements of the Venezuelan Congress: committees and individual legislators. Each house of Congress relies on a permanent committee system, by which legislation is reviewed and reported to the full chamber. Committees meet regularly, generally once each week while Congress is in session. But those who examine the actual performance of committees uniformly note their lack of staff and resources (Gabaldón and Oberto 1985, vol. 1; Kelley 1986). Within the AD at least, committee assignments are controlled entirely by the party's national executive committee, rather than by parliamentary party leaders; and committees follow executive committee guidelines in writing legislation (Coppedge 1994). Moreover, even if members of a certain committee were inclined to act, insufficient staff resources place committees at an informational disadvantage relative to central party leaders and executive ministries in terms of negotiating the details of legislation (Gabaldón and Oberto 1985: vol. 2). As a result, most substantive policy making is done not in legislative committee, but by party officers.

The same observation has been made with respect to individual legislators. Apart from party leaders and committee chairpersons, less than 20% of Venezuelan members of Congress are provided any office space or staff support (Gabaldón and Oberto 1985: vol. 1). This is in sharp contrast to Costa Rica, where every legislator has a private office in the Legislative Assembly.

A brief overview of the organization of the Venezuelan Congress, then, complements the image projected by the electoral system – that of strong central party control over rank-and-file politicians. The root of this central authority is the leadership's control over political careers. But centralization manifests itself as well in the near monopoly over information and physical resources by which politicians might exercise individual initiative.

The party system

Venezuela's party system has followed a developmental path similar to Costa Rica's in the period following the establishment of the current regime. After initial domination by the parties that founded the new regime, Venezuela experienced an increase in the effective number of parties in the system, followed by a steady trend toward the dominance of the system by two catch-all parties (see Tables 2.3 and 2.4).

In 1958, the parties that had been most prominent in opposition to the dictatorship of Marcos Perez Jimenez dominated both presidential and congressional voting. The fractionalization of the party system grew in the 1963 and 1968 elections for two reasons. First, some parties – most prominently the AD – suffered internal divisions. Second, the major parties in Venezuela had initially agreed to a coalition government, in order to moderate the stakes of political competition during the transition to democracy. Both President Betancourt and President Leoni governed with multiparty cabinets. When multiple parties had the prospect of gaining cabinet posts, there was little disincentive to cast an assembly vote for a party that was not a serious contender for the presidency. And in 1963 and 1968, the effective number of Venezuelan parties at the congressional level multiplied. But following the 1968 elections, COPEI President Rafael Caldera opted

Table 2.3. Percentage of seats won in Venezuelan Chamber of Deputies

Year	President	AD	COPEI	URD	MAS	Others
1958	AD	57(73)	15(19)	26(33)	—	3(4)
1963	AD	37(65)	23(40)	16(29)	—	24(43)
1968	COPEI	31(66)	28(59)	8(18)	—	33(71)
1973	AD	51 (102)	32(64)	3(5)	5(9)	10(20)
1978	COPEI	44(88)	42(84)	2(3)	6(11)	7(13)
1983	AD	57 (113)	30(60)	2(3)	5(10)	7(14)
1988	AD	48(98)	33(67)	1(2)	9(19)	9(18)

Note: Number of seats is in parentheses.

Table 2.4. Percentage of seats won by parties in Venezuelan Senate

Year	President	AD	COPEI	URD	MAS	Others
1958	AD	63(32)	12(6)	21(11)	—	4(2)
1963	AD	49(22)	18(8)	16(7)	—	18(8)
1968	COPEI	37(19)	31(16)	6(3)	—	27(14)
1973	AD	60(28)	28(13)	2(1)	4(2)	6(3)
1978	COPEI	48(21)	48(21)	0(0)	5(2)	0(0)
1983	AD	64(28)	32(14)	0(0)	5(2)	0(0)
1988	AD	48(22)	43(20)	0(0)	7(3)	2(1)

Note: Number of seats is in parentheses.

for a one-party cabinet. With that precedent established, voters began to cast congressional votes increasingly for the parties that are competitive at the presidential level as well. Between 1973 and 1993, the Venezuelan party system at the congressional level moved steadily toward dominance by the AD and COPEI, the two parties that also dominated presidential elections.

The 1993 elections were an electoral earthquake, at both the congressional and presidential levels. Rafael Caldera, having abandoned the COPEI and been supported by a coalition of opposition parties, captured the presidency. The AD and COPEI *combined* took only 53% of the Chamber of Deputies and 61% of the Senate, with most of the rest of the seats scattered among the parties under Caldera's umbrella. It is too soon to tell whether the 1993 election marked a single aberration or a long-term realignment of Venezuela's party system – and for the purposes of this study, it does not much matter. It is the long period of party system stability, during which legislators were able to develop expectations about the outcomes of electoral competition and the prospects for building political careers in Congress, that is important here.

Electoral reforms

For the purposes of this book, the principal observation regarding electoral reform in Venezuela is the complete absence of term limits from the agenda. This is not to imply that Venezuelan citizens, politicians, and scholars have been completely satisfied with the system's performance, nor that reformers have been inactive. Significant reforms have recently been adopted in response to persistent criticisms of the centralization of power in Venezuelan parties.

Whereas the central grievance of Costa Rican reformers in 1949 targeted the level of fraud by the pre–Civil War parties, Venezuelan elections have widely been acknowledged as largely free of corruption. Perhaps for this reason, there has been no impetus to prohibit reelection for legislators. However, there has been widespread dissatisfaction with the complete control over legislators exercised by the national party leadership, and the corresponding lack of responsiveness of legislators to the state constituencies that elect them (see especially Brewer-Carías 1989; COPRE 1988). This dissatisfaction has been expressed not only among academics and political insiders. The clearest signal was certainly the widespread rejection of both the AD and COPEI in the 1993 elections. In addition, explicit hostility toward the parties was manifest in civil unrest focused on the austerity program imposed by Carlos Andres Perez at the beginning of his second, abbreviated (1989–1993) presidential term, and in the indifference toward the Perez administration expressed in the immediate aftermath of the failed 1992 coup attempts (Freed 1992).

Recognizing the seriousness of this dissatisfaction even before the turbulent events of the early 1990s, Venezuelan party leaders embraced a series of reforms that decentralized power in the parties somewhat. In the mid-1980s, President Jaime Luscinchi established the President's Commission on State Reform (COPRE), to make recommendations on reforms. The first significant reforms, implemented in 1988, included the direct election of state governors, who had previously been appointed by the president. Also, in 1989, open party lists were used in state and local elections, giving voters an opportunity to alter slates drawn up by party leaders (Paredes Pisani 1991). In 1988, the COPRE first published its recommendation that congressional candidates be selected through primaries, as in the United States (COPRE 1988, 1990a). The COPRE has argued for the need to create a personal electoral connection between constituents and legislators, and to rely on legislators' ambition for reelection to guarantee satisfactory representation. Other academics have echoed the need to alter the electoral system so as to encourage greater responsiveness on the part of legislators to regional demands (Paredes Pisani 1991) and have pointed to single-member districts as the ideal form of representation (Rachadell 1991).

Although the parties have not been willing to do away with proportional representation and closed lists altogether, they have reached a compromise with their critics. Since the 1993 elections, the Venezuelan Chamber of Deputies has been elected according to a mixed system akin to Germany's. About half the deputies will be elected in single-member districts, while the other half will be elected from state-level closed lists (Congreso de la República de Venezuela 1989, 1992). The new system is expected to spawn a new type of legislator, whose career is directly dependent on a personal constituency, and who is therefore likely to exercise more independence from party leaders when district interests conflict with party directives.[20]

From the U.S. perspective, the Venezuelan reforms are remarkable in their call for more independence of legislators from party platforms. In the terms that Shugart and Carey (1992) use, the reforms attempt to establish a less efficient brand of presidentialism, where the coherence of national party platforms would be partially sacrificed to the ability of individual legislators to wheel and deal. This is in marked contrast to the myriad voices that have criticized U.S. political parties as too weak and argued for greater discipline among legislators, even (perhaps especially) at the expense of responsiveness to regional interests (Fiorina 1989; Robinson 1985). It is in contrast, as well, to those who have argued in favor of parliamentary government in Latin America, partly on the grounds that parliamentarism would discourage independent maneuvering by legislators whose political fortunes are not tied to those of their parties (Linz 1994; Valenzuela 1994).

Legislative organization in the United States

The literature on legislative behavior and organization in the United States is so vast that I do not presume to offer a general review of it here. The works cited in this section are all excellent sources for this purpose. Two central points are worth emphasizing, however, with regard to this comparative project. First, at the broadest level there are important similarities between the institutional structure of the United States on the one hand, and Costa Rica and Venezuela on the other, that make comparisons possible, albeit complicated. Second, with regard to legislative organization, it is important to underscore the greater importance and autonomy of standing committees in the U.S. Congress than in either of the Latin American cases. I address these points in turn.

---

[20] Of course, the degree of independence these deputies can be expected to exercise depends as well on the method of their nomination. The materials I have assembled do not refer to the nomination process under the new system.

Constitutional structure and strong legislatures

The most important institutional similarity among all three cases is a presidential system of government, guaranteeing that the legislative and executive branches are elected separately and that neither can dissolve the other before scheduled elections. This constitutional structure is relevant here primarily because presidentialism is associated with more independent and politically potent legislatures than is pure parliamentary government, for example (Lijphart 1986; Powell 1989). Reinforcing this tendency is the relative constitutional weakness of the presidencies in each of the three cases studied here. Among presidential systems there is a wide range of formal policy-making powers granted to presidents – prominently, package vetoes, item vetoes, budgetary authority, decree authority, and the right to call referenda. The U.S. president, with only a package veto, is constitutionally endowed with relatively scant policy-making powers, much like the Costa Rican and Venezuelan presidents. In terms of legislative authority, the three systems have among the weakest presidents, and correspondingly some of the most powerful legislatures, of the 41 presidential and hybrid systems evaluated by Shugart and Carey (1992).

The institutional similarities between the United States and the Latin American cases should not be overstated. Indeed, Venezuela is included in this study entirely because it is politically similar enough to Costa Rica to serve as a control on a number of factors that complicate any straightforward comparison between Costa Rica and the United States. So by mentioning institutional similarities across all three cases, I am referring only to the broadest level of institutional analysis. Nevertheless, the broad similarities are critical to the comparability of the cases because they delineate constitutional parameters that contribute to legislative effectiveness.

Although the United States, Costa Rica, and Venezuela all have legislatures that are relatively powerful vis-à-vis their executives, the United States case stands apart with respect to the importance and internal autonomy of its standing committees. As the preceding discussions of legislative organization demonstrate, legislative committees have clearly been strictly subordinate to party organizations as arenas for policy decision making in Venezuela.[21] And although some substantive legislative work is done in Costa Rican committees, the assembly chamber remains a forum of debate and negotiation over policy outcomes much more than in the United States. The instability of committee membership clearly reflects the lesser degree of im-

---

[21] This could change, if the electoral reforms that kicked in in 1993 eventually generate legislators who are increasingly independent of party leaders for their political survival and who seek to establish bases of policy-making authority distinct from national party organizations.

portance placed on the development of expertise and autonomy by committee members. In contrast, students of the U.S. Congress have overwhelmingly focused on its committee system as the most significant organizational structure. It is worthwhile to examine somewhat more closely why this is so, and what implications differences in committee systems have for this project.

The importance of committees in U.S. legislatures

The committee system of the U.S. Congress has attracted more attention by far from scholars than any other element of legislative organization, such as parties, caucuses, or even the chambers themselves. Most accounts have concurred that delegating significant policy-making autonomy to committees serves the institutional interests of the chambers as wholes, and of legislators as individuals. The specific interests summoned by various authors differ considerably, and at times are at odds with one another. Prominent explanations suggest the following motivations to create powerful committees. Committees can serve to mitigate the problem of unstable decisions, which social choice theory holds to be virtually intractable when groups of three or more individuals must choose policies along two or more dimensions of conflict (Shepsle 1979). The division of legislative labor and increasing autonomy among committees with specialized jurisdictions might be necessary for legislative chambers to cope with increasingly complex policy-making decisions (Polsby 1968). A related explanation is that granting committees significant autonomy creates incentives for committee members to develop policy expertise, which is otherwise chronically undersupplied in legislatures because individual members do not have incentives to work hard to develop knowledge that will benefit all members of the legislature equally. According to this story, the measure of autonomy granted committee members allows them to reap particularistic legislative benefits in exchange for providing specialized legislation to the entire chamber (Krehbiel 1992).

Of course, in order for committee members to develop significant policy expertise, they must serve for long periods on the same committees. Stable committee membership is in fact what we observe in the modern Congress, along with a generally respected norm of granting increased status and procedural rights to members according to their seniority on committees. The seniority norm has been seen as compatible with the interests both of legislatures in reaping the benefits of expertise and of individual committee members who can extract increasing particularistic benefits for their own constituencies as they gain seniority (Fenno 1973). Weingast and Marshall (1988) suggest that the combination of committee autonomy and the seniority norm effectively creates "property rights" for members over decision making in their committees' jurisdictions, and that these guarantees are the glue that holds together legislative logrolls.

Of course, even the property rights conferred by committee autonomy and the seniority norm would be more valuable to legislators if they could choose which committees on which to serve, and thus which policy jurisdictions they would enjoy disproportionate control over. Other studies of congressional committees argue that Congress does in fact support such a norm of self-selection, with the result that committees tend to be overpopulated by members who impose high demand for the goods that their committees distribute (Shepsle 1978). Indeed, some critics of the committee structure have argued that the combination of self-selection, seniority, and autonomy yields a structure of decision making in Congress that provides maximum electoral advantages to incumbent legislators, even while systematically hampering the institution's ability to generate efficient public policy (Fiorina 1977; Mayhew 1974).

More recent accounts of congressional organization are generally more circumspect about the extent of autonomy actually granted to standing committees, and of the sanctity of the self-selection and seniority norms. As partisan voting became more pronounced during the divided government of the 1980s, academic accounts focused on the procedural authority of the majority party leadership, especially in the House, even at the expense of committee authority (Sinclair 1989). Rohde (1991) argues convincingly that the Democratic majority in the House grew increasingly ideologically homogeneous and distinct from the Republicans during the 1970s and 1980s, and that this polarization motivated organizational reforms that shifted procedural authority from committees to the majority party caucus and its agents in the leadership. Cox and McCubbins (1993) sound a similar theme in arguing that parties have consistently had the last word over how much autonomy to afford committees, and that parties have tolerated self-selection and seniority only as long as their representatives on committees act in accord with the preferences of the party caucus as a whole. Krehbiel (1992) is likewise adamant that self-selection, seniority, and autonomy are constrained by the need for committees to serve the interests of their principals, although he differs from Cox and McCubbins in regarding the ultimate principal to be the chamber as a whole rather than the majority party caucus. All these more recent accounts offer important and convincing refinements to the picture of committee domination over policy making prevalent until the 1980s. But even these skeptics retain the basic elements of the conventional story about committee power. Committees do fill the need of legislative chambers for policy expertise. Committee membership is generally stable, and violations of seniority are exceptional. Members' requests for committee assignments are accommodated to the extent that parties and chambers can do so without creating inordinate bias in membership. And on committees whose jurisdictions are of relatively little concern to the chamber as a whole, self-selection is tolerated to an even greater extent. Most significantly, the idea that committee members extract rents from their principals (parties or chambers) in exchange for doing specialized legislative work is central to the accounts of committee skeptics. So although the importance of the committee system has been modified and qualified in recent analyses of congressional organization, committees remain central to virtually every account.

Moreover, regardless of differences in the details, the reason that committees are central to these accounts is that committee membership and committee power are recognized as important assets to individual legislators in pursuing the single goal they value most: reelection. Recall from Chapter 1 that all these theories of legislative behavior and organization share the assumption that legislators are reelection seekers. In the U.S. context, where control over party nominations and over campaign funds are highly decentralized, legislators are ultimately dependent on support in their geographical constituencies in order to win reelection. The resources that such political entrepreneurs value are those that contribute to cultivating support back in their districts. In the conventional story of committee dominance, committees certainly serve this end. Yet even for the skeptics, the rents extracted by individual legislators in exchange for committee work are regarded primarily as electoral resources. Thus, party (or chamber) control over committee assignments and autonomy are sanctions that can be wielded to elicit cooperation from individual legislators, but committee power – and the possibility of curtailing it – is valuable currency only because it is inextricably tied to the reelection incentive.

Legislative committees in the comparative context

Given the logic of the link between committee power and reelection in the United States, it is not entirely surprising that committees are less central to accounts of legislative organization in Costa Rica and Venezuela. In both countries, electoral (and in Venezuela, reelectoral) prospects for individual legislators are dependent primarily on being granted favorable positions on closed party ballot lists, rather than on eliciting personal electoral support in geographical districts. In Venezuela, for example, there has been no need for party leaders to exchange committee autonomy for committee work on behalf of the party. Individual legislators have valued access to safe list positions under party labels that are politically meaningful to voters. Thus, for 30 years they were content to accept the concentration of policy decision-making authority by the central party leadership, and absolute party discipline, as long as these provided electoral security. In Costa Rica, where term limits mean political careers cannot be built inside the legislature, there is neither the imperative for airtight party discipline in the name of electoral security, along Venezuelan lines, nor the need for committee membership and autonomy, along U.S. lines.

The distinct significance of legislative committee structure in the three cases examined here suggests a number of observations and hypotheses. First, the lesser autonomy and importance of committees in the Latin American cases than in the United States is consistent with a conclusion that term limits can be expected to reduce the importance of committees; but these three cases do not provide sufficient evidence to make a strong claim on these grounds. That is, if the general story about the electoral importance of committee assignments in the United States is correct, then *either* term limits *or* the more centralized party control of electoral resources, or both, could account for the lesser importance of committees in Costa Rica than in the United States. Along these lines, we might also expect that legislative committees will increase in importance in Venezuela, if the reforms in the electoral system implemented in 1993 produce a decentralization of control over critical electoral resources. Finally, consistent with all these claims would be a decrease in the importance of committees in U.S. legislatures – at both the state and national levels – that impose term limits. If reelection is limited, and if a principal product of committee power for individual legislators is electoral capital, then we should expect legislators to be less willing to do the hard work associated with building committee power.

The road to term limits in the United States

As this book is being written, the term limits reform process appears to be a long way from over, and the outcome far from certain. Limits on representatives to the U.S. Congress have been adopted by 22 states, and limits on state legislators by 20 of those 22 (Tables 1.1 and 1.2). An initiative on term limits is expected to be on the ballot in a 23rd state, Mississippi, in 1995. That initiative, however, will essentially exhaust the set of states for which an initiative process is constitutionally available as a means of adopting term limits.[22] Moreover, the idea of states imposing term limits on U.S. legislators has been attacked on constitutional grounds.[23] In June 1995, the U.S. Supreme Court was to have decided on the constitutionality of the Arkansas

---

[22] Illinois has a popular initiative process, but there are strong constitutional restrictions on how and for what purpose it can be used, which preclude it from being used to adopt term limits. None of the other 26 states have constitutional provisions allowing for a popular initiative process.

[23] The best review of the debates surrounding the constitutionality of state-imposed term limits is Lowenthal (1993).

term limits provision of 1992. A decision overturning state-imposed limits on U.S. legislators would be the first serious setback for term limit supporters, but it would by no means end the debate or the reform process. The next phase of the term limits strategy will involve an attempt to amend the U.S. Constitution to limit reelection for all U.S. legislators. A judicial defeat on constitutional grounds could conceivably even invigorate this effort. At any rate, in early 1995 the U.S. House moved toward a vote on a term limits amendment. So the prospect looms of an extended debate in both chambers of Congress, followed by debates over ratification of such an amendment in each of the 50 state legislatures.

The nature of the reform process in the United States means that the motivation for adopting term limits is not enigmatic, as in Costa Rica. In the first place, until 1995 at least, the question of why legislators would limit their own reelection has been moot, because term limits have been initiated outside legislatures and adopted by direct democracy.[24] Other characteristics of the U.S. reform process, in contrast to that in Costa Rica, also ensure that reformers' and opponents' motives are exposed to scrutiny. First, the process is slow and discrete, with the battle over term limits joined anew in each state where they are proposed. It began in 1990, with successful initiatives in California, Colorado, and Oklahoma. In 1991, the movement suffered a temporary setback with the narrow defeat of a retroactive term limits measure on the ballot in Washington State. One year later, however the reform moved to national prominence, passing measures in 13 states, including Washington.[25] In 1994, 8 more states adopted limits;[26] and in 1995 Mississippi and Nevada (with the second round of its constitutional amendment process) will vote. Five years after the process began, it is far from over. This is a far cry from the total of six days devoted to the establishment of all electoral rules by the Costa Rican Constituent Assembly of 1949. Not only is the pace of reform dramatically different in the United States, the process is markedly more public and deliberative. Direct democracy has meant that the term limits debate has been conducted largely over the airwaves, through political campaign commercials. Repeat initiatives in Washington, California, Colorado, and Nevada has meant that voters in those states have confronted the issue in the voting booth on two separate occasions. Court challenges at both the state and federal level have placed term limits among the highest profile subjects of judicial review in the mid-1990s. Moreover, during the 1994 electoral earthquake in which the Republican Party gained

[24] The one exception was the adoption of term limits by the Utah state legislature. This action was taken, however, to preempt a popular initiative on term limits.
[25] One of the 13 was California, again, which added limits on its congressional representatives to those already imposed on state legislators.
[26] One was Colorado, amending its 1990 limits on its congressional delegation.

control of both chambers of Congress, the party's House candidates prominently included term limits as part of their Contract with America platform. In short, term limits may be a radical electoral reform in the United States, but their arrival is not marked by the element of surprise, as it was in Costa Rica.

Notwithstanding the differences in process, the motives and expectations behind term limits reform in the United States appear to be broadly complementary with those in Costa Rica. In both cases, supporters have been perfectly clear as to whom their reform is aimed against: entrenched incumbent legislators. In both cases, incumbency is portrayed as the enemy of fairness, competitiveness, and a level electoral playing field.[27] In both countries, term limit supporters have equated political professionalism and careerism with corruption, and have extolled the idea of the amateur legislator. Beyond the common attack on incumbency, however, the impact of term limits on the representation expected among their adherents has been less clear. In Costa Rica, this may be due to the lack of public debate on the reform. In the U.S. case, it is because the claims made for term limits have been so diverse, and at times even inconsistent (Chapters 1 and 7). The clearest consensus, among supporters and opponents, in Costa Rica and the United States alike, is on the general point that term limits can be expected to alter significantly the behavior of legislators. The next move, then, should be to examine in more detail the empirical evidence as to whether and how this is so.

Looking ahead

This chapter has provided the necessary background information on the three cases considered here to proceed with a more thorough analysis of the impact of term limits on congressional representation. The basic electoral framework of Costa Rica and Venezuela has been explained, and the structure of the national assemblies reviewed. The strong similarities between these two systems underscore the degree to which the presence of term limits in Costa Rica offers an opportunity for fruitful comparison with Venezuela. The important similarities, and equally important differences, between the Latin American and U.S. cases have also been reviewed.

This background material suggests the following strategy for comparison. First, the most straightforward comparison will clearly be between Costa

---

[27] Some Republicans appear to be backing away from this theme in the wake of their stunning victories in 1994, not only at the congressional level, but also in many state legislatures. Nevertheless, to abandon term limits after riding the issue to electoral victory would appear highly opportunistic. Most Republicans, therefore, remain wedded to the issue, albeit with dampened enthusiasm.

Rica and Venezuela, so the next three chapters pursue this comparison along three principal lines. Chapter 3 contrasts the manner in which legislators build political careers through patronage in Costa Rica with the prospects for legislative careers in Venezuela. Chapter 4 establishes that the presence of term limits in Costa Rica does not mean that legislators there refrain from activities, such as constituent service and the distribution of pork, that legislative theory has generally attributed to the drive for personal reelection. Chapter 5 argues that the prohibition on immediate reelection in Costa Rica hampers the ability of national party leaders to coerce rank-and-file legislators, generating party discipline in the Assembly that is significantly looser than in Venezuela. Each of these comparisons focuses primarily on the Latin American cases because the major institutional variables – apart from term limits – can be held constant. In these chapters, the prospects for generalizing the conclusions to the U.S. case will be discussed only briefly. Chapters 6 and 7 then shift the focus directly to the U.S. case, examining the robustness of the conclusions suggested by the comparison of Costa Rica and Venezuela.

Part II

The Latin American cases

3

Term limits and political careers

Term limits on legislators alter political careers, but do not eliminate them. Chapter 2 offers some evidence of the importance of career interests in shaping Constituent Assembly decisions in Costa Rica, even despite the lack of explicit debate over the adoption of term limits in 1949. This chapter explores in detail the nature of political careers in Costa Rica and Venezuela. I argue that term limits redirect, but do not diminish, the impact that legislators' personal ambition has on political behavior.

To build a career in public office, politicians in democratic systems are dependent on at least two principals: voters and political party leaders. To some extent, assembly candidates in any system must build support among both principals to secure election. But variations in electoral rules structure the extent to which electoral success is dependent on the support of assembly constituents, or of party leaders. In the absence of term limits, the relative dependence of legislators on these two principals is determined by the strength of party leaders' control over candidates' access to ballots, whether voters cast ballots for parties or for individual candidates, whether votes cast for any member of a party are pooled across all candidates of that party in a district, and the number of seats available in each electoral district (Carey and Shugart in press).

The qualities of these four variables determine the extent to which legislators must build support among their two main principals in order to further their careers. Where the control of party leaders over an individual's electoral prospects is weak, legislators are relatively more dependent on the direct support of their constituents. Where the control of party leaders over electoral prospects is strong, legislators are relatively more dependent on leadership support for their career prospects. In such a system, politicians may spend their entire careers in the assembly, or they may circulate among government posts and party posts, but their career survival depends primarily on the support of party leaders.

Term limits eliminate the prospect for assembly careers. Thus, regardless of the qualities of the electoral incentive variables, term limits eliminate the possibility of direct dependence on constituents for career prospects. Under term limits, then, political parties can become potentially more important to the career prospects of legislators. But term limits also constrain the resources that party leaders have available to feed the ambition of legislators. Legislators cannot be rewarded with assembly careers, nor sanctioned by being denied such careers. If parties are to control political careers, then they must be able to provide other positions for legislators who are proscribed from continuing to serve in the assembly.

This chapter demonstrates that term limits in Costa Rica have virtually eliminated Legislative Assembly careers. This is true even though Costa Rican term limits are not lifetime bans on reelection.[1] Nevertheless, the absence of Assembly careers does not eliminate the prospect of political careers for Costa Rican deputies. Political careers subsequent to Assembly service are built through appointments to government posts. The likelihood of securing such appointments, moreover, is directly tied to the subsequent electoral success of a deputy's party. Costa Rican deputies understand the connection between the party's success and their individual political careers, and career interests largely drive the behavior of representatives in office.

The manifestations of this electorally motivated behavior are the subject of Chapters 4 and 5. The project here is to establish, first of all, that Assembly careers are not viable prospects for Costa Rican deputies, despite the legal possibility of staggered reelection. I compare rates of reelection and professionalization of the Assembly in Costa Rica's current regime with those of the pre-1949 regime in that country, and with the current Venezuelan regime. The comparisons demonstrate that under an electoral format similar in every respect but for the presence of term limits, congressional careers are viable for legislators. Next, I demonstrate that political careers in both Costa Rica and in Venezuela are dependent on the support of national party leaders. This conclusion is supported by interview material, by data on the political backgrounds of legislators, and by analysis of the nomination process for assembly candidates in both Costa Rica and Venezuela. Finally, I provide archival data on political appointments to demonstrate that, in Costa Rica, a deputy's political future is immediately dependent on the ability to secure a presidential appointment to a government post. This prospect, in turn, is dependent on the success of the deputy's party in the next presidential election. I conclude with a discussion of the implication of this indirect electoral connection for legislative behavior, and the responsiveness of deputies to changing principals.

---

[1] Costa Rican term limits merely require that incumbent deputies to the Legislative Assembly cannot be immediately reelected. There is no limit on the total number of four-year terms legislators may serve, provided no two terms are consecutive.

Table 3.1. Number of terms served in Venezuelan Congress.

Terms	COPEI	AD	MAS	Others	All parties
1	108 (49)	126 (44)	6 (40)	187 (88)	385 (54)[a]
2	62 (28)	83 (29)	7 (47)	22 (10)	173 (24)
3	28 (13)	51 (18)	2 (13)	4 (2)	94 (13)
4	14 (6)	20 (7)	0 (0)	0 (0)	38 (5)
5	5 (2)	6 (2)	0 (0)	0 (0)	12 (2)
6	3 (1)	3 (1)	0 (0)	0 (0)	6 (1)

Note: For all legislators elected from 1963 to 1988, excluding those whose first term was 1988. Deputies and senators pooled. Percentages are in parentheses, and are calculated by party.
[a] Sums of figures across rows may be slightly greater than the figure for "All parties," because in a few cases, members of Congress were elected by different parties in different years. In this case, they are counted separately for each party.

Reelection rates

Assembly careers are possible, and from 1958 to 1993 were increasingly likely, in Venezuela. In Costa Rica, rotation-style term limits leave open at least the possibility of a politician serving alternate terms. Nevertheless, multiple terms for Costa Rican deputies are rare. Even a staggered Assembly career, in short, is not a good prospect for an ambitious Costa Rican politician.

Reelection rates without term limits: Venezuela

Data on reelection rates to the Venezuelan Congress demonstrate two things: first, assembly careers are possible; and second, the Venezuelan Congress has grown increasingly professionalized since the foundation of the current regime in 1958. The first point is underscored by Table 3.1 and Figure 3.1. The data here are rosters of each Congress elected from 1963 through 1988.[2] Those legislators elected for the first time in 1988 are excluded from the data, because the data on rosters extends only through the 1988–1993 Congress, so I cannot determine their rate of subsequent reelection. Columns break down the data by party, with the farthest right column aggregating across all parties. Rows indicate the number of terms served by legislators. Thus, of all those elected to the Venezuelan Congress as deputies or senators, 385 (54%) have served only one term; 173 (24%) have served two terms, and so on. The rate of reelection for legislators from the AD and COPEI, the two parties that have dominated the Congress through the early

---

[2] I was unable to secure a roster for the 1958 Congress.

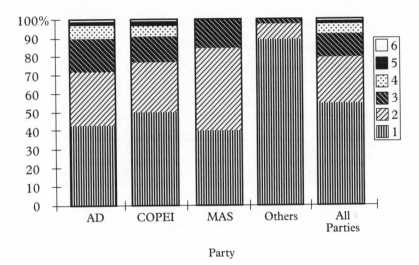

Figure 3.1. Professionalization of Venezuelan Congress, by party. *Note:* Gray tones mark the cumulative number of congressional terms served by percentages of each party's cohort for all those elected from 1963 to 1988, excluding those whose first term was 1988.

1990s, is markedly greater than that for the cross section of all legislators. Data for the Movement to Socialism (MAS) are also displayed independently, because this party has maintained a viable electoral presence over four consecutive elections now.[3] Deputies from other parties, as well as those for whom party label data are unavailable, are grouped in the column labeled "other."

The prospects for reelection are illustrated more clearly in Figure 3.1, which graphs the percentages of each partisan cohort according to the number of terms served. The number of terms is indicated by gray-tone codes embedded in the figure's right-hand side. More than half of all legislators elected from the AD, COPEI, and MAS have returned to Congress to serve subsequent terms. Deputies from minor parties, on the other hand, are overwhelmingly likely to be one-term legislators.

The shape of Venezuelan assembly careers is further clarified by data on successive reelection. Figure 3.2 shows the likelihood not only of serving multiple terms in Congress, but of being reelected to the immediately following Congress, for the members of each Congress elected from 1963 through 1988. The variance among rates of immediate reelection is large, but the overall trend is toward greater likelihood of reelection.

[3] The MAS has secured more than five seats in Congress in each election from 1973 to 1988. Other minor parties have either won fewer seats or have demonstrated less longevity.

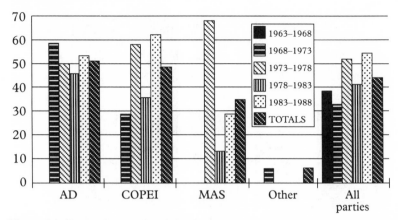

Figure 3.2. Rates of successive reelection to Venezuelan Congress. *Note:* Breakdown of the 1963 Congress by party was not possible, because party label was missing for many observations. It was possible to calculate the successive reelection rate across all parties for that cohort, however.

Increasing rates of immediate reelection to the Venezuelan Congress are due at least in part to the steady growth of the AD and COPEI as dominant assembly parties during the period under examination. For AD legislators in particular, the rate of immediate reelection has not grown over time; it has always been relatively high. But as the AD has controlled an increasing share of all legislative seats, the rate of immediate reelection across all parties has grown. Conversely, as minor parties have faded in the Venezuelan Congress, their generally low rates of immediate reelection have had less impact. Increasing rates of reelection have produced an increasingly professionalized Venezuelan Congress. This is illustrated by data providing a "snapshot" of the institution in the 1988–1993 term (Figure 3.3). Only 38% of Venezuelan legislators in the last Congress were freshmen. Another 30% had served one previous term; and another third had served two or more previous terms. Overall, at the beginning of the Congress, the mean number of years of congressional experience for a Venezuelan legislator was 6.19. Given that Venezuelan terms are 5 years in duration, the average legislator had over 11 years of experience by the end of the term in 1993. By comparison, the mean length of previous experience for U.S. legislators in the 102nd Congress was 9.4 years.[4] Clearly, then, the Venezuelan Congress is highly professionalized by comparative standards.

Next, I discuss the electoral dependence of legislators on central party leaders. For now, the point is that assembly careers are possible in Venezuela and have grown increasingly likely since the 1960s. Venezuelan politicians,

---

[4] From Benjamin and Malbin (1992: Appendix B-3).

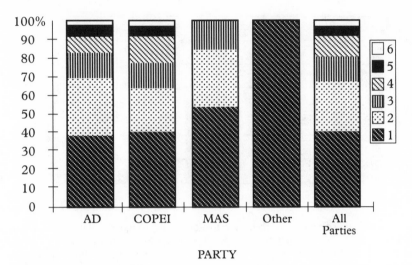

PARTY

Figure 3.3. Professionalization of 1988 Venezuelan Congress. *Note:* Gray tones mark the cumulative number of congressional terms served by percentages of each party's cohort. Data for senators and deputies are pooled.

once elected to the legislature, have good reason to believe they can remain in that office.[5]

Term limits and Legislative Assembly careers: Costa Rica, 1949–present

In Costa Rica, the prospects for Assembly careers are comparably bleak. This is not surprising, given the prohibition on immediate reelection. What is somewhat surprising, however, is the infrequency with which former deputies are able to return to the Legislative Assembly, even after sitting out a term. Table 3.2 shows the number of terms served in the Assembly for all those elected from 1949 through 1990.[6] The columns break the data according to political parties. Under "Major opposition" are included all depu-

---

[5] The year 1993 marked a critical turning point in Venezuelan politics, with the election of Rafael Caldera as president heading a coalition ticket outside the traditionally dominant AD and COPEI parties. At the congressional level, the elections were the first held under a mixed system, combining single-member districts and PR. I do not have congressional rosters for the 1994–1999 Congress, and so am not able to provide data on rates of turnover, although it is likely they were significantly higher in 1993 than in other recent elections. However, the AD and COPEI remain the largest two partisan cohorts in the current Congress, and the reforms implemented in 1993 did not include any restrictions on reelection.

[6] The data on Costa Rican reelection rates was calculated from a database consisting of rosters of each Legislative Assembly dating back to 1920. Assembly rosters, as well as data on the parties and provinces represented by deputies, were gathered from documents at the archives of the Legislative Assembly and the TSE.

Table 3.2. Number of terms served in Costa Rican Legislative Assembly by those who have served since 1949. Service in 1949 Constituent Assembly not included

Party / Terms	All	PLN[a]	Major Opposition[b]	Christian Democrats (PUSC)[c]	Others
1	495 (87)	233 (87)	225 (90)	169 (90)	59 (89)
2	60 (11)	29 (11)	20 (8)	17 (9)	6 (9)
3	14 (3)	5 (2)	4 (2)	2 (1)	1 (2)
Total	569 (100)	267 (100)	249 (100)	188 (100)	66 (100%)

[a] Includes Social Democrats of 1949, prior to formation of PLN.
[b] Includes PUN deputies, as well as those included in Christian Democrat category.
[c] Includes remnants of Calderon Guardia's Republican Party, and those parties in coalition that went on to form PUSC.

ties from the major coalitions or parties opposed to the PLN, grouping those from Otilio Ulate's PUN with the *calderonistas* and Christian Democrats. I also display separately just the *calderonistas* and Christian Democrats who coalesced to form the PUSC, which is currently the dominant adversary to the PLN. All other, mostly regional and leftist, deputies are grouped as "Others." Rows indicate the number of terms served by deputies. Thus, of 267 politicians who have served for the PLN in the Assembly, 233 have served only one term, 29 have served two terms, and only 5 have served three terms. The prospects for multiple terms are remarkably similar across parties.

Not only are multiple assembly terms a rarity, but unlike in Venezuela, there is no trend toward increasing professionalization in the Costa Rican Assembly. Figure 3.4 shows the number of terms of Assembly experience among members of each cohort since 1949. Terms served prior to 1949 are not included in this data, because service before that date does not pertain to the likelihood of reelection under rotation-style term limits. For the first two cohorts, of course, all deputies were serving their first term; and for the first four cohorts, third-term deputies were a constitutional impossibility. Indeed, up through 1966, the election of experienced former deputies increased. After that election, however, the number and ratio of experienced deputies in each cohort drops off some and stabilizes. From 1970 on, at least 80% of each cohort consists of rookie deputies, with a small minority of veterans, and perhaps a handful of third-term legislators.

Yet another cut on the data provides more information on the pattern of Assembly careers, such as they are, in Costa Rica. For all those who served more than one term, I determined how many intervening terms had passed

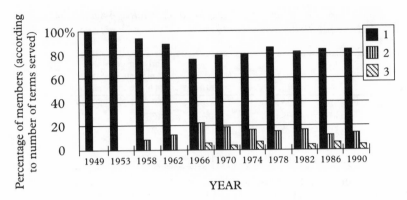

Figure 3.4. Number of terms of experience among members of each cohort to Costa Rican Assembly.

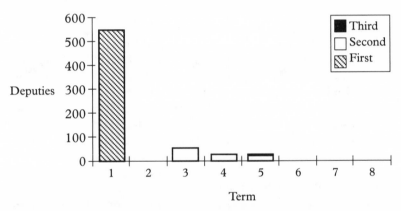

Figure 3.5. Patterns of reelection to Costa Rican Legislative Assembly aggregated across all deputies, 1949–1982.

before the deputy returned to the Assembly. Figure 3.5 shows the rate at which former deputies were reelected, according to how many terms had elapsed since their original service in the Assembly. Only the 1949–1982 cohorts are included here, because when these data were collected reelection had not yet been a legal possibility for subsequent groups. Thus, at Term 1, all deputies are serving their first term, and at Term 2 none is eligible to be serving again. At Term 3, on the other hand, all are again eligible for reelection to a second term, but only 7% (38 of 541) actually return at that time. Likewise, at Term 4, all those who have not been reelected remain eligible. By Term 5, those who were elected to a second term at Term 3 are now eligible for a third term.

The most important point illustrated by these data is that rotation-style term limits in Costa Rica have not produced a systematic pattern of rotation in and out of the Legislative Assembly. If rotation were systematic, we might imagine an Assembly with effectively two cohorts of deputies that rotate between being "Ins" and "Outs." Death and other forms of attrition would mandate that somewhat less than 100% of those who served at Term 1 could return at Term 3, but rotation-style limits need not preclude high rates of staggered reelection. This is not the case, however. Reelection is rare in Costa Rica, and those who are reelected do not necessarily return according to an orderly rotation scheme. Of those who serve second terms, 49% do not return until at least two interim terms have elapsed, and 22% not until three or more terms have passed. The handful who serve third terms are even more dramatically spread over time.

The conclusion drawn from the data presented here on reelection rates is that Costa Rican politicians cannot expect Assembly careers. Although Costa Rican term limits formally allow for staggered reelection, this is the exception rather than the rule. And even the Assembly recidivism that does occur does not follow any predictable pattern over time. Thus, Costa Rican legislators aspiring to build political careers need to look elsewhere besides the Assembly.

Costa Rica before term limits, 1920–1948

The current electoral system of Costa Rica and the Venezuelan system through the 1980s are strikingly similar, apart from the existence of term limits in the former. Thus, I am prone to attribute the stark difference in reelection rates between the two countries to term limits. This is only one comparison, however, and more data can refine these results. It is possible to compare reelection rates under the current Costa Rican regime with those of its predecessor.

The Costa Rican party system was far less institutionalized prior to 1949 than it is currently (Lehoucq 1991b; Mainwaring and Scully 1992). Other things being equal, the greater fluidity and personalization of the party system in the pre-1949 period should be expected to depress the stability of congressional membership, due to the large variance in the share of seats won by each party from election to election (Coppedge 1992b). Reelection rates, then, may not be as high as they would be in a more institutionalized system with unlimited reelection. Nevertheless, employing data from the preceding Costa Rican regime allows for comparison between systems without requiring cross-national analysis.

Costa Rican deputies have been elected from closed party lists since 1897 (Lehoucq 1993), so the data from before 1949 are based on an electoral

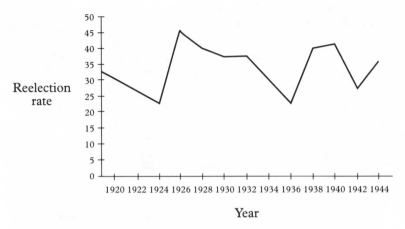

Reelection
rate

Year

Figure 3.6. Reelection rates for deputies to Costa Rican Congress, 1920–1944.

system fundamentally similar to the current one.[7] One significant difference, however, is that before 1949 the National Congress[8] was renewed by halves every two years. The congressional rosters available for this period do not distinguish those deputies who were just reelected from those who were in the middle of their terms at each election. Therefore, among those deputies whose names turn up on successive rosters, it is not possible to identify precisely which were reelected as opposed to those who were simply continuing their terms. However, for any given Assembly cohort, it is possible to determine the number of deputies who served subsequently. Given that at the end of each Congress exactly half of each cohort was midway through its term, it follows that the number of identical deputies above half on the subsequent roster must have been reelected.

Immediate reelection rates to the Costa Rican Congress from 1920 through 1944, calculated in this manner, are presented in Figure 3.6. Recall that the average rate of immediate reelection to the Venezuelan Congress since 1963 is 44%. This is substantially greater than the 34% average found here, but the difference is not surprising, given the greater stability and institutional-

[7] A 1946 electoral reform reduced the number of votes that minor parties had to obtain before being eligible to win seats based on their remaining votes, once all possible seats had been distributed by quota. The bottom line of the reform was that it reduced the advantage that large parties have over small ones. The reform also created an independent commission – a precursor to the current TSE – to oversee elections, in order to reduce fraud (Lehoucq 1991b). These reforms aside, the pre–Civil War electoral system of translating votes into seats was formally much like the current system.

[8] Until 1948, the national legislature was called the Congress. After 1949, it has been called the Legislative Assembly.

ization of the Venezuelan party system. Rates of reelection in both systems are far above rates of staggered reelection under the current Costa Rican regime.

Rates of reelection under the pre-1949 system cannot be broken down according to party, because party affiliation data are not available from congressional rosters. Nevertheless, it is reasonable to assume that reelection rates were higher among deputies whose party (or coalition) controlled the presidency. Historical discussions of this period consistently point out that presidents used fraud and manipulation of the electoral process to engineer congressional majorities and to provide patronage (Aguilar Bulgarelli 1986; Arguedas 1992; Lehoucq 1991b, 1993; Volio Jimenez 1992). Moreover, it is precisely this alleged manipulation of congressional elections by President Calderón Guardia, and corresponding charges that Congress was controlled by entrenched *caciques*, that prompted demands for both electoral reforms in 1946 and legislative term limits at the Constituent Assembly of 1949 (Asamblea Nacional Constituyente, May 2, Acto 58; Lehoucq 1991b).

Finally, although simple rates of immediate reelection do not show a consistent pattern of change over this period, it is clear that the incidence of lengthy individual congressional careers was increasing by the time the regime was toppled. The Congress elected in 1946 had 13 members serving their second term, whereas previously the greatest number of second-term deputies had been 6; 6 deputies were serving their third term, whereas the previous high had been 4; 4 deputies were serving their fourth term, whereas the previous high had been 1; and 1 deputy was serving his fifth term.

In short, during the period prior to 1949 in Costa Rica, congressional careers were a possibility. The instability of the party system, along with high levels of fraud and manipulation, implied that congressional membership would not be as stable as under a highly institutionalized party system. Nevertheless, an average of 34% of those deputies eligible for reelection at any given time won, and deputies in the president's party or coalition could expect greater levels of success. Finally, by the mid-1940s, congressional careers of three, four, and five terms were becoming possible for the first time.

Comparisons with Venezuela and with the previous Costa Rican regime indicate that Assembly careers under the current Costa Rican regime are strikingly less common, shorter, and less predictable. Given the presence of term limits, these conclusions are not particularly surprising. Nevertheless, it has been important to document the nature of the Assembly career in Costa Rica under term limits, and to place it in comparative perspective, before proceeding to assess the nature of Costa Rican political careers more broadly.

Citizen legislators or professional politicians?

The preceding section demonstrated that Costa Rican politicians do not build careers in the legislature. This section begins to build the case that this lack of Assembly careers does not imply a lack of political careers altogether. The distinction is important, particularly in light of claims made by term limit advocates in the United States, who argue that legal prohibitions on congressional careers will generate citizen-legislators, whose political decisions are not driven by personal career interests. I begin by providing interview results as well as data on the personal backgrounds of Costa Rican deputies, suggesting that legislators under term limits are not – and do not consider themselves to be – political amateurs. Then I present data on post-Assembly political careers that confirm this belief.

The most straightforward – and perhaps least effective – way to determine whether Costa Rican deputies are political professionals is simply to ask them.[9] I asked 42 incumbent deputies, "Do you view politics as your career?"[10] The responses are reviewed in Table 3.3. Among the no answers, a few deputies offered term limits as the reason politics could not be a profession. More frequently, negative replies were based on loftier ideals, in "No, it's merely a way I can contribute to preserving and strengthening our democratic regime" (Interview 93-18),[11] or even noblesse oblige, as in "Better to say it's my obligation" (Interview 93-41). Answers identified as "Waffles" were cautiously vague. For example, "I have had broad experiences in politics for the last 22 years" (Interview 93-10) or "I like politics very much" (Interview 93-24) are not quite affirmative, but are definitely not negative.

This initial set of responses does not yield a clear conclusion. A majority of deputies claim not to see politics as a profession. Yet many appeared to use a negative reply as a means of posturing. What is more surprising, in light of these data on Assembly careers, is that nearly half the respondents either waffled on the question or said yes outright.

Rather than rely on a query where legislators had good reason for evasiveness, it is better to look to deputies' personal backgrounds and their responses to some less direct questions in assessing whether politics is a viable profession in Costa Rica. I begin by looking at the political experience

[9] I recognize that quite possibly the worst way to determine what politicians are up to is to ask them. Politicians – especially professionals – have good reason to be less than candid in explaining their motivations. Remaining aware of this, however, one can derive useful information from interviews. What is most remarkable about Costa Rican deputies, in fact, is the degree to which they frankly state their plans and ambitions for a political career.

[10] During January, February, and March 1992, I conducted interviews with 45 of the 57 Costa Rican deputies.

[11] The format "Interview 93–00" denotes an interview with some deputy (identified by number, for confidentiality) in the 93rd Costa Rican Legislative Assembly.

Table 3.3. Responses by Costa Rican deputies to the question:
"Do you consider yourself a professional politician?"

Yes	14 (33)
No	22 (52)
Waffle	6 (14)

Note: Percentages are in parentheses.

Table 3.4. Prior political experience of Costa Rican deputies, 1974–1990 cohorts

Positions/year	None listed	1 or 2	3 or more	Prior elected office[a]	Missing data[b]	Total
1974	4	8	7	22	7	48
1978	5	9	5	12	12	43
1982	3	4	10	17	21	55
1986	5	7	6	21	1	40
1990	2	4	10	9	6	31
Total	19	32	38	81	47	217

Note: "Political experience" refers to holding political appointments or party office. Prior to service in the National Assembly, "political appointments" are generally low-level positions: local customs official, membership on local directorate of roads, local administrator for some executive ministry program (e.g. veterinary affairs). Higher-level political appointments, such as ministerial appointments, however, are also included here. "Party offices" refer to positions such as cantonal-level or provincial-level director of the party, campaign coordinators, and members of party sectoral committees, such as youth affairs or women's issues.
[a] Prior elected office can refer to those previously elected to the National Assembly, but generally refers to membership on city councils (regidores municipales). These officials are elected at the cantonal level on closed party lists. There are no provincial level elected officials in Costa Rica. Regidores, then, are the only elected offices below the National Assembly level.
[b] In each cohort, deputies were issued curriculum vitae forms, the first page of which requested specific data on things like age, address, number of children. Highest degree earned was included on this first sheet. The second page of the form requested more open-ended data, including a list of prior political service. In each cohort, some deputies returned only the first sheet. For these, political experience is regarded here as "Missing data."

that deputies bring to the Legislative Assembly. For every cohort since 1974, some curricula vitae were available in the Assembly archive. Most of these vitae contain information on prior political service. These data are summarized in Tables 3.4 and 3.5.

The difference between the tables is simply that the second excludes those vitae for which prior political experience data are missing. There is no reason to believe that such vitae are systematically different from those that include prior experience data, so this gap in the data should not distort the picture

Table 3.5. Prior political experience of Costa Rican deputies, 1974–1990 cohorts

Position/year	None	1 or 2	3 or more	Prior elected office	Total
1974	4 (10)	8 (20)	7 (17)	22 (54)	41
1978	5 (16)	9 (29)	5 (16)	12 (39)	31
1982	3 (9)	4 (12)	10 (29)	17 (50)	34
1986	5 (13)	7 (18)	6 (15)	29 (54)	39
1990	2 (8)	4 (16)	10 (40)	9 (36)	25
Total	19 (11)	32 (19)	38 (22)	81 (48)	170

Note: Missing data are excluded. Percentages are in parentheses.

presented here of deputies' backgrounds. Likewise, in each cohort, some deputies did not provide vitae to the Assembly archive, but there is no reason to expect that these missing vitae would differ systematically from those that are available.

These data demonstrate that Costa Rican legislators by and large are not rank political amateurs. An average of only 11% report having held no political appointment or party office prior to election to the Assembly. These 11% might be considered the prototypical citizen-legislators – although it is possible that even some of these previously held such posts, but did not list them on their vitae. Another 19% list one or two appointments or party offices, and 22% list three or more.

Simply counting offices clearly does not yield much information on the substance of political backgrounds. The nature of deputies' experiences certainly varies substantially, even within these groups. Some were national political actors, even ministers, while others were strictly local appointees or party operatives. But even merely counting positions provides some idea of the effort and time that these deputies devoted to building political connections and support before arriving in the Assembly. Clearly, this level of involvement is high, as suggested by the fact that 48% of Costa Rican legislators from these cohorts have held elected office prior to their Assembly terms. For 16%, there was a prior term in the Assembly itself. The other 36% served as *regidores municipales* (city councilors).[12] Across all five cohorts,

---

[12] *Regidores* are elected at the cantonal level. Apart from the national legislature and the presidency, the cantonal councils are the only elected political offices in Costa Rica. Almost all of those who served as *regidores* also held numerous appointed and party posts. And given the extremely limited scope of local governmental authority in Costa Rica, nonelected posts are likely to have entailed greater political power. Nevertheless, I distinguish those who have held elected office from those who have not, and regard the former group as more experienced politically. The rationale for why previous electoral experience should be regarded as the most important single measure of political experience is spelled out in Jacobson and Kernell (1983).

the overwhelming majority of deputies have some political experience before their election to the Assembly. An average of 70% are highly experienced, having held elected office, or at least three nonelected posts, or both.

In addition to building substantial political resumes before service in the Assembly, deputies exhibit a general desire to continue their political careers after their terms are up. In interviews with the 1990–1994 cohort, I asked 44 deputies the question, "How many terms do you intend to serve?" Of these, 20 (45%) stated that they would like to serve at least one more term, and 12 (27%) said that their response depended on unknown factors, most commonly their level of future political support. Taken together, over 70% of interviewees indicated interest or intention to serve again. This number is remarkably high, given the data on actual reelection rates, which suggests that only 13% will succeed.

Even more striking than this set of responses was the near uniform response to another interview question: "If you serve your party well in the Assembly, what compensation can you expect?" I initially included this question in the interview format not to garner information about political careers, but to learn about party discipline. Of 33 deputies asked this question, however, fully 30 stated that if they served their party well, they hoped to receive a future political appointment. Invariably, they mentioned either ministries, the foreign service, the autonomous corporations, or some combination of these institutions as desirable appointments. The consistency with which deputies offered the same information in response to a fully open-ended question suggested two things. First, political careers are a primary concern for most Costa Rican legislators; and second, career prospects are largely shaped by political parties. These conclusions are supported by the following quotation from former deputy Juan José Echeverría Brealey (1974–1978), criticizing the combination of closed-list elections and term limits: "It creates a loyalty between the representative and the party superstructure that he must satisfy; it is the party leaders that will be able subsequently to place the representative in posts, if he has served well in the parliament" (Casas Zamora and Briceño Fallas 1991: 348).

In the following sections, I provide clear evidence to support Echeverría's argument. For now, however, it is important to sum up the data presented in this section. Although slightly more than half of the deputies interviewed stated they do not consider politics to be their career, the clear majority of those elected to the Assembly since 1974 have had extensive political experience. Likewise, a clear majority indicates interest or an intention to serve subsequent terms in the Assembly. And 91% of those interviewed expressed interest in post-Assembly political appointments. Despite term limits, and the near absence of Assembly careers, Costa Rican legislators look and think like political professionals, not amateurs. Moreover, interview data suggests that Costa Rican parties control the extent to which these professional aspirations can be realized. In the next two sections, I turn to the subject of how parties control political careers – through nominations for assembly candidacies in both Venezuela and Costa Rica, and through post-Assembly appointments in the latter country.

Nominations and ballot lists

I return now to the comparative perspective with which this chapter opened. The goal of the chapter is to illustrate the nature of political careers in Costa Rica and Venezuela, and to determine the principals on which legislators in each country are dependent for career advancement. In the Venezuelan case, the task is relatively straightforward. The data on reelection rates demonstrates that congressional careers are viable. In this section, I simply demonstrate that control over nominations and list position are the basis of strong control by national party leaders over legislators' career prospects. In the Costa Rican case, political careers are more complex. The absence of Legislative Assembly careers makes necessary the careful analysis of the career paths of deputies before entering and after leaving the legislature. Ultimately, I argue that control over nominations to Assembly lists is effectively centralized in the hands of each party's designated presidential candidate.

Venezuela: Centralization despite reform

Control over legislative candidates' electoral prospects is entirely centralized in the national leaderships of Venezuela's parties. Central executive committees dictate not only which aspiring politicians are nominated to run under a party's label, but also the rank order of candidates on party lists. Moreover, national party leaders control lists at the state, as well as national, level.

As indicated in Chapter 2, Venezuela adopted important electoral reforms in September 1989 and again in May 1992. The most critical change to the electoral law, in 1989, was the shift from pure closed-list proportional representation to a mixed system akin to that of Germany, where single-member districts (SMDs) are combined with proportional representation. Under the new system, voters cast ballots both for party lists at the state level and for deputies to the lower house in SMDs. SMD seats are won by plurality, but the total number of seats that a party wins in each state is determined by the statewide vote for party lists. Compensatory seats are distributed at the state level to ensure that SMD elections do not produce disproportional distributions of seats.[13]

[13] Congreso de la Republica de Venezuela, *Ley de sufragio*, Title II, Chap. IV, Art. 8. September 14, 1989: 22–23.

This new system will likely create some incentive for those deputies elected in the SMDs to respond to district demands and pressures. Nevertheless, it is critical to note that the reforms to the electoral code do not alter the complete control exercised by national party leaders over who runs under party labels – whether on lists or in SMDs – in the first place. In 1980, Henry Wells noted that the Venezuelan regime's original electoral code contained a chapter entitled "Nominations," which was entirely silent as to how the process of naming candidates to congressional lists was to be conducted. He concluded that this statutory silence on nominations left complete discretion to national party leaders to determine the electoral prospects of aspiring legislators (Wells 1980).[14] Other Venezuelan authors have concurred that control over nominations and list positions is the basis of party strength, and that this strength generates obedience by legislators to national party leaders, even at the expense of responsiveness to voters in their own districts (Brewer-Carías 1989; Rachadell 1991).

The degree to which central party leaders dominate the nomination and list construction process is perhaps best illustrated by the insignificance of individual legislative candidates to voters in Venezuelan elections. Voters cast a single ballot in Venezuelan legislative elections for both chambers of the national Congress, as well as for state legislatures. Voters simply mark their preferred party; lists of candidates' names do not appear on the ballot. In fact, most Venezuelan voters do not even know who the candidates are. Lists are generally not published anywhere until the day before the election, and even then they are merely printed on the back pages of newspapers (Wells 1980). The nearly complete absence of individual candidates from campaigns is indicative of their irrelevance to voters. Where legislators are so tightly controlled by their parties, it is only party label that carries meaning for the electorate.

Despite the putative intention of the reforms of 1989 and 1992 to strengthen the direct connection between legislators and voters, those sections of the electoral code dealing with nomination procedures were unchanged. The new version of the law retains an entire chapter devoted to nominations, but this is limited to detailing the bureaucratic protocol parties must obey in registering their selected lists with the CSE. There is still no mention of how the lists are to be selected in the first place.[15]

---

[14] The leverage that control over lists gives to party leaders, of course, is dependent on other factors as well – notably the barriers that individual politicians face in breaking with their parties and running as independent candidates. Venezuela's highly proportional electoral formula makes the formal barriers to creating new parties relatively low (see Shugart 1988). Nevertheless, competition for votes among minor parties is fierce, and most do not win seats over any series of elections, as the reelection data presented earlier demonstrate. Therefore, Venezuelan legislators – even those with marginal list positions – generally face better career prospects staying within their parties than striking out on their own.

[15] Congresso de la Republica de Venezuela, Ley de sufragio, 1992, Title IV, Chap. II, Art. 102–111. See *La Gaceta Oficial*, May 7, 1992: 18–20.

In short, Venezuela's powerful legislative parties were willing to compromise their control over rank-and-file members of Congress slightly, by altering the electoral law and establishing SMDs. But they proved unwilling to interfere in the process that precedes elections: nominations and list creation. Continued statutory silence in this area suggests that central party control over legislators will remain strong.

Costa Rica: Centralization despite the law

The letter of the electoral law in Costa Rica suggests that control over Legislative Assembly nominations is strongly decentralized. Unlike in Venezuela, the electoral code in Costa Rica is quite specific in detailing the formal procedures by which parties can put together Assembly lists. Nevertheless, politicians and observers of Costa Rican politics uniformly state that national party leaders – especially presidential candidates – tightly control the nomination process. This discrepancy between formal rules and observed practices presents a puzzle. I argue here that the observers are correct: despite the formal decentralization of the process, presidential candidates are able to exercise control over nominations, by virtue of their expected monopoly on future political appointments.

The first step in resolving this puzzle is to establish the formal rules of decentralized control over nominations. The Organic Electoral Code states that all provincial lists of candidates for the Legislative Assembly for each party shall be selected by a majority vote of delegates to that party's national assembly, or convention. But delegates to each party's national assembly are the products of a series of lower-level assemblies. The process begins at the subcantonal level, in 510 districts nationwide. Each party is to hold an assembly (effectively a caucus) open to all registered partisans[16] in the district, at which 5 delegates to a cantonal-level assembly are selected by majority vote. These delegates then attend cantonal level assemblies, where 5 delegates are likewise selected to provincial assemblies. Each provincial assembly then selects 10 delegates to the party's national assembly, where all provincial lists are drawn up and must by approved by majorities.[17]

This process appears to establish clearly the independence of those who decide nominations from control by central party leaders. Nevertheless, Costa Rican political scientists state without exception that nominations are controlled from the top of the parties' hierarchies (Sojo Obando 1992). Ventura Robles writes, "It is certain . . . despite legal provisions, that the

---

[16] Registering as a partisan is a simple matter of declaring party preference when registering to vote, and does not require payment of party dues.

[17] Ley Orgánica del Tribunal Supremo de Elecciones y del Registro Civil y Código Electoral y otras disposiciones conexas, Title IV, Arts. 58, 60, 61, 63.

presidential nominee . . . can influence the parties' national assemblies to choose specific candidates for deputy lists" (Ventura Robles, 1984: 57). Eduardo Ortiz is less reserved in his assessment of the party assemblies at all levels:

Neither the Constitution nor the law succeeds in providing effective state supervision of the internal electoral process in each party . . . permitting all kinds of fraud, including the fabrication of "paper assemblies," consisting of the acts of assemblies that were never held, providing the signatures of the supposed delegates, as ordered by the leaders of the party in the capital. (Casas Zamora and Briceño Fallas 1991: 323)

The means by which party leaders are able to retain control over the nomination process, in spite of formal decentralization, range from the use of patronage, to procedural tricks and manipulation, to outright fraud. The first of these provides the single most compelling explanation for central leadership control. Nevertheless, a broad array of strategies is important to national leaders. I review those that primarily affect district-, cantonal-, and provincial-level assemblies first, then discuss those that provide control over national party assemblies.

Controlling the lower-level assemblies. Among the more mundane factors frequently cited as contributing to central leadership control is the simple inability of the TSE to monitor the hundreds of district- and cantonal-level assemblies held by each party. Costa Rica has 510 districts and 81 cantons. Even monitoring only the assemblies of the two main parties, then, would require the TSE to oversee almost 1,200 assemblies prior to each election. Clearly, this is impossible for the 5 members of the tribunal and their staff of less than 20. A number of Costa Rican writers argue that this lack of direct oversight allows party leaders to rig local assemblies and vote counts to ensure that the delegates sent to provincial and national party assemblies are obedient to central directives (Muñoz Quesada 1981; Ventura Robles 1984).

Lack of direct oversight may allow the possibility of corruption, but it by no means guarantees it. Students of the U.S. Congress and of bureaucratic oversight have argued convincingly that the presence of "fire alarms" in administrative procedure can generate effective oversight even in the absence of direct monitoring (McCubbins, Noll, and Weingast 1989; McCubbins and Schwartz 1984). The argument is generalizable to the Costa Rican nomination process, provided that rank-and-file partisans have the incentive and ability to petition the TSE to sanction malfeasance by central party leaders.

The argument that the lack of direct monitoring allows illicit central party control over nominations, then, depends on the absence or ineffectiveness of

such fire alarms. In fact, party leaders, in manipulating the assembly process, take precisely the types of actions that would prevent fire alarms from
being pulled. One former deputy states that a favorite trick of party leaders
is to convoke district-level assemblies at seven in the morning, informing
only loyal party activists in advance of the time. The assembly would then
vote on delegates to the cantonal assembly and have completed its business
by 8 A.M. (Casas Zamora and Briceño Fallas 1991: 325n). Party members
who were not present, of course, might complain after the fact about the
scheduling procedure, but the low profile of the original district assembly
itself is designed not to attract attention. Moreover, the parties in the Legislative Assembly have recently taken action to provide even more leeway in
scheduling lower-level assemblies. Up until 1988, the electoral code man-
dated that no assemblies could be held more than one year prior to the
general election. In 1988, the Legislative Assembly amended the code to
eliminate this restriction starting with the 1990 elections, allowing the parties
to hold assemblies at any time.[18] District-level assemblies for the 1994
elections were being held in February and March 1992 – more than two
years in advance of the general election. The Costa Rican media quite
reasonably pointed out that party leaders were attempting to establish the
delegates to provincial and national assemblies early, before most voters
began to pay attention to the campaign. Once loyal and obedient delegates
are chosen by district and cantonal assemblies, central leaders can dominate
the nomination process (Roverssi 1992a, 1992b).

Dominating the national party assemblies. In addition to the manipulation of
lower-level assemblies, there are various procedural means by which central
party leaders exert influence over decisions by the national party assemblies
that make final decisions over nominations and lists. The first relevant factor
is precisely that national party assemblies are sovereign over provincial
assembly lists.[19] That is, despite the fact that assembly lists are voted on in
the general election at the provincial level, the provincial party assemblies
do not determine their own lists; rather, they recommend lists to the national
party assemblies. Given the level of central control over lower-level assemblies, these lists generally reflect national leadership preferences. When they
do not, however, they are altered by the national assemblies (Sojo Obando
1992; Ventura Robles 1984).

The national party assemblies as well have traditionally been extremely
responsive to central leadership demands. Although delegates elected
through the district, cantonal, and provincial assembly processes are gener-

---

[18] Tribunal Supremo de Elecciones (1989), Organic Electoral Law, Title IV, Art. 74, and
Transitorio II and III.
[19] Tribunal Supremo de Elecciones (1989), Organic Electoral Law, Art. 74.

ally loyal to central directives, national leaders have taken the precaution of expanding the size of national party assemblies to dilute the power of elected delegates. In addition to the 70 elected delegates, since the 1982 elections, the two main parties have expanded their national assemblies with appointed sectoral delegates. Sectoral delegates have been appointed by each party's executive committee – the president, general secretary, and treasurer – as representatives of organizations within each party, such as youth, women's, labor, business, agriculture, church, and student groups. The electoral code is silent on the appointment of additional sectoral delegates, so their number has not been fixed by law; but the parties have generally appointed 40 to 70, such that national party assemblies have included almost as many appointed delegates as elected ones.

Critics of the process have charged that national party leaders handpicked sectoral delegates to be absolutely obedient to central leadership decisions, thus rendering irrelevant any independent positions that might be taken by elected delegates. In 1992, a faction of the PLN led by party maverick and presidential candidate Jose Miguel Corrales challenged before the Supreme Court and the TSE the practice of appointing sectoral delegates, on the basis that sectoral appointments violated the principle of "one person, one vote" in intraparty decision making (Corrales 1992). The Court and the TSE upheld the challenge, thus forbidding the practice of expanding the national party assemblies beyond the 10 elected delegates from each province.[20] Thus, in the future, the ability of national party leaders to control nominations – and indeed, to control all intraparty decision making – is likely to be somewhat compromised relative to the level of control over the past 12 years.

Even the elimination of sectoral delegates, however, does not exhaust the means that central party leaders have employed to influence national party assembly decisions. Corrales has long insisted that blatant fraud is used when less heavy-handed means of influence fail. Before his break with the central leadership, Corrales had served two terms as a deputy, including two years as Assembly majority leader during his second term, so he is able to offer an insider's perspective. Even in 1990, prior to his most recent clash with the national leadership, he stated:

The situation has reached intolerable extremes in the major parties. For example, there was one case where the leadership had an interest in the election of X and not Y. The delegates voted, and X got 50 votes and Y 60. But the balloting was done on little pieces of paper, handed up to the leaders at the head table. So the leaders simply inverted the result, reading: "X 60 votes and Y 50." (Casas Zamora and Briceño Fallas 1991: 333)

[20] See "Sectoriales fuera de asamblea del PLN," in *La Nación*, March 14, 1992: 6A; and "El Registro Civil respalda las distritales del PLN," in *La República*, March 12, 1992: 6A.

Corrales's story suggests that whatever oversight TSE officials perform, even at national assemblies, may not be perfect. Nevertheless, most observers of party politics place more importance on the subtle use of patronage than on outright fraud to apply pressure on delegates. The current chairman of the TSE, Rafael Villegas Antillón, has stated that "the national party assemblies are highly manipulable. In practice, the presidential candidate, with a look, can tell any delegate how to vote" (Casas Zamora and Briceño Fallas 1991, fn. p. 332; Villegas Antillón 1992; Sojo Obando 1992; Interview 93-04).[21]

The consensus that presidential candidates have such enormous and universal influence over delegates seems odd on the surface, given the internal party struggles that surround presidential nominations. But the logic of the candidate's authority is straightforward and consistent with the focus of this study on career interests: presidential candidates are expected to control government patronage in the near future, and political appointments are a primary concern for party assembly delegates. Miguel Angel Rodriguez, a two-term deputy and president of the Legislative Assembly, makes the case the most clearly:

Nothing is more important in the nomination process than loyalties to the presidential candidate. All the delegates know that if their party wins the election, the future president ultimately controls all government posts. This is the source of the loyalty they profess, because they know this loyalty can be rewarded sooner or later, and all of the delegates are at the national assembly with an eye toward an ambassadorship, an advisory post, or a position in a ministry, etc. Under these circumstances, it is clear that the power of the candidate over the delegates is almost absolute. (Casas Zamora and Briceño Fallas 1991: 337)

Moreover, the president's patronage powers are not limited to the prime appointments that Rodriguez mentions by name. While some government workers are protected from the spoils system by civil service protection, Costa Rican presidents fill posts all the way down to local police chiefs and chauffeurs for government vehicles. Scanning issues of *La Gaceta* during the early weeks of any administration, one can find literally hundreds – maybe thousands – of notices for presidential appointments to jobs at all levels of government.

The main conclusion from this section is that national party leaders, and presidential candidates in particular, exercise enormous influence over the process of nominating assembly candidates and drawing up ballot lists. Party leaders have managed to subvert the formal decentralization of this process in the electoral code through a number of procedural maneuvers, most

---

[21] In the past three elections, the major parties have selected their presidential candidates in national primaries, well before the national party assemblies. Even before that, however, when presidential candidates were elected by the party assemblies, the presidential candidate was determined before the assembly lists.

significantly through the use of patronage. The recent Supreme Court prohibition on sectoral delegates to national party assemblies might reduce the influence of central party leaders somewhat, but the main carrot with which presidential candidates can persuade delegates – appointments – remains.

Control over nominations and ballot lists, and thus over electoral prospects, in Costa Rica is similar in Venezuela in that it is centralized in national party leaders. A key difference between the two countries concerns which party leaders control the process. In Venezuela, the party leaders who control nominations and lists are long-term fixtures in the official hierarchy of each party, and they prominently include the leaders of the party's caucus in the Senate and the Chamber of Deputies. In Costa Rica on the other hand, presidential candidates have the most influence over career prospects, and so the most influence over delegates' behavior. But in Costa Rica, the tenure of presidents is limited even more strictly than that of legislators – to a single four-year term. So although presidential candidates can exercise ex ante control over who secures election to the Legislative Assembly, once in office their control over the future career prospects of legislators is limited. This fact will be critical in Chapter 5, on party discipline in the Costa Rican Assembly. The next step for now is to demonstrate that ex post control over deputies' careers is exercised through the control by subsequent presidents over political appointments.

Appointments and political careers

This section demonstrates that political appointments are the primary source of post-Assembly careers for Costa Rican politicians. In contrast, I do not present data on appointments in Venezuela. Given the comparative nature of this chapter, the inattention to Venezuela in this section warrants some explanation.

Venezuela

In Venezuela, the presence of legislative careers means that the party leaders who control nominations and ballot lists exercise control over politicians' career prospects. Appointments to executive branch positions may be a significant route to political careers in Venezuela. I do not have the data on executive appointments to test this proposition. Nevertheless, the high rates of reelection to the Venezuelan Congress show that for those already in Congress, the *primary* route for extending a political career is to remain in Congress. Any explanation of legislative behavior based on career motivations, then, must focus on who controls congressional reelection prospects. These are the party leaders who control nominations and ballot lists. The lack of term limits in Venezuela allows legislative party leaders to remain in Congress indefinitely. Thus, the leaders who exercise ex ante control over electoral prospects for congressional candidates also exercise ex post control over reelectoral prospects for congressional incumbents.

The point is that the political careers of Venezuelan legislators are controlled by stable cadres of career politicians and their supporters. Those who control nominations and ballot lists in one election are likely to be the same party leaders who control these processes in the next election. The fact that Venezuelan law stipulates neither term limits nor specific processes by which nominations and lists must be established allows for stable control over Venezuelan political careers over time. It is precisely the lack of such stability in the control of Costa Rican political careers that mandates an examination of post-Assembly appointments in that country.

Costa Rica

This section presents data that clearly demonstrate two points. First, the absence of Legislative Assembly careers in Costa Rica does not imply an absence of political careers. Political appointments provide the most promising route to a post-Assembly political career. Second, the prospect for political appointment depends directly on the electoral fortunes of a legislator's party in presidential elections. Thus, incumbent legislators can improve their post-Assembly career prospects by enhancing their party's chance of winning the presidency.

Costa Rican presidents dominate post-Assembly career prospects, much as the preceding section argued that presidential *candidates* control ex ante Assembly electoral prospects. The key to presidential control in both cases is patronage. However, presidential control over political careers in Costa Rica does not imply stable control over political careers, as in Venezuela, because Costa Rican presidents are prohibited from reelection for life. For any given politician, X, control over X's electoral prospects to the Assembly and over X's post-Assembly career prospects are exercised by different principals. A presidential candidate, Y, might dominate nominations and the formation of lists that determine X's initial prospects for election to the Assembly. If Y wins the presidency, Y serves his or her term concurrently with X's term in the Assembly. But X's post-Assembly political career is dependent on an appointment by the president who serves after Y. Thus, ex ante control over electoral prospects, and ex post control over career prospects, are exercised by different principals.

Aggregate appointments. The first task in building this case is to demonstrate that post-Assembly political careers in Costa Rica are possible, and that they are built on presidential appointments. Recall that among deputies asked "If you serve your party well in the Assembly, what compensation can you expect?" over 90% mentioned appointments to executive ministries, the foreign service, or posts as directors of the country's autonomous institutions. With this in mind, I undertook to determine how many ex-deputies actually receive presidential appointments to one or more of these posts.[22] Of course, it is likely that some deputies received presidential appointments to institutions other than those included in this study.[23] Thus, the rate of post-Assembly appointments established in this analysis is almost certain to underestimate the actual post-Assembly appointments. Nevertheless, the consistency with which the three sets of institutions included here appeared in deputies' interview responses indicates clearly that these are plum appointments. The rate at which ex-deputies are given these posts serves as a good, albeit conservative, indicator of the rate at which deputies' career ambitions are rewarded.

Because no records are kept as to what deputies do after their service in the Assembly, it was necessary to compile databases of all presidential appointments to the relevant institutions, and then check these lists against Assembly rosters to determine the rate of appointment. Assembly rosters were easy to obtain; complete data on presidential appointments was more difficult. Complete data on ministerial appointments was available at the Legislative Assembly Archive.[24] Nearly complete data on foreign service appointments since 1982 were also available. However, no data on foreign service appointments were available prior to that date. As for appointments to autonomous institutions, I was able to obtain complete data for 11 of the 25 such institutions from 1949 to 1990, and for 18 of 25 for the 1990–1994 administration.

The data on post-Assembly political appointments that I have documented are presented in Table 3.6. Columns represent the number of appointments received by politicians *after* their service in the Assembly. The rows break down the data according to party. All those who served in the 1949 through

---

[22] Appointments to all such posts are strictly presidential prerogatives. The Assembly has no confirmation authority analogous to the U.S. Senate's power of advice and consent over executive appointments.

[23] The most likely such appointments would be in the judiciary, and possibly in law enforcement. These appointments are not included in the database constructed here for two reasons. First, they were not mentioned by most deputies as preferred appointments, as were appointment to ministries, ambassadorships, and posts in the autonomous institutions. Second, I did not have sufficient time in the Costa Rican government archives to conduct searches of all judicial and law enforcement appointments to identify ex-deputies. Ideally, of course, all these appointments would be included in this study.

[24] Appointments at the level of vice-minister, however, were not included here. Thus, if any ex-deputies received appointments at the level of vice-minister or below – which is virtually certain – then the rate of ministerial appointment is inevitably underestimated here.

Table 3.6. *Distribution of appointed posts among former Costa Rican deputies,*
1949–1986 cohorts

Number of Appts per deputy / party	0	1	2	3	4	5
PLN	168 (67)	54 (22)	17 (6)	5 (2)	3 (1)	2 (1)
Main opposition[a]	215 (81)	33 (12)	10 (4)	4 (2)	2 (1)	2 (1)
Christian Democrats	133 (77)	26 (15)	6 (3)	4 (2)	1 (1)	2 (1)
Other	44 (83)	5 (9)	3 (6)	1 (2)	0 (0)	0 (0)
All	425 (74)	96 (17)	30 (5)	11 (2)	4 (1)	5 (1)

Note: Columns represent number of documented appointments for each deputy. Percentages
are in parentheses.
[a] Main Opposition includes all *calderonistas* and Christian Democrats, as well as all members
of the PUN. The former two groups are also counted in the Christian Democrat category,
however, to illustrate career patterns in what has become the unified main opposition to the
PLN. Because of this format, double counting occurs, and column totals do not sum to the
total for "All" parties. A few other cases are also double counted because deputies served in
the Assembly under different party labels in different terms.

the 1986 Assembly cohorts are included.[25] Thus, of 571 deputies to serve
during this period across all parties, I document no post-Assembly appointments for 425, or 74%; one appointment for 17%; two appointments for 5%;
three appointments for 2%; and four and five appointments each for 1%. I
document a greater rate of appointments for those who served in the Assembly for the PLN – not surprisingly, given that appointments are controlled
by the president, and that the PLN has controlled the presidency during 6
of the 10 administrations studied here. Deputies from the main opposition
parties to the PLN, and from the Christian Democratic coalition that has
gained parity with the PLN, have fared somewhat worse. And deputies from
minor parties are the least likely to continue their political careers outside
the Assembly.

The documented appointments demonstrate that post-Assembly political
careers are possible, but the lack of complete data on appointments to
the foreign service and the autonomous institutions means that these data
inevitably underestimate the likelihood of post-Assembly appointments. To
account for the unavailability of complete data on appointments, and to
provide a more accurate assessment of post-Assembly prospects, I calculate
estimates of the actual numbers and rates of appointments. These estimates
are extrapolations based on the documented appointments as follows. For
foreign service, I calculated the average ratio of foreign service to ministerial
appointments across the three administrations for which data on foreign

[25] The 1990–1994 cohort of incumbent deputies is not included, as incumbent deputies are
ineligible for concurrent service in executive branch appointed positions.

service appointments are complete: 1.3 foreign service appointments to each domestic ministerial appointment. Then, for the period for which no foreign service data were available, I estimate a number of appointments equal to 1.3 times the number of ministerial appointments. For autonomous institutions, the process is more straightforward, because documented appointments to these agencies exist across the entire period under study.[26] For administrations before 1990, I simply multiply the number of autonomous institution appointments in each administration by 2.3 to arrive at the estimate. For the administration beginning in 1990, I multiply the appointments by 1.4.

The total estimated number of appointments is distributed across the total number of deputies and across parties according to the same distribution as reflected in the documented appointments. That is, there is no reason to believe that actual appointments are distributed any more densely among deputies (i.e., more multiple appointments for individual deputies, with fewer deputies overall receiving appointments) or more diffusely than are documented appointments. The same is true for the partisan distribution.

The estimated data on post-Assembly appointments (Figure 3.7) provide a far more realistic evaluation than do the data on documented appointments of the likelihood for securing post-Assembly appointments.

Across all parties, I estimate that 54% of those who served in the Assembly cohorts of 1949 through 1986 received no appointments to ministries, foreign service, or autonomous institutions, 30% received one appointment, 9% received two, and 6% received three or more appointments. The relative likelihood across parties of receiving an appointment is the same as with the documented appointments, but the absolute likelihood is higher.

---

[26] Most of the autonomous institutions have been created in the years since the establishment of the current Costa Rican regime in 1949. The major exceptions are the banks, the social security administration, and a handful of utilities. Social security directors have been appointed by the president since before the current regime. The bank and utility directors have been presidential appointees since the nationalization of these institutions during the junta of 1948–1949.

As for the other autonomous institutions, my data on appointments begins with their creation. Thus, complete data on 11 of 25 institutions throughout the entire current regime does not imply that there were presidential appointments to all 11 institutions during every administration since 1949. Rather, as more institutions were created, there have been more appointments.

I use the ratio of 11 of 25 (44%) institutions to estimate total appointments to the autonomous institutions throughout the entire period, however, for the following reason. For the institutions on which I lack appointments data, I also lack data on their dates of creation. I have no reason to expect that the institutions for which I have data were created systematically any earlier or later than were those for which I lack appointments data. Therefore, I retain the 11 of 25 ratio as the basis for my estimation of autonomous institution appointments for the entire period 1949 through 1990. For the administration beginning in 1990, I have appointments data on 18 of the 25 existing autonomous institutions, and so for this administration, I estimate that I have documented 72% of actual appointments.

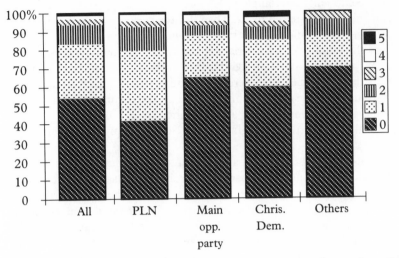

Figure 3.7. Estimated distribution of appointed posts among former Costa Rican deputies, 1949–1986 cohorts. *Note:* Gray tones represent number of appointments for each former deputy.

The estimated data on appointments reinforce the point that political careers are possible in Costa Rica, and provide an accurate assessment of their likelihood. On this count, the comparison with Venezuelan political careers is most striking. Recall that of Venezuelan members of congress across all parties since 1963, 54% had served one term, 24% had served two terms, 13% three terms, and 8% four or more terms. The likelihood that a Venezuelan deputy is reelected to Congress is virtually the same as the likelihood that a Costa Rican deputy receives a plum political appointment after Assembly service.

Appointments and the electoral connection. The aggregate estimates on post-Assembly appointments make clear that political careers are viable in Costa Rica. But for the purpose of explaining how political careers affect legislative behavior, a more relevant cut on the data examines the likelihood of a deputy receiving an appointment immediately after service in the Assembly. This is the critical cut for two reasons. First, term limits give Costa Rican deputies short time horizons. Deputies know exactly when their tenure in office will end, and that without exception they will need to secure other employment after that date. Therefore, the prospects for appointment during the *immediately subsequent term* are the most relevant appointment data in explaining the behavior of incumbent legislators. Second, incumbent deputies can affect their own prospects for appointment in the immediately successive term if they can help their party to win the presidency. Their ability to influence their party's prospects in more distant elections is tenuous, but their actions as incumbent deputies might well influence whether one of their own partisans – rather than an opponent – is dispensing patronage as they leave the Assembly.

Party control over patronage is critical in establishing the existence of an "electoral connection" between the performance of Costa Rican legislators and their career prospects. This electoral connection has been studied at length in the U.S. Congress, and there is abundant evidence that legislators struggle mightily to serve the interests of their electoral constituency in order to be reelected.[27] But in Costa Rica, only the party can be reelected at the end of a term; none of the national elected officials can be so rewarded. So if there is to be an electoral career connection for Costa Rican politicians, it must be channeled through the party. And because the positions coveted by deputies are appointed by the president, the critical arena for party success is the presidential election.

To determine the link between party electoral success and immediate post-Assembly appointments, I examine the likelihood that a deputy receives an appointed post in the term immediately succeeding Assembly service. For each Assembly cohort up to 1986, I divide those deputies whose party or coalition won the next presidential election from those whose party lost. For each group, I determine the rate at which the ex-deputies received political appointments during the next administration (see Table 3.7 and Figure 3.8).

The data illustrate a number of points clearly. First, for a deputy whose party or coalition wins the next presidential election, the prospects for securing a political appointment during the next administration are bright. An estimated average 48% of this group has been able to continue in national politics in the term immediately following Assembly service. Second, these prospects have grown considerably brighter over time. Whereas the estimated rate of appointment for winning partisans in the 1953 to 1974 period was 30%, the rate from 1974 to 1990 was 64%. This is largely due to the growth in the size of the Costa Rican government. There are more ministries and more autonomous institutions now than at the beginning of the current regime, and thus more appointed positions. Third, for deputies whose party loses the next presidential election, the prospects for receiving an appointment during the successive administration are close to nil, with no change in the pattern over time.

---

[27] Classic works on this behavior include Mayhew (1974), Fiorina (1977), and Fenno (1978), as well as Cain, Ferejohn, and Fiorina (1987). Statistical analyses of the compatibility of voting records with constituent interests of members of Congress include Peltzman (1984) and Lott (1987).

Table 3.7. Estimated appointments of former deputies to executive positions during term immediately following Assembly service

Cohort	Party won next presidential election	Party lost next presidential election
1949	2/3 (67)	0/60 (0)
1953	4/20 (20)	1/38 (3)
1958	7/21 (33)	0/40 (0)
1962	8/25 (32)	0/33 (0)
1966	12/24 (50)	0/33 (0)
1970	7/36 (19)	0/26 (0)
1974	11/19 (58)	2/42 (5)
1978	25/29 (86)	0/33 (0)
1982	14/34 (41)	0/25 (0)
1986	18/25 (72)	0/33 (0)
Average	124/258 (48)	3/363 (1)

Note: Percentages are in parentheses.

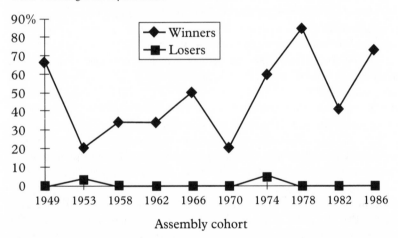

Figure 3.8. Estimated appointments of former deputies to executive positions during term immediately following Assembly service according to party's fortunes in next presidential election.

These data tell a clear story about political careers in Costa Rica. They confirm the interview data suggesting that the primary route to a post-Assembly political career is through political appointments. The reliance of deputies on appointments generates an electoral connection for deputies that is dependent on the party's electoral success, and in particular, through the party's ability to win the presidency. Those deputies whose party wins the next presidency have excellent prospects for continuing their careers in politics; conversely, those whose party loses are – at least for the time being – finished. This fact suggests that the presence of term limits in Costa Rica has not removed the imperative for legislators to seek electoral success in order to further their own careers. If anything, the all-or-nothing prospects for appointment in the immediate post-Assembly term imply that the electoral connection is extraordinarily stark for Costa Rican legislators precisely *because of* term limits. But the measure of electoral success is partisan instead of personal.

Conclusion

Political careers are possible in both of the countries examined. In Venezuela, those who manage to secure election to Congress tend increasingly to stay there. Congressional careers are the norm, as indicated especially by the experienced cohort who formed the 1989–1994 Venezuelan Congress – the most recent for which I have data. In Costa Rica, term limits stunt Assembly careers, but ex-deputies nonetheless build political careers based on presidential appointments.

The remarkable thing about the comparison between Venezuela and Costa Rica is the subtlety of the effect of term limits on political careers. Political careerism is the primary motivating force driving legislative behavior in both countries. In both countries the career prospects of legislators are primarily dependent on party leadership decisions. In Venezuela, this is because of the centralized control that legislative party leaders exercise over nominations and ballot lists. In Costa Rica too, control over nominations and lists is centralized in the leadership. So far, it seems that the two systems are similar despite term limits.

The effect of term limits, however, is in altering the nature of centralized party control over careers. Because of term limits, there is no route to a political career in Costa Rica besides patronage. Expected control over patronage gives presidential nominees control over party nominating conventions and the structure of lists. Presidential candidates in Costa Rica exercise vast control over electoral prospects for Assembly candidates. But once in office, term limits mandate that Assembly members are no longer dependent on the president (or unsuccessful candidate) who was responsible for their nomination. Rather, they are dependent on the country's *next* president for post-Assembly appointment. Because the identity of the next president is unknown to deputies throughout most of their Assembly term, they cannot simply curry the favor of the next president in order to improve their odds of receiving appointments. However, deputies can and do work doggedly to improve the prospects for their party to win the next presidential election. And parties, in turn, serve as appointment cartels, distributing plum positions among their own members and denying appointments systematically to opposing partisans.

In Venezuela, those responsible for legislators' election also control their prospects for reelection, and thus for a political career. The electoral connection for Venezuelan legislators runs through the party, and only weakly to voters. In Costa Rica as well, the electoral connection runs through the party. But term limits add the twist that the principal responsible for legislators' election is not the same principal responsible for their possible appointment.

The shifting dependence of legislators for their career prospects lends a fascinating complexity to representation in Costa Rica. It also suggests a solution to a potential problem for political parties as collective actors under term limits. The interest of parties is to win elections. To do so they need to build reputations for providing the goods and services that voters want. Parties need politicians who are willing to do the hard work of building and maintaining party reputations. But where politicians cannot be reelected, the question arises of what incentive they have to work hard maintaining their party's reputation. Parties in Costa Rica face a collective action problem in ensuring that a legislator under term limits will act in the party's interest. The data presented here suggest that patronage is the solution to this problem. Despite term limits, Costa Rican deputies depend on their parties for their political futures. The electoral connection is not gone in Costa Rica; it is just indirect.

The next two chapters explore in greater detail two aspects of Costa Rican legislative representation as they are affected by term limits. In particular, I explore the extent to which political parties in Costa Rica have solved the collective action problem just described. The subject of Chapter 4 is legislative particularism; that of Chapter 5 is legislative party discipline. In both cases, I argue that the behavior and performance of Costa Rican legislators are directly related to their career prospects. Having outlined the nature of political careers in this chapter, I turn attention now to legislative behavior and performance.

4

Term limits and particularism

Particularism is the provision of goods and services that exclusively benefit a specific set of recipients, even when the collective costs of providing the goods and services outweigh the collective benefits. Political scientists have argued that two conditions are necessary to generate particularistic behavior by legislators: personal votes and the desire for reelection. With regard to the first condition, certain electoral rules generate incentives for legislators to cultivate personal reputations, which, in turn, can encourage legislators to provide particularistic goods to their personal supporters, even at the expense of the programmatic policy concerns of their parties (Carey and Shugart in press; Myerson 1993). The second condition is logically inseparable from the first: the incentive to cultivate personal constituencies is driven by the desire to secure reelection. Political scientists are in such widespread agreement on this point that it has reached near axiomatic status. Academics who differ on fundamental issues nevertheless concur that legislative behavior is driven by the desire for reelection (Cox and McCubbins 1993; Downs 1957; Fenno 1978; Mayhew 1974). This unusual consensus is a product of the scarcity of political systems in which legislators are prohibited from reelection. In short, political science has rarely considered the nature of legislative behavior in lieu of an electoral connection because so few legislators in any political systems are barred from reelection.

The assumption that reelection is allowed, however, is logically necessary to any explanation of particularism based on electoral rules.[1] The existence of legislative term limits, in turn, renders useless any such electoral explanation of particularism. Where legislators cannot be reelected, they have no

---

[1] Even where electoral rules seem to preclude any personal electoral payoff from particularism, this has been the case. The Israeli Knesset is elected in a single, nationwide district, from closed party lists. The system provides minimal incentives for members – at least those from large parties – to cultivate personal support. Yet in explaining why Knesset members engage in casework, Eric Uslaner (1985) argues that members believe in its marginal electoral benefits, and that many cultivate personal reputations in the expectation that the electoral system will eventually be changed to one that more directly rewards personal support.

direct electoral incentive to build personal support among voters through particularism, regardless of how the electoral system is organized. This prima facie insight is the basis of the confidence among term limit supporters that restricting reelection will reduce particularism among U.S. legislators. In this light, however, the behavior of Costa Rican deputies is doubly puzzling. Most deputies spend more time providing particularistic goods than on any other task. Yet neither of the necessary electoral conditions for particularism exists in Costa Rica. In the first place, deputies are elected from closed party lists in large-magnitude districts. And in any case, incumbent deputies cannot be rewarded by voters with reelection.

This chapter addresses the issue of why Costa Rican legislators provide particularism when the conditions normally regarded as necessary for this behavior do not exist. More specifically, the chapter addresses two questions: Why are particularistic goods provided without personal electoral incentives, and how are the suppliers of particularism under these conditions motivated? I answer these questions by arguing, first, that particularism can generate electoral support for parties. If individual politicians cannot be reelected, a party nevertheless can benefit from the favors done for voters by its agents. Second, I argue that suppliers of particularism under these conditions are motivated by career interests, but not through a personal electoral connection. Post-Assembly careers for Costa Rican legislators are dependent on presidential patronage, which, in turn, is contingent on partisan electoral success. Although I demonstrate that Costa Rican Assembly parties organize so as to ensure the provision of particularism, I am unable to demonstrate conclusively that those deputies who best provide particularism are most frequently rewarded with patronage appointments after their Assembly terms. Deputies interviewed, however, clearly believed this to be the case. Finally, the relationship between particularism and post-Assembly careers in Costa Rica is complicated by competition within parties over presidential nominations. I demonstrate that intrapartisan jockeying among deputies and presidential hopefuls is another factor influencing career prospects under term limits. Before presenting the main arguments of the chapter, however, it is necessary to establish the basic empirical fact of particularism by deputies in Costa Rica, and more briefly to remark on its absence in Venezuela.

Particularism observed: Small favors

Recall from Chapter 2 that in both Costa Rica and Venezuela, legislators are elected from closed party lists in large-magnitude districts. If the possibility of reelection and an electoral system that rewards personal reputation were both necessary for legislative particularism, then neither Costa Rican nor Venezuelan deputies should be expected to engage in particularism. In both countries, the second condition is absent. And indeed, Costa Rican deputies should be even less prone toward particularism given legislative term limits. In practice, the behavior of Venezuelan deputies has been consistent with the theory of electoral incentives: they have not engaged in particularism.[2] Costa Rican deputies, on the other hand, are diligent suppliers of such goods and services to constituents. I focus on two critical types of particularism provided by Costa Rican deputies: constituent service, and small pork-barrel appropriations called *partidas específicas* (PEs).[3] These are the most small-scale and locally (sometimes *personally*) specific types of particularism. They are akin to the errand boy activities and local pork-barreling for which U.S. legislators are so often criticized (Ehrenhalt 1991; Fiorina 1977). These are precisely the types of small favors to local petitioners that legislators without electoral incentives should be least likely to engage in, according to an electoral theory of particularism.

Making the collective personal: Costa Rican bailiwicks

The first fact of Costa Rican legislative particularism that needs explanation is how geographically specific benefits are distributed by deputies who have no geographically exclusive constituencies. Under the closed-list proportional representation electoral system, Costa Rican deputies are elected by votes cast across entire provinces; but in the provision of small favors, they focus attention on mutually exclusive subdistricts within their province that necessarily encompass only a fraction of the constituents who elected them, and that do not have any official stature within the electoral system. I refer to these subdistricts as bailiwicks, in keeping with the language used by Ames (1992) to describe the bastions of particularism and electoral support for individual Brazilian legislators within multimember districts. Indeed the bailiwick phenomenon has been noted as well in the United States, most notably in municipal politics, where urban party machines coordinate the distribution of small favors to neighborhoods by city officials elected at large in multimember districts (Caro 1974; Riordan 1963).

The division of provincial electoral districts into multiple bailiwicks for

---

[2] It is important to keep in mind that the 1989 and 1992 electoral reforms were designed to encourage Venezuelan deputies to be more attentive to district constituencies. The reforms went into effect in the 1993 elections.

[3] *Partidas específicas* translates literally to "specific projects." These are not the only type of budgetary pork in Costa Rica, and in all likelihood are not the largest in terms of funds appropriated. But whereas most large particularistic appropriations, such as highways, dams, harbors projects, are included in the budgets of the executive departments, PEs are set aside in a separate part of the annual budget. The PEs budget is unique in that each appropriation is attributable to a specific deputy and can be traced to a specific geographical location. For this reason, the distribution pattern of PEs can be documented relatively accurately. Securing and delivering PEs also occupies a disproportionate amount of deputies' time, relative to the PEs' share of the entire budget. Thus, although PEs are not a large proportion of overall spending, they do account for an inordinate amount of deputies' activity.

the provision of small favors takes place within each of the two major parties in the Legislative Assembly – those that secure representation in all the nation's provinces. After elections, each party divides each province into as many bailiwicks as it has won seats in the province. Each deputy is personally charged with providing small favors – constituency service and PEs – to a geographically exclusive bailiwick (Arias Sanchez 1979; Casas Zamora and Briceño Fallas 1991; Taylor 1992; Ventura Robles 1984).

Thus, once the election results are in, Costa Rican legislative representation takes something of the appearance of a system with single-member legislative districts. Henceforth, deputies refer to themselves as representing Liberia and Santa Cruz Counties, for example, rather than Guanacaste Province, or Perez Zeledon County rather than San José Province. The press also refers to deputies matter-of-factly according to their bailiwicks, as do constituents. One critical difference from single-member districts, of course, is that each citizen effectively has two representatives – one from each major party – not one. But this is not the same as saying the country is divided into two-member districts, because the bailiwicks carved up by the parties do not necessarily coincide. And at any rate, the division into unofficial districts is primarily of consequence for majority party deputies, whose access to pork and influence with the bureaucracy make them proficient providers of small favors. Deputies of the major opposition party also divide their provinces into bailiwicks and act as interlocutors between constituents and government agencies, but without pork to distribute and with less clout over bureaucrats, they are far less influential than their majority counterparts.

In addition to dividing the work of representation geographically through bailiwicks, Costa Rican parties also divide labor functionally. Political observers and politicians alike distinguish between national and local deputies (Ventura Robles 1984; Interview 93–09; Interview 93–13). The former are generally those who occupied the top five or so positions on each of the major parties' San José list, so their election is virtually guaranteed. They are generally nationally prominent figures even prior to their election, and their names are expected to attract votes to their parties' lists (Interview 93–04). In office, they focus on national policy, and it is from among these deputies that the Assembly leadership is generally selected. The rest of the Assembly members are considered local deputies. They elect the Assembly leadership, attend committee meetings, and vote in caucuses on party positions on key issues, but most of their day-to-day work focuses on servicing their bailiwicks.

Even acknowledging this functional division of labor, it should be noted that national deputies are not entirely exempt from particularistic responsibilities. An examination of budgets demonstrates that all deputies, local and national alike, are individually responsible for distributing PEs to specific areas. The difference between national and local deputies on this count likely has to do with staffing. National deputies holding party and Assembly leadership positions are allotted more staff support than are local deputies. In these offices, staffers provide small favors to constituents, allowing the deputies to attend to national legislation. At any rate, the budgetary data indicate that PEs are distributed by all majority party deputies.

Partidas específicas: A clearer look at particularism

The format of the annual budget legislation makes it possible to piece together a fairly precise picture of Costa Rican bailiwicks and to identify their personal representatives in the Legislative Assembly. PEs, small pork-barrel appropriations targeted at specific communities, are recorded in a separate section of the budget, and each individual line item (each PE) is identified by the county in which the money is to be spent, the recipient organization and the nature of the project, and the deputy responsible for securing and distributing the PE.[4] Rather than being disbursed through executive agencies, PEs are delivered directly and personally by deputies to community groups. If Costa Rican bailiwicks have budgetary substance, then, they should be identifiable as geographical areas in which communities are exclusively dependent for PEs on a single deputy. This is precisely what I find in the budgets.

Partisan distribution of PEs. PEs are distributed almost exclusively among majority party members, and denied to deputies of the main opposition altogether. In the two years for which the data are available, majority party deputies received 98% and 96% of all PE funds, while those of the main opposition received virtually nothing (Table 4.1).[5] Members of minor parties, a few of which generally win seats in the Legislative Assembly, are given a few PEs in exchange for supporting the majority party on key votes,

---

[4] The deputy responsible for each PE is identified in each line item only in the most recent budgets – during the Arias Sanchez and Calderón Fournier administrations. In earlier budgets, only the project, county, and amount of the PE were noted. The current form of budget annotation makes analysis of the distribution of PEs easier for recent years. Nevertheless, the job of securing and delivering PEs predates the current budget format.

[5] Data on PEs broken down item by item are available for the years 1983, 1988, and 1991. These data had to be input to the computer by hand, with between 5,000 and 10,000 observations on each variable (county, amount, and, in the latter two years, deputy). Loading each year required about one week of labor. Moreover, research budget constraints seriously limited the amount of time I was able to spend in Costa Rica. Therefore, I was able to load only three years of data – one from each of the past three assemblies. Because the distribution of PEs by deputy was included only in the 1988 and 1991 budgets, the breakdown by party is available only for those years.

Table 4.1. Partisan distribution of small pork from two Costa Rican budgets

Partidas Especificas	1988		1991	
Colones to majority party deputies	1,135,145,000	(98)	1,351,630,000	(96)
Colones to main opposition deputies	50,000	(0.0004)	300,000	(0.02)
Colones to independent deputies	22,635,000	(2)	50,480,000	(4)
Total colones appropriated	1,157,830,000	(100)	1,402,410,000	(100)

Note: Percentages are in parentheses.

when some majority deputies are absent, or occasionally when a handful of majority deputies break party discipline. The most opportunistic party in this manner during recent assemblies has been the Unión Agrícola Cartaginés (UAC), which competes only in Cartagena Province, and has won one seat in four of the five assemblies elected from 1974 to 1990. The UAC has regularly been willing to exchange its support on broad national policy issues for a share of PEs, regardless of whether the PLN or PUSC controls the Legislative Assembly (Villanueva Badilla 1992; Volio Guevara 1988). In the 1990–1994 Legislative Assembly, the similarly nonideological Partido Unión Generaleña (PUGEN) deputy has secured PEs for his loyal supporters by supporting the national policy platform of the majority PUSC (Interview 93–20). In 1991, the UAC and PUGEN deputies each received C25 million each in PEs. The other minor party deputy, on the other hand, was from the socialist Pueblo Unido Party. He was fundamentally at odds with the PUSC economic program of austerity and privatization. Not surprisingly, he received no PEs in 1991. Likewise, during the previous Legislative Assembly, the UAC deputy was willing to trade his vote to the majority PLN for a share of pork. In 1988, he received C23 million. The other two minor party deputies in that Legislative Assembly, both Socialists and opposed to PLN policies almost as vehemently as to PUSC policies, received nothing.

   Within the majority party itself, PEs are distributed remarkably equitably. Table 4.2 shows summary statistics on the total funds per deputy within Assembly majorities in the 1988 and 1991 budgets. In both cases, the standard deviation in total funds per deputy is less than 20% of the mean funds across all majority party members, and in the 1991 budget the figure is below 10%. The data overall indicate that there is very little variance in the ability of majority party deputies to secure small pork-barrel appropriations for their bailiwicks. Based on two budgets, during two assemblies with different majorities, in each case majority party deputies were all allotted pretty much the same resources to distribute among their communities.

   The strictly partisan division of PEs in Costa Rica demonstrates clearly

Table 4.2. Distribution of PE funds among majority party deputies, 1988 and 1991

Total PE funds per majority party deputy	1988	1991
Mean	39,142,800	44,490,600
Minimum	30,000,000	35,500,000
Maximum	57,785,000	60,505,000
Standard deviation	6,533,820	4,307,320
Standard deviation as percentage of mean	16.7	9.7

that small pork is a tool used by the majority party to cultivate party support. The intrapartisan distribution of PEs, however, suggests that a rule of equality is used by Assembly majorities in spreading funds among members. Parties compete for small pork, but individuals within parties do not. The lack of intrapartisan competition for funds is sensible, given that Costa Rican deputies are not in direct competition with each other for votes. In the first place, vote pooling across party lists and the lack of personal votes means that personal reputations among voters matter little in elections. More significantly, the lack of immediate reelection means that the incumbents who deliver PEs will not be judged by voters relative to their fellow deputies at the end of their terms.

Using PEs to identify bailiwicks. I have claimed that, within parties, deputies divide multimember electoral districts into single-member bailiwicks to deliver small favors personally. In this section, I use PE data to demonstrate that these bailiwicks have budgetary substance. The key point is that the distribution of PEs across Costa Rican counties demonstrates that majority party deputies are each responsible for delivering small pork to geographically exclusive constituencies.

Each PE is recorded in the budget according the county in which the project is located, as well as the deputy responsible for delivering the funds.[6] These data make it possible to cross-tabulate total funds appropriated to deputies and counties to determine how much each deputy and county received in total, as well as what share of each county's total funds were delivered by each deputy. Imagine first that representation is purely national; no deputy is responsible for any particular geographical subdistrict. If this is the case, then each county's total PEs should be delivered about evenly by all the majority party deputies. Now imagine that representation is purely provincial – the level at which deputies are elected. In this case, each county's PEs should come about evenly from the majority party depu-

---

[6] Counties (in Spanish, cantons) are subprovincial units. Each province is divided into between 6 and 20 counties; there are 81 counties in all.

ties elected from that province. No deputies from outside the province should deliver PEs in the province, but there should be no pattern to the delivery of PEs among provincial deputies. Finally, imagine the expected distribution of PEs under a bailiwick system. There are always more counties than majority party deputies in a province.[7] Bailiwicks, then, should encompass more than one county, and in turn, each county should be dependent on a single deputy for the delivery of PEs. The delivery of PEs approximates this last scenario remarkably closely.

The fact that bailiwick boundaries do not necessarily fall precisely along county lines mitigates the perfect dependence of each county on a single deputy. There are a couple of reasons for this incongruence. In the first place, counties are fixed geographical units that are noted in PE budgetary line items and so make possible a rough identification of where funds are spent. But bailiwicks are informal divisions drawn for each Legislative Assembly by the majority caucus. Counties generally demark distinct communities of interest, particularly in rural areas, and so county lines are often salient references to follow in drawing bailiwicks. But this need not always be the case. Second and more important, counties vary by factors of almost 100 in population. Although the average bailiwick encompasses two to three counties, the largest urban counties contain enough voters to warrant division into more than one bailiwick. Where this is the case, of course, the county will not be entirely dependent on a single deputy for PEs.

Despite these qualifications, the degree to which most counties are dependent on a single deputy is striking, as shown by the Herfindahl–Hirschman (HH) index scores for the concentration of each county's PEs across deputies. The HH index for each county is calculated as follows:

$$HH = \Sigma P_d^2,$$

where P_d is the proportion of the county's PEs delivered by each deputy. Thus, if a county received 40% of its PEs from one deputy, 30% from another, 20% from another, and 10% from a fourth, its HH index would be

$$(.4)^2 + (.3)^2 + (.2)^2 + (.1)^2 = .3.$$

If it received 75% from one deputy and 25% from another, its HH index would be

$$(.75)^2 + (.25)^2 = .62.$$

If it received all its PEs from a single deputy – perfect concentration – its HH index would be 1^2, or 1. Across all 81 cantons for the years 1988 and

---

[7] The majority cohorts during the two assemblies for which I have complete budgetary data each included 29 deputies, responsible for the country's 81 counties.

Table 4.3. Dependence of Costa Rican counties on individual deputies for PEs

Hirfindahl–Hirschman Index	1988	1991
Mean	.83	.81
Minimum	.25	.14
Maximum	1.00	1.00
Standard deviation	.19	.19
Mean, excluding provincial capitals	.84	.83
Standard deviation, excluding provincial capitals	.18	.16

1991, summary statistics on the HH index scores for concentration of PEs by deputies are listed in Table 4.3. The mean HH index scores of .83 and .81 indicate a high concentration of dependence of almost all counties on a single deputy. For example, if a county received 90% of its PEs from a single deputy and 10% from another, its HH index score would be .82 – exactly the mean score across all Costa Rican counties over the two years. Moreover, in each case, if the seven, primarily urban, provincial capitals are removed from the data, the mean HH score climbs slightly, supporting the hypothesis that these counties drag HH scores down by encompassing more than one bailiwick.

Overall, the concentration scores illustrate a systematic division of Costa Rica's multimember districts into bailiwicks that are serviced by individual majority party representatives.[8] Although party lists are elected by votes cast across entire provinces, deputies' day-to-day work entails personal representation of mutually exclusive geographical districts.

The job of providing small favors: Pork and service

Having established the existence and the partisan content of the bailiwick system, I turn now to describing in more detail the substance of the relationship between Costa Rican deputies and their bailiwicks. Deputies' work on behalf of their bailiwicks falls into two general categories: the distribution of PEs, and the provision of constituency service. I address these activities in turn.

PEs: What types of projects? PEs are invariably for small projects, ranging in cost from a few hundred to a few thousand U.S. dollars. These funds are

---

[8] Main opposition party deputies also divide their districts in an effort to provide constituency service; but this phenomenon is less relevant to constituents, and more difficult to document, for the same reason: main opposition deputies are excluded from pork. Without PEs, identifying opposition party bailiwicks is difficult and imprecise. Moreover, without PEs, and with less access to government patronage, as well as less influence in the bureaucracy, opposition deputies' ability to provide small favors to constituents is slight.

targeted occasionally at municipal governments or at dioceses of the Catholic Church, but the overwhelming majority are delivered to community groups that are organized to carry out specific local development projects. The local recipients – whether municipal governments, churches, or community groups – generally supply the labor in such projects, and the national government supplies funds to buy materials. Typical examples of such projects from the 1991 budget[9] include: U.S.$1,600 to repair the church steps in the San Rafael neighborhood of San José; U.S.$5,600 to build a bridge over the Turrubares River between two villages; U.S.$4,000 to build a sports field in Barrio San Andrés; U.S.$400 to buy uniforms for a Perez Zeledón soccer club; U.S.$12,000 to buy equipment for a Perez Zeledón hospital; U.S.$4,800 to repair a school in Cahuita; U.S.$800 to build a little park opposite the cemetery in Barrio Los Angeles; and U.S.$600 to enclose a sewage pipe in El Guarco.

All together, PEs generally amount to around 2% of annual appropriations in Costa Rica. In the years for which data are available, 1974–1990, PEs account for a mean of 1.8% of total appropriations. The centrality of PEs to the work of most deputies, however, far outweighs their relatively small share of total annual appropriations. The majority of the budget is consumed by fixed outlays, such as servicing foreign debt, subsidizing the semiautonomous institutions, and social security payments, over which individual deputies can exercise little influence and, more significantly, can claim no credit.[10] Likewise, for appropriations disbursed through executive departments, funds are ultimately spent by executive bureaucrats. But the PE belongs entirely to the individual deputy identified in the budget as its patron.

Delivering PEs to the bailiwick. PEs are generally born of requests made by constituents to deputies either during the deputies' office hours or on trips back to their bailiwicks. Deputies prioritize requested projects and in turn make requests for their lists of PEs on the Legislative Assembly Budget Committee, which draws up the annual budget legislation. Once funds are appropriated, deputies then turn to the task of petitioning for the disbursal of funds for each PE from the Budget Ministry. The equal division of PE funds among majority deputies, and the faithfulness of the executive in disbursing PE funds in recent years, both indicate that the work of providing

---

[9] Costa Rican colones were converted to U.S. dollars at the exchange rate prevailing in mid-1991: C125 = $1.00. Exchange rates were provided by the Costa Rican Central Bank.

[10] A PUSC deputy and member of the party leadership estimates that only about one-third of the government budget is subject to the Legislative Assembly's discretion through legislation. The rest is fixed outlays (Interview 93–38).

small pork is not so much in *securing* funds as in *delivering* them. And deputies in fact labor to ensure that the delivery of PEs attracts attention.

Checks for PE projects are delivered personally by deputies to community group leaders. Deputies frequently hold meetings in their bailiwicks, at which constituents can make requests of the deputy, but where the central event is the delivery of PE checks. In one case where his good works evidently were not widely enough recognized, a deputy purchased a full page in a San José daily with text extolling the importance of PEs to the economic health of the bailiwick, reviewing the public works projects he had person-ally delivered, and showing a photo of the deputy in front of a crowd of people during a recent visit to the bailiwick, handing over a check for school repairs to the leader of a local community group (*La Nación*, May 27, 1984: 3E). Maximizing the fanfare surrounding PE deliveries is not without its risks, however. On a February weekend in 1992, the city of San Isidro in southern San José Province was hosting the National Youth Games. The PUSC deputy whose bailiwick included San Isidro had planned a meeting to deliver PEs during the Games, while the city was full of media and constit-uents. While driving out from the capital on Friday evening, after stopping at a restaurant for dinner, the deputy emerged to find his car broken into and his briefcase full of PE checks stolen from the trunk. The deputy succeeded in attracting media attention, but not for conscientious service to his bailiwick. Although the checks could not be cashed by the thief, and so no government funds were lost, the deputy was lampooned for days in the papers for having bungled the mainstay of a deputy's job – delivering loot to the bailiwick.

Constituent service and home style. In addition to delivering pork, deputies act as government ombudsmen and patronage brokers on behalf of their constituents. Constituent service consumes more time than any other task for most deputies. For a group of PLN deputies interviewed during the 1986–1990 Legislative Assembly, the estimated share of their time spent on constituent service ranged from 35 to 90% (Taylor 1992). Most deputies have office hours posted – usually a few afternoons each week – during which any constituent from their district can come to ask for help. Better-connected constituents arrange meetings outside office hours.

Deputies uniformly stated that they return to their communities regularly to visit and meet with constituents. Of 25 deputies asked about how much contact they have with constituents, 24 regarded their level of contact as high. Deputies frequently referred to their constituent contact as "constant," with more than one pointing out that all the people sitting in the office waiting room during our interviews were there to place requests for special government assistance (Interview 93–43). Many deputies pointed out that they return to their bailiwicks to meet with constituents each weekend, even when this requires a substantial amount of travel time (Interview 93–46).

The substance of constituent meetings is personal and local problems, rather than national policy questions. When asked about contact with constituents, a typical (although unusually concise) answer was, "I have lots of contact. The people I see are looking for three things, generally. First, jobs; second, funding for community projects; and third, housing. In that order" (Interview 93–08). From another: "I visit my communities, my constituents come here to my office, I meet with organized groups, I have written contact. More than anything, constituents are looking for resources for public works" (Interview 93–10).

Another deputy was more descriptive of the substance of her home style:

At times, deputies fulfill functions that are closer to that of a city council member. We keep very close ties to the communities. This is especially true for those of us who represent areas outside San José. My constituents come to my house at all hours to make requests. This is a difficult part of the job – it takes a lot of time. But it's part of the democratic system, right? Some come to talk of legislation, and others come to talk about the condition of the roads, housing, jobs, school repairs, sports facilities, church repairs. These are the most common.

And later, "I receive plaques, flowers, mariachis sent to my house on my birthday – all from those to whom I provide PEs, or who are looking for them" (Interview 93–22).

Many deputies' descriptions of their home life seem so familiar to students of the U.S. Congress that they could almost have been lifted from the pages of Fenno's classic work:

(Constituents) visit me on weekends, or I go to the communities. They share many very simple requests and needs with me, and also much more complex problems. Also I go to socialize. The people love to have their deputy show up at local fiestas, to come and ride a horse, to drop by the house, come into the kitchen and have lunch, things like that. (Interview 93–28)

Another straddles the border between the mundane and the bizarre:

Let me give you an example. Last year, I had a traffic accident – pretty serious. I was in the house for about 12 days, recovering. One afternoon, about 1 o'clock, I get a phone call from the principal of a high school. He's calling to tell me the plumbing is backed up, to see what I can do. This is what it's like. (Interview 93–24)

Majority deputies almost always referred to the goods they could deliver to constituents as dominating the substance of these meetings. Opposition deputies were more reserved, more often than not pointing out that although they meet with constituents, they have no means by which to satisfy local demands. As one PLN deputy from the 1990–94 Legislative Assembly told me:

I visit the constituents in my communities on weekends, hear their problems, exchange ideas. I make personal visits, and many come personally to see me. But there is a big difference between being an opposition deputy, as opposed to a government deputy. We do not have access to PEs, and so are not as attractive to constituents. So there are somewhat fewer demands placed on us. (Interview 93–29)

Costa Rican particularism: Empirical conclusions

Up to this point, this chapter establishes a clear picture of particularism among Costa Rican legislators. Despite the lack of individual incentives provided by the electoral system, providing small favors and pork to constituents in a specific geographical area occupies most Costa Rican deputies on a daily basis. For citizens or local communities seeking special consideration from the government, the bailiwick system puts a personal face on partisan representation. There is a single, acknowledged representative in the Legislative Assembly for each community to solicit for government assistance, and that individual is regularly available to hear constituents' petitions. For the party, the bailiwick system provides part of a solution to the collective action problem of how to supply particularism in the absence of direct electoral incentives. It allows a division of labor whereby individual members can be held responsible for providing small favors to identifiable sets of constituents. For the deputy, the bailiwick system entails responsibility for contributing to the party's collective effort. Whether an individual deputy shirks on this effort, or delivers small favors effectively, the results can be identified and personally attributed.

Venezuela: Electoral incentive theory redeemed

The discussion of Venezuela in this empirical section on particularism is brief, for a straightforward reason. In Venezuela, despite the possibility of reelection and the existence of congressional careers (Chapter 3), national legislators do not engage in systematic particularism. In this section, I (1) establish that legislative particularism is basically nonexistent in Venezuela, (2) note the connection between this lack of particularism and electoral reform, and (3) underscore the consistency of Venezuelan legislative behavior with electoral incentive theory.

The lack of responsiveness to individual and local petitions by Venezuelan legislators would likely have escaped entirely without comment by students of Venezuelan politics if it were not for the recent debate in that country over electoral reform. This is because the absence of particularism does not present a puzzle to electoral incentive theories of political behavior. In Venezuela, ballot access is controlled by national party leaders, all copartisans candidates from a given district benefit from the same partisan pool of votes, voters cannot distinguish on their ballots among members of the same party; and district magnitude is generally large enough that individual candidates on lists are secondary to party reputations in determining voter preferences.[11] All of these conditions minimize direct electoral incentives for individuals to cultivate personal reputations among voters. Without such incentives, electoral theories predict that legislators will not devote time and energy to providing small favors – and in Venezuela, legislators have not.

In the first place, Venezuelan budgets lack any analog to Costa Rica's PEs. Of course, the mere absence of such a convenient (from an academic's perspective) accounting device as the PE is not evidence that pork does not exist in Venezuela.[12] The important point, however, is that all appropriations are channeled through executive departments, and in no instance can specific line items be attributed to individual legislators. Moreover, academic accounts of the distribution of pork in Venezuela consistently dismiss any role for national legislators in securing funds for local projects. Rather, decisions on what public works and local jobs programs to fund, as well as contracting decisions with local firms, are handled by national party leaders in Caracas (Arroyo Talavera 1986; Myers 1986; Rangel 1978).

To the extent that any politicians act as sponsors for specific local interests, this responsibility is borne by municipal councilors and state legislators, even when their petitions for local causes are directed at bureaucrats from the federal government. On one account, "District and state politicians and administrators commonly make biweekly pilgrimages to the capital city to obtain funds and lobby for local projects" (Arroyo Talavera 1986: 224). Arroyo Talavera notes that this phenomenon underscores the weakness of state and local governments relative to the national government. More important for the purposes of this study, however, is the fact that national legislators are not the primary lobbyists on behalf of regional interests, even at the level of government in which they serve.

The failure of Venezuelan legislators systematically to serve their constituencies or to respond to specific communities is noted most clearly in the debate conducted during the late 1980s and early 1990s over electoral reform (Chapter 2). In 1985, Gabaldón and Oberto noted the widespread criticism that "the system of closed lists with proportional representation undermines any tight link between the electors and the elected, to the detriment of representativeness and candidate quality" (1985, vol. 1: 10). In 1988, the

---

[11] Note that the discussion of legislative behavior and of the Venezuelan electoral system here refers to that prior to the electoral reforms put into effect in 1993.

[12] Even in Costa Rica, there is much pork in the annual budget beyond just PEs. It should also be noted that PEs are not just a Costa Rican phenomenon. In Colombia, a country in which particularism dominates legislative behavior, there is likewise a distinct section of the budget, labeled *auxilios*, that is set aside for pork-barrel projects attributable to individual legislators (Shugart and Nielson 1993).

President's Commission on Reform of the State initially recommended the adoption of a mixed PR–SMD system along the lines of Germany's, in order to create a personal vote in congressional elections. In the Commission's words:

The possibility of choosing among candidates is an important means of encouraging responsiveness . . . The reforms [will] alter the parameters that guide elections such that the legislator who aspires to be reelected will take an interest in ensuring that his personal work is considered valuable in the eyes of his constituents. (COPRE 1988: 114)

Academic authors resoundingly concur with the proposition that legislators have been negligent in attending to constituent and community demands, and that the election of half the Chamber of Deputies from SMDs will improve representation (Vanderdijs and Torres 1981). According to Edgar Paredes Pisani, the reforms "will improve the quality of responsiveness to the demands of local communities, which will be the basis of better control by society over this part of the government . . . The obligation of a deputy, of whichever party is elected to a seat, will be increasingly to the community that elected him" (1990: 199). And Manuel Rachadell reports:

Elected representatives ought to act in the interests of those who elected them, ought to attend to their complaints and demands, ought to respond to their correspondence . . . The SMD system does not guarantee the proportional representation of parties, but in exchange it is the best at allowing the representation of the interests that really stir society. (1991: 208)

The enthusiasm of these authors for an electoral reform that establishes SMDs is driven largely by the conviction that a commitment on the part of legislators to local and community interests is essential to good legislative representation, and that this commitment has been lacking in Venezuela. The irony for U.S. observers, of course, is that the commitment to local interests generated by SMD elections – the very cornerstone of particularism – is roundly criticized by reformers as generating government waste and uncohesive parties. The lesson from Venezuela seems to be that legislative representation entirely without particularism is disagreeable to constituents. At any rate, the groundswell of support behind reform, and the arguments of reform adherents, underscore the fact that Venezuelan legislators have failed to provide the small favors of pork and constituency service observed in Costa Rica.

Particularism explained: An effort to connect behavior to elections and careers

The preceding section describes the effects of particularism as observed in Costa Rica and, more briefly, the absence of particularism by national legislators in Venezuela. There are, however, a number of logical connections that remain concealed. To explain the puzzle of Costa Rican legislative behavior requires an explanation for why and how parties provide particularism in the absence of personal electoral incentives for legislators. Any general explanation to this puzzle must answer two fundamental questions: Why do parties want particularism, and how are legislators to be coerced to provide particularism? In this section, I suggest hypotheses in response to these questions and make an effort to test these hypotheses, despite some serious limitations in the available data.

Two hypotheses

I offer a straightforward hypothesis in response to each of the two questions. First, I propose that parties can reap electoral gains from particularism. Second, I propose that parties can use control over future careers to force legislators to provide pork.

The extent to which parties might gain from particularism is largely ignored in studies that focus on the electoral incentives of individual politicians. These works argue, correctly, that where electoral systems reward personal reputations, providing pork and constituency service are means by which politicians cultivate voter support on grounds independent from the programmatic policy debates that define party reputations (Anagnoson 1983; Clarke 1978; Fenno 1978; Fiorina 1977; Maheshwari 1976; Mayhew 1974; McCubbins and Rosenbluth 1995). Moreover, this behavior actively undermines the coherence of party reputations, because pork and constituent service are provided and advertised by politicians as alternative bases on which to evaluate the quality of representation, and because providing pork frequently undermines the economic policy goals of parties (Ames 1992; Shugart and Nielson 1993).

I do not contest this portrayal of systems that reward personal reputations. The point here, however, is that the electoral benefits of particularism need not accrue only to individuals (Cain, Ferejohn, and Fiorina 1987). Parties can benefit from particularism when voters associate particularism with partisan, as opposed to individual, reputations. The ability of voters to make this association is enhanced, in turn, when copartisans do not compete for votes on the basis of which individual best provides pork and constituency service. The very absence of intrapartisan competition for votes makes interpartisan competition based on particularism possible. Costa Rica's lack of individual incentives to compete over pork, then, opens the door for particularism to take on partisan content. The strict majority party monopoly over PEs demonstrates that parties value pork in Costa Rica. Nevertheless, to evaluate the hypothesis that particularism benefits parties, it is also worthwhile to test whether the distribution of PEs has an impact on partisan electoral success. I attempt such a test later.

To evaluate the second hypothesis, that parties use control over future careers to force legislators to provide particularism, I combine the data on executive appointments from Chapter 3 with Costa Rican electoral data broken down according to bailiwicks. The basic proposition is as follows: deputies are uniquely responsible for providing particularism in identifiable bailiwicks. Particularism generates partisan votes. Therefore, whether deputies do a good job providing particularism or not should be reflected in their party's electoral fortunes in the bailiwicks. Deputies' likelihood of being rewarded with post-Assembly appointment, then, should be connected to their diligence and effectiveness at providing particularism, and thus generating votes.

Previous work on the Costa Rican case

Before presenting the tests of these hypotheses, it is necessary to note one analysis of the Costa Rican case in particular, which addresses quite directly some of the questions posed in this chapter. The focus on particularism by Costa Rican legislators is identified as a puzzle by Michelle Taylor (1992). Taylor notes that Costa Rica's closed-list PR offers little incentive relative to an SMD system – for example, like that of the United States. She also notes that Costa Rican term limits largely eliminate Assembly careers, such that direct electoral incentives cannot reasonably explain Costa Rican particularism. Taylor's explanation for Costa Rican particularism is entirely in line with the two hypotheses I offer. She argues that parties benefit from pork and constituency service, and that post-Assembly appointments are the rewards motivating deputies to provide particularism.

Although Taylor's general conclusions are solid, her analysis is incomplete on some key points. First, she does not provide any data on the actual distribution of PEs, either by party or among individual deputies, or on election results. Second, in evaluating career prospects for deputies, Taylor assesses the prospect of long-term political careers (10 years or more), but the relevant factor in Costa Rica is *immediate* career prospects. Where term limits force all incumbents out of office at the end of each term, time horizons are uniformly short. Taylor's argument is that Costa Rican deputies work for their parties' electoral success; but the only election they can reasonably expect to affect is the one immediately following their term in the Legislative Assembly. This focus contributes to the most important shortcoming in Taylor's analysis: the failure to link deputies' career prospects to the immediate electoral success of parties.

Even without identifying the bailiwicks of individual deputies with PE data, it is possible to link post-Assembly career prospects to partisan electoral fortunes at a national level. In Chapter 3, I show that immediate post-Assembly appointments are quite likely for deputies whose party wins the successive presidential election, but virtually nonexistent for deputies whose party loses. Taylor does not cut her appointments data to test for the effects of partisan electoral success, and as a result she presents a uniformly bleak picture for appointments across all deputies. Given this scenario, she puzzles over the proposition that appointments have any effect on incumbent behavior at all. If the argument is to be made that particularism wins parties elections and deputies are rewarded for contributing to partisan success, however, then the data must be cut to account for partisan success. As Chapter 3 shows, the relationship between partisan success and individual career prospects is strong.

These criticisms of Taylor's work are directed at details. She fails to specify some of the logical links in her argument and to provide data to test some of the connections that are made explicit. In spite of these shortcomings, however, I agree with her general argument. Her analysis traverses some logical gaps, but arrives at solid conclusions. Moreover, even the attempts I will make to test our common hypothesis are hampered by gaps in data that, although more extensive than Taylor's, remains incomplete.

The electoral impact of PEs

It is possible to evaluate the impact of PEs on party electoral fortunes because data on both the distribution of PEs and on election returns are broken down according to county. Tests of the electoral impact of PEs, then, are based on comparisons of county PE receipts against county voting returns.[13] Nevertheless, there are serious difficulties in establishing the impact of PEs on elections. First, the data on the distribution of PEs by county

---

[13] All the electoral data used here are *presidential* election returns. These are the most relevant data for testing the hypotheses that particularism generates electoral payoffs, which in turn generate post-Assembly careers. The reason is that all the appointments that are used as indicators of post-Assembly careers in this analysis are made solely by the president (Chapter 3). Thus, for incumbent deputies interested in political careers, the relevant election is for the presidency, not the Legislative Assembly.

At any rate, the difference between vote percentages for the presidency and Legislative Assembly for the two main parties over the elections analyzed here was less than 5% on average (presidential votes uniformly higher than Assembly votes). More significantly, for both parties, presidential and Assembly votes vary uniformly, because the parties lost votes to minor parties in Assembly elections at similar rates. Thus, the difference *in the gap* between the major parties in presidential and Assembly elections averages less than 1% over the elections analyzed here.

The central points are that the presidential returns used here are the most relevant for what is being tested. But if Assembly returns were used, the results would be essentially unchanged.

has been available only for budgets during the past three electoral cycles, so the number of cases for analysis is limited. Second, because of the prohibitive cost of data collection, I am able to provide detailed country distributions of PE data for only one year out of four in each of the three electoral cycles. If the year included is unrepresentative of the complete distribution of PEs for a given electoral cycle, then the results here are distorted accordingly. On the other hand, there is no reason to believe that the distributions of PEs across counties for the years included here differ systematically from the complete distributions, so I take the incomplete data to be representative of the complete data.

There are other, more theoretically troublesome difficulties in evaluating the impact of PEs on elections. One is that the direction of causality between the distribution of PEs and election returns is far from clear. Imagine two different scenarios: (1) a party that monopolizes PEs distributes them strategically and enjoys increased electoral support in the next election in those counties that receive disproportionate shares of PEs; (2) a party rewards those counties that contribute disproportionately to its victory in the preceding election with disproportionate shares of PEs. In either of these cases, there should be a positive correlation between a party's electoral success in a county and that county's share of PEs, but the direction of causality between these variables may not be clear. One way to untangle this problem is to specify a dependent variable that encompasses two electoral cycles, for example, by testing for whether a party that distributes a disproportionately high share of PEs to a given county during one electoral cycle makes electoral gains in that county over the party's share of the vote in the preceding election. This approach eliminates direction of causality problems for the specific electoral cycle, but it is hampered by the fact that any electoral gains generated by PEs must face diminishing returns over time, so the value of PEs will likely be underestimated for counties where the party already enjoyed success in the first election. Put another way, this approach detects any electoral support *gained* by PEs from one election to the next, but it does not detect electoral support *maintained* by PEs over time.

Another difficulty is that party strategies with regard to PEs may vary. For example, a party might use PEs for damage control, rather than to reward supporters. Imagine a scenario in which a party distributes a disproportionate share of PEs to counties in which it has done poorly (perhaps precisely because it believes the returns on this investment will be higher than in its "safe" counties). In this case, high shares of PEs would correlate with poor electoral returns for the party, giving the appearance that PEs hurt the party electorally when in fact they may be producing gains from a low base point. Again, this problem could be addressed by measuring the effect of PEs on *changes* in a party's fortunes in each county from one election to the next. Nevertheless, this method is not perfect. Imagine a scenario in which a party identifies counties in which it expects to suffer electoral losses from past levels, for reasons unrelated to pork. The party might concentrate PEs in those counties to mitigate electoral losses. Here, high shares of PEs would correlate with electoral losses from one election to the next. In short, various plausible partisan strategies in the distribution of PEs can generate markedly different apparent effects of PEs on elections. The goal here is to assess the effects of PEs, remaining aware of the various possible strategies of distribution and how these strategies might affect test results.

The first test evaluates the simple hypothesis that counties receiving disproportionate shares of PEs reward the party monopolizing PEs accordingly. The relevant OLS regression is

(EQ. 4.1)   PARTY VOTE% = a(CONSTANT)
             + b(SHARE OF PEs),

where PARTY VOTE% is the percentage of valid presidential votes cast in a county for the party monopolizing PEs in the election after the distribution of PEs, CONSTANT is set equal to 1, and SHARE OF PEs for each county is calculated as (%PEs/%Population) − 1. This is an indicator of the county's share of all PEs appropriated in a given year, adjusted according to the county's population. SHARE OF PEs is centered on zero and is derived from the ratio of a county's percentage share of all PEs to the county's percentage share of population. For example, SHARE OF PEs equals 0 if a county receives a share of PEs exactly proportionate to its population; it equals 1 if the county's share of PEs is twice its share based on population; and it equals − 0.5 if the county's PE share is half its share based on population.

Data are available to test equation 4.1 for two electoral cycles. The data cannot be combined across cycles because the dependent variable is being driven by a host of factors exogenous to the model that differ in their effects between the cycles. Within each election, however, these factors are picked up by the CONSTANT term. The results are shown in Table 4.4.

Results in the middle column show no correlation at all between the distribution of PEs in 1983 and the PLN's electoral success in 1986. The right-hand column, on the other hand, shows some effect of PEs in 1988 on PLN returns in 1990. For example, a county that received twice its share of PEs proportional to population in 1988 could be expected to give an additional 1.16% of its vote to the PLN in 1990. Likewise, a county that was "shortchanged" by the PLN in 1988 could be expected to punish the party in 1990. Even during this second electoral cycle, however, the impact of PEs appears to be modest: fairly dramatic deviations from proportionality in PE

Table 4.4. Impact of PEs on party vote shares in counties

Dependent variable: Percentage of valid presidential votes cast in a county for party monopolizing PEs in the election after the distribution of the PEs.		
Independent variables	1983 PEs/1986 PLN Vote	1988 PEs/1990 PLN Vote
Constant	51.82 (79.74)	46.41 (71.03)
Share of PEs	0.00 (0.00)	1.16 (1.55)
N	81	81
Adjusted R^2	0.01	0.17

Note: OLS regression; t-statistics are in parentheses.

Table 4.5. Impact of PEs on electoral gains between elections in counties

Dependent variable: Percent gain between elections in each county in the vote share of the party controlling PEs.		
Independent variables	1982 – 1986 elections	1986 – 1990 elections
Constant	-7.42 (-17.17)	-5.13 (-25.09)
Share of PEs	-1.97 (-4.58)	0.29 (1.23)
N	81	81
Adjusted R^2	.20	.01

Note: OLS regression; t-statistics are in parentheses.

distribution produce relatively small effects at the polls, and the coefficient for SHARE OF PEs falls somewhat below conventional significance levels.

Moreover, equation 4.1 is subject to the direction of causality problem discussed earlier. It may be that counties receiving PE windfalls in 1988 rewarded the PLN in 1990; but it may also be true that these counties were PLN strongholds that are regularly regaled with PEs when the party monopolizes pork. The next test attempts to disentangle this problem:

(4.2)   DIFFERENCE $=$ a(CONSTANT) $+$ b(SHARE OF PEs),

where DIFFERENCE is the percentage gain between elections in each county in the vote share of the party controlling PEs. For example, from 1982 to 1986, DIFFERENCE is the PLN's vote percentage in 1986 minus its percentage in 1982. CONSTANT is set equal to 1, and SHARE OF PEs is measured the same as before (see Table 4.5).

Once again, the test is run separately for each electoral cycle. The CONSTANT coefficients illustrate the PLN's declining electoral fortunes overall. From Carlos Monge's sweeping victory in 1982 to Oscar Arias's narrow victory in 1986, the PLN's expected vote share in a county receiving a proportionate share of PEs fell 7.42%. Then from Arias's victory to Carlos Manuel Castillo's defeat to the PUSC's Rafael Calderón in 1990, the PLN's expected vote share in such a county fell another 5.13%. The coefficients for SHARE OF PEs, however, show no clear pattern. There is actually a negative correlation between PEs and electoral shifts to the PLN during the first electoral cycle, and a positive, but quite modest, effect during the second.

The results so far are decidedly mixed. In both sets of equations, the evident effects of PEs differ from one electoral period to the next. Neither set demonstrates unequivocally that PEs have any effect on partisan fortunes at all, and it is impossible from these results to determine what strategy, if any, the PLN used to distribute PEs. I make one further effort to identify partisan strategy

(4.3)   PCT PEs = a(CONSTANT) + b_1(PCT VOTES)
          + b_2(PCT OF PLURALITY),

where PCT PEs is the percentage of all PEs in a given year that were appropriated in a given county, CONSTANT is set equal to 1, and PCT VOTES is the county's percent share of all valid votes cast in a given election. This serves as a control for county population; and PCT OF PLURALITY calculated as COUNTY DIFFERENCE/NATIONAL DIFFERENCE, where COUNTY DIFFERENCE is the vote margin in a county of victory (or loss) by the party winning the presidential election over the second-place party, and NATIONAL DIFFERENCE is the vote margin nationally – that is, the size of the winning party's plurality. PCT OF PLURALITY measures the percent contribution of each county to the winning party's overall margin of victory over the main opposition. If the winning party loses in a given county, of course, the value of PCT OF PLURALITY is negative. This variable estimates the degree to which any given county is worthy of being "rewarded" by the winning party with excessive PEs.

Equation 4.3 tests the hypothesis that a county whose contribution to the winning party's victory is disproportionately large, relative to its population, will receive a disproportionately large share of PEs during the next electoral cycle. Because the dependent variable is not obviously driven by factors exogenous to the model that vary from cycle to cycle, data from three electoral cycles can be pooled. The results in Table 4.6 include data from the elections of 1982, 1986, and 1990, as well as the budgets of 1983, 1988, and 1991. The coefficient on the CONSTANT shows that small counties receive a disproportionately large share of PEs; and the coefficient on PCT VOTES demonstrates that for every additional share of all valid votes cast in an election, a county could expect a two-thirds' share increase in PEs. But the coefficient on PCT PLURALITY shows that across all three electoral

Table 4.6. Impact of electoral support on PEs received by counties

Dependent variable: Percentage of all PEs in a given year that were appropriated in a given county.	
Independent variables	1982, 1986, 1990 electoral cycles
Constant	0.42 (7.73)
Percentage of valid votes cast in county	0.67 (19.32)
Percentage of winning party's overall plurality contributed by that county	-0.01 (-0.55)
N	243
Adjusted R^2	.84

Note: OLS regression; t-statistics are in parentheses.

cycles, contributions to the winning party's plurality did not gain counties any expected PE "reward," once population was controlled for.

In sum, the tests here of the effects of PEs on electoral results in Costa Rica are indeterminate. I have tested three separate hypotheses: first, that counties receiving more PEs will generate higher overall levels of support for the party monopolizing PEs; second, that PEs benefit the monopolist party in a county from one election to the next; and third, that parties reward supportive counties with more PEs. The results are suggestive for some electoral cycles, but in no case do they illustrate a consistent pattern. In short, based on this evidence it is impossible to show that PEs yield electoral payoffs for parties in counties, or that parties distribute PEs among counties systematically to cultivate electoral support.

In evaluating these results, it is worth bearing in mind the shortcomings in the data discussed at the beginning of this section. With incomplete data and a limited number of electoral cycles, discerning broad patterns in the effects of PEs is difficult. Moreover, given the multiple plausible strategies that parties might use in distributing PEs, it is necessary to exercise caution in interpreting any patterns that are detected. Finally, recall that the broad question addressed here is whether particularism pays dividends for parties. Particularism can include both constituency service and budgetary pork. I am unable to measure constituency service across counties in such a way as to include it in tests for electoral effects. And as for pork, recall that PEs account for a relatively small amount of Costa Rica's annual budget, and large pork-barrel projects are included in other parts of the budget that cannot be broken down by county. Once again, if the distribution of PEs is representative of the distribution of particularism generally, then PEs are good indicators of the electoral impact of particularism on elections. And there is no reason to believe otherwise. But it is worth bearing in mind that the indicator of particularism used here is based on incomplete information.

Even without clear quantitative evidence of PEs' electoral impact, it is important to note that Costa Rican politicians *believe* that particularism generates electoral support for parties. The partisan monopoly on PEs demonstrates this fact, as does the emphasis that deputies place on particularism in evaluating their jobs. In interviews, 20 of 21 majority deputies mentioned constituency service and distribution of PEs – usually first – when asked what is the most important way they serve the public. Even among opposition deputies, 10 of 22 noted that it is difficult for them to serve, given their lack of access to PEs and lack of bureaucratic clout. Clearly, to these politicians, doing a good job as a deputy means effectively providing particularism. Moreover, over 90% of these same deputies linked good service to the party to receiving post-Assembly appointments (Chapter 3), drawing a clear link between particularism and partisan electoral success.

When asked to describe the representation he provides and the motivation for providing it, one majority deputy stated:

The typical means of serving constituents is by providing pork for communities – PEs, specifically . . . This is a spoils system. The majority deputies take everything, and the opposition gets nothing . . . If the party wins the next election, you can be named a minister, or an ambassador. If the party loses, you're out on the street. (Interview 93–08)

Taylor's (1992) work confirms this belief among legislators. Among her interview responses from deputies are the following remarks:

If someone is a "do-nothing" deputy, it will be hard for his party in the coming election. (1066)

If a deputy is elected and then is not seen in the (bailiwick) it makes his party look bad. (1066)

The people of Costa Rica think they are electing "little presidents" not deputies, and they expect them to bring projects and public works to the district. But this expectation also allows the deputy to fortify the image of the PLN in his district. (1067)

The quantitative data examined here are stubborn in yielding clear conclusions regarding the electoral effects of PEs. Inconclusiveness on these tests, however, is not grounds to reject the hypothesis that particularism generates votes for Costa Rican parties. More complete data might well have illustrated the electoral effects of particularism more clearly. With better data, for example, a recent study of the Programa Nacional de Solidaridad (PRONA-SOL) public works program in Mexico shows clear partisan electoral benefits from the distribution of pork (Molinar and Weldon 1993). In terms of explaining political behavior, in particular, the important point here is that Costa Rican politicians believe that particularism pays off electorally.

Party-administered rewards for effective deputies

The second central hypothesis to be tested in this chapter is that parties use control over post-Assembly appointments to create incentives for deputies to provide particularism in their bailiwicks. Chapter 3 established that presidents control appointments to the most desirable posts for ex-deputies, and that appointments among ex-deputies are given almost exclusively to members of the president's party. Thus, incumbent deputies have a collective incentive to contribute to the electoral success of their parties' presidential candidate by providing particularism. Of course, they also have individual incentives to free ride on the efforts of others in providing particularism (Cain, Ferejohn, and Fiorina 1987; Taylor 1992). However, the Costa Rican bailiwick system provides a solution to this free-rider problem among copartisans. Bailiwicks allow those who control post-Assembly careers to identify the contribution of individual deputies to their party's electoral fortunes.

In this section, I test whether deputies who perform well for their parties (and so, for their parties' presidential candidates) in their bailiwicks improve their chances of being rewarded with post-Assembly appointments. The small variance in PEs among majority party deputies suggests that the amount of pork secured by a given deputy will not explain much about post-Assembly appointments as an independent variable, and also that there is not much to explain by positing this distribution as a dependent variable. Rather, the equilibrium in distributing PE funds within majority parties in Costa Rica is universalism. Given this situation, this section assumes that a test of strong performance by deputies is not how much pork they bring back to the bailiwicks, but their effectiveness in parlaying that pork, and their constituent service work, into electoral gains for the parties. If this assumption is valid, then it might be possible to discern some pattern of success in securing post-Assembly appointments, based on the electoral fortunes of a deputy's party in his or her bailiwick.

The first task, of course, is to estimate deputies' performance in bailiwicks. Certainly, informal mechanisms exist for party leaders and presidents to do so. These leaders regularly travel to meetings with local party organizations and actively seek feedback from activists on the attentiveness of deputies to local needs. During election years, presidential candidates campaigning throughout the country gather such information (Taylor 1992). Moreover, party leaders do not always have to seek feedback on a deputy's performance; local opinions regularly pursue deputies straight to the capital.

The San José daily newspapers have sections devoted to short reports on local issues submitted from the provinces. This space is frequently used to applaud or chastise deputies for their work on behalf of their bailiwicks. One example – more harsh than most – comes from a mayor in Guanacaste Province:

> With all the respect that you deserve, Ms. Provincial Deputy, it worries me that a representative of Guanacaste in the Legislative Assembly would suggest that her constituents could wait longer for the construction of a Tempisque River bridge. With this type of attitude, it seems you are not a *guanacasteca* at all, or at least that you are not interested in the problems of Guanacaste, especially the bridge construction, which is a necessity for everyone in the province. We cannot wait anymore. I would very much like you to rectify your position and unite yourself with all *guanacastecos* on this project, and many other badly needed projects of which you seem unaware, given how infrequently you are seen in those places where subjects relevant to our province are discussed. No wonder you are out of touch. What a shame. (*La República*, March 14, 1992)

Clearly then, informal communications make it impossible for deputies to hide entirely from their local reputations. Nevertheless, there is no way to estimate systematically the bailiwick performance of each deputy based on such communication. Besides, the basic premise here is that good bailiwick performance yields electoral payoffs for parties. The best estimators of deputy bailiwick performance, then, are electoral returns. Specifically, for deputies whose party wins the next presidential election, I calculate the difference between the party's presidential vote share in a given bailiwick from the beginning to the end of the deputy's term. I then test for whether deputies' likelihood in securing post-Assembly appointments are related to these changes in their parties' fortunes. The structure of the test is straightforward, although once again, the results are inconclusive and subject to complications based on insufficient data.

Before presenting the results, it is unfortunately necessary to review the shortcomings in the data used for this test. There are two critical problems. The first is that data on the dependent variable – whether a deputy receives a post-Assembly appointment – is incomplete. Recall from Chapter 3 that archival data were not available for appointments to all autonomous institutions, or to the foreign service, for many administrations. In Chapter 3, it was possible to estimate the level of total appointments by extrapolating from documented levels. In this case, the relevant information is whether specific deputies received appointments, so no such manipulation of the data is possible. Therefore, I rely on documented appointments – an incomplete account.

The second problem has to do with identifying deputies' bailiwicks accurately and thoroughly. Ideally, it would be possible to identify each deputy's bailiwick by identifying the counties reliant on that deputy for PEs. The problem, however, is that only the bailiwicks of majority party deputies can be identified in this manner. If the Assembly minority party in one term wins the presidency for the next term, then those deputies in line for appointments cannot be linked to bailiwicks by PEs, simply because they controlled no PEs as opposition deputies. This condition makes precise identification of bailiwicks for the relevant deputies impossible for most electoral cycles, because the Costa Rican presidency has changed partisan hands in three of the five cycles for which I have electoral data. Moreover, for the two cycles in which the Assembly majority party retained the presidency, PE items are not attributed to individual deputies in budgets. Therefore, in none of these cycles is precise identification of bailiwicks possible.

There is, however, a second-best alternative. An appendix to a law school thesis at the University of Costa Rica provides rosters of all deputies since the 1970–1974 term, identifying each as either a national or a local deputy (see the earlier section on "Making the Collective Personal"), and for local deputies, listing the main county for which they were responsible (Casas Zamora and Briceño Fallas 1991, Anexo II). This appendix does not provide precise identifications of bailiwicks for a number of reasons. First, counties are attributed to deputies not by systematic budgetary data, but rather through interviews and reminiscences of past party leaders. Second, those deputies listed as national are not linked to any specific counties, whereas PE data, when it is available, clearly shows that all deputies have local responsibilities. Third, even for local deputies, only one county is identified as the district for each, whereas PE data shows that most bailiwicks consist of multiple counties. In short, the only data that can feasibly be used to identify the bailiwicks of all deputies over an extended period provides only an impressionistic sketch of the bailiwick system. On the other hand, this is the only sketch available, so it is worthwhile to extract from it whatever information is possible.

The probit analysis used to test the relationship between deputy performance in the bailiwick and the likelihood of appointments is as follows. The dependent variable, APPOINTMENT, is a dummy, scored 1 if the deputy received a documented appointment to either a ministry, an autonomous institution, or the foreign service during the administration immediately following his or her service in the Legislative Assembly; and scored zero otherwise. The independent variable is DEPUTY'S DIFFERENCE – the percent gain in overall presidential vote share by the deputy's party in his or her bailiwick, from the beginning of the deputy's term to the end. Thus, if the PLN won 46% of the presidential vote in a deputy's bailiwick in the year the deputy won office, and 54% in the election marking the end of the deputy's term, DEPUTY'S DIFFERENCE = 8%. The idea behind the probit analysis is that the better deputies serve their parties in their baili-

Table 4.7. Effects of deputies' performance in their bailiwicks on prospects for post-Assembly appointments

Dependent variable: Equal to 1 if deputy received an executive appointment during the term immediately following Assembly service, 0 otherwise.

Independent variables	1970–1974 PLN deputies	1974–1978 PUSC[a] deputies	1978–1982 PLN deputies	1982–1986 PLN deputies	1986–1990 PUSC deputies
Constant	-0.10 (1.35)	0.19 (0.87)	4.02 (2.75)	-0.28 (0.58)	2.71 (1.68)
Deputy's difference	0.10 (0.12)	-0.04 (0.04)	-0.26 (0.18)	0.05 (0.07)	-0.43 (0.28)
N	30	26	23	33	24

Note: Probit analysis; t-statistics are in parentheses.
[a] The PUSC was not formally established until 1982. The coalition of parties that eventually formed the PUSC, however, was stable much earlier. Thus, the deputies included in this group are from the pre-PUSC coalition and supported the successful presidential candidacy of Rodrigo Carazo in 1978.

wicks, the higher should be the DEPUTY'S DIFFERENCE value, and that presidents should be more likely to reward such deputies with appointments. If this is the case, then the coefficient for DEPUTY'S DIFFERENCE should be positive.

Because the Casas Zamora and Briceño Fallas appendix identifies bailiwicks for all Assembly cohorts since 1970, it is possible to run this test for five separate electoral cycles. This seeming data windfall, however, does not guarantee clear and consistent results, as demonstrated by Table 4.7. The coefficient for DEPUTY'S DIFFERENCE is positive for two electoral cycles, negative for three, and does not reach conventional levels of statistical significance for any. The data clearly fail to support the hypothesis that presidents systematically reward deputies for producing at the polls. This is particularly noteworthy given the strong belief, expressed by deputies themselves, that presidents use appointments as rewards for deputies who contribute to their parties' electoral success.

The very inconclusiveness of this test, then, suggests that other factors besides partisan electoral gains could be influencing appointments in Costa Rica. Given the president's control over appointments, the most promising area to consider is the political relationship between presidents and the former deputies whose career prospects they control.

Jockeying for appointments in Costa Rica

It is possible that more complete and precise data would show a positive relationship between bailiwick electoral results and post-Assembly appointments. But the straightforward connection between partisan competition and rewards is complicated in Costa Rica by internal partisan politics that precedes presidential elections. In this section, the premise remains that presidents reward those former deputies who contributed to their elections. But the focus shifts from deputies' contribution to presidents' success against other parties to deputies' alliances in internal partisan competition. It is in the struggle for the presidential nomination that deputies most clearly distinguish themselves from their copartisans in the eyes of presidential candidates. Prior to the nomination, deputies are pressured to make clear their personal loyalties by openly supporting one candidate or another. Upon inauguration, a new president making cabinet appointments may consider a deputy's contributions in her bailiwick to the party's general election victory; but the president most certainly will remember the deputy's early willingness to support his presidential candidacy.

Costa Rica's post–Civil War electoral code initially stipulated that presidential candidates were to be nominated by party conventions (Tribunal Supremo de Elecciones 1989, Art. 74; hereafter TSE). That provision has since been broadened to allow for nationwide primaries, which have been adopted by the PUSC in the most recent elections (Sojo Obando 1992; TSE 1989, Art. 74 Trans. III). The PLN continues to rely formally on a convention comprised of the members of the party's national assemblies in addition to a number of party officials from all levels, local to national (PLN Statutes, Arts. 93, 95). Even in the PLN's case, however, the convention's deliberative capacity has been steadily weakened over time. Presidential hopefuls now take their appeals directly to partisans in the electorate, presenting lists of committed delegates as early as the district-level elections for county party assemblies. PLN district elections took place, for example, in March 1992, more than two years before the 1994 general election, with district lists supported by and committed to specific presidential candidates (*La República* March 16, 1992: 2A). Moreover, these district party elections are perceived as personal referenda on presidential candidates. Preceding the 1992 district elections, newspaper coverage focused on opinion polls that asked voters to choose among various presidential hopefuls, with the question format, "If the Convention were today, who would you support: A, B or C?" regardless of the fact that at the Convention, delegates would be doing the voting (*La República*, February 14, 1992).

The important point here is that the popularization of nominations makes early support from incumbent deputies important to the establishment of credible presidential candidacies. Prior to the PLN district elections, 16 of the party's 25 deputies signed a full-page newspaper advertisement supporting the candidacy of José María Figueres, proclaiming in part, "The Figuerista deputies urge all PLN members to vote in the district elections on March 15" (*La República*, February 14, 1992). These deputies may have risked

burning bridges to other possible PLN candidates, but their move appeared
to pay off. Three days later, Figueres's district lists won 85% of the seats in
the county-level assemblies (*La República*, March 16, 1992: 2A). In 1994,
Figueres was elected president. In sum, in both major parties, candidacies
are announced extremely early in each electoral cycle, and incumbent deputies are forced to begin jockeying early to build alliances with candidates
who may ultimately control post-Assembly careers.

Ideally, it would be possible to gather precise data on which deputies had
supported which presidential hopefuls over the years, and then compare the
rate of appointments among those who supported nomination winners versus
those who supported losers. However, if data on pork and bailiwicks is
characterized as sketchy, data on such alliances is virtually nonexistent. In
the first place, not all alliances are systematically and publicly advertised.
Second, alliances necessarily shift over the course of nomination campaigns,
as candidates enter and abandon races.

In lieu of solid data on prenomination alliances, however, it is nevertheless
possible to demonstrate the importance of personal support for the party's
presidential candidate to deputies' post-Assembly career prospects. One
incident in 1985, known as the Mayo Negro (Black May), illustrates this
point most clearly. The Mayo Negro will be discussed at further length in
Chapter 5 on party discipline. For now, the relevant information is that in
April 1985, Oscar Arias Sanchez had already won the PLN nomination for
president in the 1986 elections. Arias broke party precedent by interfering
in the selection of a deputy to serve as president of the Legislative Assembly
for the last year of the 91st Assembly.[14] The PLN caucus divided over
Arias's chosen candidate, with 17 deputies favoring the choice and 16 voting
against in the caucus vote. Arias regarded the caucus vote as binding on all
PLN members, but on the Assembly floor the 16 mavericks joined with
most of the opposition to elect an alternative PLN deputy as president of the
Legislative Assembly for the final year of the term.

The Mayo Negro was a widely publicized fiasco for the PLN and Arias.
For this study, however, it provides useful data, because the alliances with
and against a presidential candidate were explicit (ALCR 1985a; Villanueva
Badilla 1992). Moreover, the post-Assembly fates of those deputies involved
in the Mayo Negro strongly suggest that personal support for presidential
candidates is critical in determining prospects for executive appointments.
Of the 17 deputies who supported Arias, 7 received documented appoint-

---

[14] Recall from Chapter 2 that the Assembly presidency generally rotates among four different
deputies during the four-year term. Each year, the majority party caucus selects a candidate
for president by majority vote. The entire caucus then supports that candidate in what has,
in every year besides 1985, been a pro forma floor vote.

ments. Of the 16 who opposed Arias, only 1 received a documented appointment.

In the one case where preelection alliances between deputies and a presidential candidate are known, the candidate's supporters were rewarded with appointments at a far greater rate than his opponents. Unfortunately, it is not possible to test whether this pattern of incentives exists across all campaigns, but the actions of deputies and presidential candidates strongly suggests that it does. This does not imply that the contributions deputies make to their parties' electoral strength in their bailiwicks are unimportant; and deputies state that they believe this work does matter to post-Assembly prospects. But this section demonstrates that personal alliance building and jockeying *within* the party also matters to political careers. This condition hinders our ability to analyze incentives to provide particularism solely on the basis of data on interpartisan competition. But it confirms the basic argument that legislators subject to term limits will be responsive to those who control their careers once their terms are up.

Conclusion

This chapter began with the puzzle of why legislators provide particularism in Costa Rica, even where standard, electoral explanations for particularism do not apply. The basic argument of the chapter is that the electoral conditions by which legislative particularism is conventionally explained may be sufficient for particularism, but they are not necessary. The evidence for this claim is clear in Costa Rica, where deputies diligently provide constituency service and small pork, despite closed-list PR and term limits. The evidence raises new questions, however, regarding why and how particularism is provided in the absence of personal electoral incentives.

I suggest in this chapter that particularism is desired by parties because it benefits parties collectively at the polls; that Costa Rican parties organize deputies such that the contribution of each to the party's electoral goals can be measured independently; and that deputies who contribute to their parties' electoral well-being are rewarded systematically with post-Assembly appointments. Deputies' comments in interviews overwhelmingly indicate that they believe all of these arguments to be accurate. Nevertheless, with the budgetary, electoral, and appointments data available, it has proved difficult to demonstrate any consistent relationship either between this kind of pork and electoral support, or between electoral support and post-Assembly appointments in Costa Rica. There are some likely explanations for this ambiguity. In all cases, there are serious shortcomings in the data available. In the case of partisan payoffs from PEs, the multiple plausible partisan strategies in distributing pork imply that simple regression analysis might well turn up no single pattern of distribution, and no consistent correlation between pork and partisan support. In the case of electoral support and appointments, the presence of intraparty competition for presidential nominations, and the alliances that this competition fosters between deputies and presidential hopefuls, obscures the relationship between partisan support in deputies' bailiwicks and their likelihood of gaining post-Assembly appointments. I have shown the impact of alliances between deputies and a presidential candidate on post-Assembly appointments in the only case in which these alliances are explicit.

Where more subtle and precise data on legislative behavior and more complete data on post-Assembly career paths are available, it is possible to demonstrate that legislators no longer dependent on their constituents for reelection are increasingly responsive to those who do control career advancement (Chapter 6). For now, the story must remain that where personal incentives to provide particularism do not exist, those who stand to benefit electorally can create incentives for particularism. By this, I do not mean to imply that political parties will always organize effectively to capture electoral gains from particularism, much less that legislators will always be the agents designated to provide particularism. The Venezuelan experience related in this chapter demonstrates the first point, that where direct personal incentives do not exist, parties do not inevitably respond by creating alternative incentives for politicians to provide particularism.[15] The second point is a reminder that other agents besides national legislators can supply small favors to individuals and communities. Where local or state (or county, provincial, etc.) governments have sufficient resources, elected officials below the national level may cater to local and individual demands, perhaps even by lobbying the national government on behalf of such interests.[16] Alternatively, in a number of systems official state ombudsmen have been created to provide the bureaucratic assistance described here as constituent service (Caiden 1983; Cain, Ferejohn, and Fiorina 1987; Elder, Thomas, and Arter 1988; Marshall 1993). Of course, where small favors are provided by a nonpartisan state bureaucrat, parties cannot reap electoral benefits by

[15] Of course, the recent Venezuelan electoral reforms suggest that constituent demands for responsiveness by legislators to local concerns eventually did prompt a restructuring of electoral incentives expressly to encourage responsiveness to local demands. Whether the reforms succeed on this count remains to be seen. The point here is that Venezuelan parties waited 30 years under the current regime before responding to voter demands for local representation.

[16] To the extent that local petitions in Venezuela were presented to national government officials prior to the electoral reforms, the work was done by state and municipal officials (see the earlier section entitled "Venezuela: Electoral Theory Redeemed"). Evidently, however, these traffickers in particularism were unable to meet the level of demand for small favors generated by their constituents.

providing them. It is not within the scope of this work, however, to explain specifically how small favors will be provided in all systems. The point here is that where electoral incentives for legislators are absent, parties can create them.

Costa Rican deputies regard the provision of small favors as a central element of their job. Parties in the Costa Rican Legislative Assembly organize their deputies to provide small favors and to be accountable to geographical constituencies distinct from their broader electoral constituencies. Deputies, in turn, associate their effectiveness in serving their parties with the prospect of receiving post-Assembly appointments, and so of continuing their political careers despite term limits. However, exclusive presidential control over appointments, coupled with intrapartisan alliances and competition over party nominations, complicate any straightforward relationship between deputies' service to their party and their prospects for appointment. The structure of political careers under term limits, then, introduces an element of divisiveness into Costa Rican legislative parties. The effect of term limits on party cohesiveness is the subject of Chapter 5.

5

Term limits and legislative party cohesiveness

Parties in the Costa Rican Legislative Assembly are less cohesive than those in the Venezuelan Congress, and legislative term limits are the principal cause of the difference. By cohesiveness, I mean the tendency of copartisan legislators to vote together on policy. All Venezuelan deputies who intend to continue their political careers are dependent on a stable cadre of party leaders who determine candidate positions on ballot lists; so all ambitious Venezuelan deputies are responsive to the same set of directives. Costa Rican deputies, on the other hand, face uncertainty over (1) whether any post-Assembly appointments will be available to members of their party, and (2) who within their party might control post-Assembly appointments. In the first place, if a Costa Rican deputy's party loses the next presidential election, no amount of party loyalty will gain the deputy a post-Assembly appointment. Second, party caucuses in the Legislative Assembly are likely to be divided among supporters of various aspirants for the party's presidential nomination. Thus, legislative term limits in Costa Rica mandate that the prospects for sustaining a political career based on party loyalty are more bleak than in Venezuela, and the criteria for party loyalty themselves are much less clear.

This argument should be qualified by noting that Costa Rican parties have been organized so as to mitigate the damage to party cohesiveness caused by term limits. Chapters 3 and 4 have been largely devoted to outlining measures that parties have taken to this end. The strict partisan distribution of patronage, as well as monitoring of deputies' performance in serving their constituents, are elements of party efforts to control political careers, and so to be able to coerce deputies to act cohesively in the Legislative Assembly. Nevertheless, these organizational structures are second-best solutions for parties. The patronage-based system of control over careers is complicated by the winner-take-all nature of patronage, and by the existence of *presidential* term limits, which guarantee continuous uncertainty and instability in who controls political careers. The most effective means of enforcing cohesiveness is direct control by a stable party leadership over potential careers in the Legislative Assembly. Such a solution is precluded by term limits in Costa Rica, so Costa Rican parties have done what they can within their constitutional constraints to maintain cohesiveness among deputies.

The conclusion of this chapter is that legislative term limits reduce the resources available to party leaders in Costa Rica to impose discipline on deputies, as compared with the ability of leaders in Venezuela to do so. In making this case, the chapter proceeds as follows. The first section presents empirical evidence of the differences in levels of party cohesiveness in Venezuela and Costa Rica. In Venezuela, cases of indiscipline by legislators on important votes are extremely rare, and sanctions imposed by party leaders on maverick legislators are harsh. In Costa Rica, intraparty divisions by legislators on important votes are not unusual, and party sanctions are less certain. The next section of the chapter explains the link between legislative term limits and party discipline. With regard to Venezuela, I review the consensus among scholars that control over party ballot lists, and so over political careers, by party leaders is the principal source of party discipline. With regard to Costa Rica, I demonstrate that intraparty politics is made much more complex by the lack of certainty over who controls political careers. Extensive interviews with politicians and party officials illustrate the conditions under which Costa Rican Assembly parties establish formal party positions on issues, the motivations of deputies for breaking party discipline, and the prospects of receiving punishment from the party if voting discipline is broken. Finally, I sum up the deleterious effects of term limits on party discipline and cohesiveness in the Costa Rican case. I then draw the broader conclusion that the effects of term limits on party cohesiveness can vary, depending on the incentives for cohesiveness generated by the electoral system to which term limits are applied.

Observing levels of party cohesiveness

The most straightforward way to measure party cohesiveness in assemblies is to examine data that identifies how individual legislators voted on specific pieces of legislation. In the U.S. Congress, where most significant votes are roll calls and computer records are kept, there are no barriers to precise quantitative analysis of cohesiveness. Methodological debates remain, of course, primarily over how cohesiveness, or party discipline, should be identified, and so over what types of partisan vote patterns should count as cohesive and what types should count as undisciplined (Brady, Cooper, and Hurley 1979; Collie and Brady 1985; Cox and McCubbins 1993; Rohde 1991). In Venezuela and Costa Rica, debates over how to interpret voting data would be a luxury. In these countries, almost no legislative votes are taken by roll call, although the reasons for this differ. In Venezuela, roll calls are unnecessary because breaches of party discipline are so rare that once the positions of party leaders are known, vote totals are generally derived simply from the attendance of various party cohorts. In Costa Rica, where party discipline is not so regular, roll calls are still unnecessary because the small size of the Legislative Assembly (57 members) allows party leaders to determine the votes of all deputies simply by watching them.

Venezuela

Perhaps the most striking testament to the regularity with which Venezuelan legislative parties vote as disciplined blocs is the 1985 report of two congressional aides, who were commissioned by the Congress to submit suggestions for improving the administrative organization of the legislature and its technical support services (Gabaldón and Oberto 1985). One of the technologies considered in the report was electronic vote-counting machines. But the report notes that such technology only improves the efficiency of voting if legislators cast individual votes, as opposed to when party blocs simply declare their positions on legislation. It concludes:

> In both houses of Congress, roll call votes are rare . . . The party caucuses tend to vote as blocs, and it is not common that there has been dissidence by any member – such cases have been very rare . . . From this, it's clear that there would be little value in having automatic electronic registration of individual votes. (Gabaldón and Oberto 1985, vol. 1: 46)

It is remarkable that aides assigned to make proposals for technical improvements in a legislature with over 200 members[1] should dismiss the need for electronic vote counters because the need to count individual votes at all is virtually unnecessary. But this is also clear testament to the regularity with which copartisans vote as blocs.

This conclusion is supported by other students of the Venezuelan Congress as well. Among U.S. scholars, Michael Coppedge is probably currently the most familiar with the Venezuelan Congress. Within the AD and CO-PEI, between the mid-1940s and 1993, he identifies only two cases of voting indiscipline among legislators. In 1992, following a failed military coup attempt, President Carlos Andres Perez (AD) suspended some constitutional guarantees, including habeas corpus. When the COPEI subsequently voted to ratify this move in Congress, the ex-president and then-COPEI Senator Rafael Caldera abstained from the vote. Caldera's vote was not pivotal, and he was not formally punished. Coppedge suspects that Caldera was able to act independently without sanction in this case because of his national

---

[1] The Chamber of Deputies generally has over 200 members. The Senate has 46.

stature, which is independent of his current position as senator, and that his refusal to support Perez's maneuver was an exercise in posturing in preparation for his presidential bid in 1993.[2]

Apart from this exceptional case, what is noteworthy about voting indiscipline in Venezuela is its rarity, and the swiftness with which it is punished. For his other case of indiscipline, Coppedge reached all the way back to the constitutional assembly during Venezuela's three years of civilian government in the 1940s. In 1947, seven AD delegates to the assembly voted against the party and in favor of direct election of governors. They were expelled from the party immediately.[3]

More recently, the February 1992 coup attempt was the cause of another intraparty division, this within the AD over support for Perez's cabinet. The coup attempt was launched in the context of widespread popular discontent with Perez's economic austerity policies. January 1992 opinion polls indicated that 80% of Venezuelans had no confidence in Perez (Reuters News Service March 23, 1992). In March 1992, after the failed coup, opposition parties launched an effort in Congress to oust Perez's planning, finance, and agriculture ministers. Removing the ministers would have required a two-thirds vote in each chamber, and the AD held 48% pluralities in both, so to remove the ministers would have required the support of at least some AD legislators. On March 25, Reuters reported that "two [AD] legislators were applauded during a heated Chamber of Deputies debate when they said some economic ministers must leave and threatened an unprecedented break with the party line." The AD majority leader publicly promised disciplinary action against any deputy who broke party ranks, drawing the defiant response, "Do what you want to me and to my political career," from AD Deputy Luis Matos Azócar (Reuters News Service March 25, 1992). As expected, the motion to oust Perez's ministers failed (Reuters News Service March 26, 1992). But his independence cost Matos Azócar and the one other AD deputy who voted against party. Both were expelled from the party by the AD executive committee within days of the vote. A spokesman for the AD explained: "They had distanced themselves from the party line and they took a position that challenged the party. If no sanction is applied now, there could be a situation of anarchy in the parliamentary wing of the party" (Reuters News Service March 30, 1992).

The dearth of cases of voting indiscipline in the Venezuelan Congress is striking. The cases reviewed here are the only ones I have been able to

---

[2] Personal communication with Professor Michael Coppedge, April 13, 1992. Coppedge's broader suspicion about Caldera's goals proved to be right on the mark. Caldera left the COPEI to run for president in 1993, and won, at the head of a coalition of small parties opposed to both the AD and COPEI.

[3] Personal communication with Coppedge, April 13, 1992.

document. One predates the current Venezuelan regime and the other two are the direct results of the current regime's most severe crisis of confidence. In two of the three cases, punishment against the wayward legislators was immediate expulsion from the party. The scant evidence of party indiscipline, moreover, accords with the consensus among students of Venezuelan politics that parties in the Congress are extraordinarily strong (Combellas 1986; Coppedge 1994; Gil Yepes 1981; Kelley 1977; Levine 1978, 1987; Stambouli 1988; Karl 1986). I discuss the logic of Venezuelan party cohesiveness in more detail later. For now, however, the next task is to demonstrate that Costa Rican legislative parties are clearly less cohesive than their Venezuelan counterparts.

Costa Rica

In Costa Rica, like in Venezuela, recorded roll call votes are extremely rare.[4] Despite the absence of comprehensive voting data, however, incidents of partisan divisions on important legislative votes are abundant and can be documented from floor speeches, occasional recorded committee votes, press accounts, partisan disciplinary procedures, interview accounts, and even the rare recorded roll call vote. I now review a number of examples of recent intraparty divisions on important votes, and the responses taken by party organizations. The point is to illustrate the persistence of divisions, the types of motivations behind breaks with party lines, and the ability of party organizations to discourage indiscipline.

Mayo Negro. The Mayo Negro was described briefly in Chapter 4, to illustrate the connection between deputies' support for presidential candidates and prospects for post-Assembly appointments; but the case warrants further treatment in this chapter as an example of contentiousness over what constitutes a strict party position in Costa Rica. The division within the PLN in the Mayo Negro case was primarily over the party's selection for president of the Legislative Assembly, but it was also over the means

---

[4] My original intention in studying party cohesion in Costa Rica was to gather data on roll call voting. My inquiry into the availability of such data at the Legislative Assembly Archives, however, was met with bemusement. I was escorted to the Assembly chamber, and shown the single long table where legislative floor procedures are conducted. Deputies from the two main parties sit along either side of the table, with party leaders at the head, and minor party deputies at the other end. As I was later told by the Assembly majority leader, "Roll calls are not necessary for the party leadership in enforcing discipline, because there are so few deputies, and all the members of a given party sit together along one side of the room. They generally vote by standing up or remaining seated, and their position can easily be seen, and noted, by the leadership" (Interview 93–04). Roll calls are taken perhaps two or three times per year, according to Leo Nuñez Arias, of the Legislative Assembly Archives, and not necessarily on important legislation.

by which the party caucus reaches decisions that bind deputies to vote as a bloc.

In 1985, having won the PLN presidential nomination for the 1986 election, Oscar Arias Sanchez undertook to build a coalition among incumbent PLN deputies to elect Matilde Marín Chinchilla as president of the Legislative Assembly for the 1985–1986 term. The Assembly had never had a woman as president, and Arias's motivation was at least in part to rectify this inequity (Villalobos 1992). He circulated a letter among all PLN deputies suggesting the choice of Marín Chinchilla (ALCR 1985b). The caucus divided bitterly over this suggestion, in part because some deputies resented the interference of the presidential candidate in the selection process, but also because many strongly objected to the selection of a woman to the position of president of the Legislative Assembly.[5] Ultimately, the caucus vote was 17 to 16 in favor of Marín Chinchilla. On the Assembly floor, however, the 16 dissident PLN deputies joined with most of the PUSC deputies to elect Guillermo Vargas Sanabria (PLN) to the post. The maneuver set off an open and acrimonious debate over the requirements of loyalty to the party, the manner by which the party caucus could establish positions that bind all deputies, and what the repercussions of breaking with the party should be.

The central procedural point of contention was whether a simple majority vote in caucus bound all PLN deputies to observe a party line. The dissidents' defense was that PLN party statutes set a two-thirds majority in the Assembly caucus as necessary for decisions pertaining to internal organization of the caucus (PLN Statutes, Art. 100), so the 17 to 16 vote was not binding. Arias's loyalists contended that the two-thirds rule had never been applied for any caucus decision, and that all decisions previously taken by simple majority vote had been honored. As Carlos María Chajud Calvo put it in the floor debate:

[Majority rule] has always been respected, and it is not as one deputy from my party has put it, that it was half against half. It was 17 against 16, and the decision was taken to support the leadership, and one has to respect that, because in the PLN we have always done everything by voting and not by decree. (ALCR 1985a, Tomo 405: 18)

Of course, by this time, the point of whether the caucus vote was binding or not was moot with regard to the election for president of the Legislative Assembly. But the question remained relevant for those PLN members who sought disciplinary action against the dissident deputies. The case was brought before the PLN's internal Ethics Tribunal, which is authorized to

---

[5] Villanueva Badilla (1992); Villalobos (1992); see also ALCR (1985a and b), Ugalde Alvarez's speech on p. 16, and Curling Rodriguez's speech on p. 30.

impose sanctions on party members who break with party protocol. The Ethics Tribunal expelled Vargas Sanabria on the grounds that he had accepted the post of president of the Legislative Assembly, and so benefited personally from the party's division (Villanueva Badilla 1992). It failed to expel the other 15 renegade deputies, however, for a series of reasons. The stated explanation of the Tribunal was that there had been no roll call vote on the election, so there was no evidence as to how individual deputies had voted. This, however, was a clear rationalization, as each deputy's position on Marín Chinchilla's candidacy was publicly known. According to José Miguel Villalobos, there was no consensus, even within the Tribunal, as to whether the two-thirds rule on caucus votes should have applied in this case. Moreover, there was a serious reluctance formally to expel so many prominent PLN members from the party (Villalobos 1992).[6]

In the end, despite the lack of formal expulsion, the renegade deputies were largely denied executive appointments by President Arias during his administration, whereas Arias's supporters were rewarded for their loyalty (Chapter 4). Moreover, the connection between loyalty to the party's presidential candidate and post-Assembly appointments was not lost on the PLN mavericks. Benjamin Muñoz Retaña, for example, appeared to be perfectly aware of the implications that his indiscipline could have on his post-Assembly prospects. After casting his vote for Vargas Sanabria, Muñoz Retaña acknowledged another deputy's suggestion that to break the party line on this vote jeopardized one's political future:

Possibly among this Group of 16 there are many who have no political futures, who have just terminated their political careers. This could be. Perhaps some of us have come here to serve the country briefly, without any interest in our futures. But I prefer it this way, I prefer to return to my house at peace, and not depend on the opinion of any other person for what he might give to me in the future. (ALCR 1985a, Tomo 405: 40)

Muñoz Retaña proved to be an accurate, if melodramatic, prophet of the post-Assembly fates of the PLN mavericks. The case of the Mayo Negro, however, also suggests that Costa Rican deputies are more willing than their Venezuelan counterparts to challenge party leaders, and that party organizations are not as adept at providing deterrents to such behavior. Further examples of indiscipline underscore this point.

---

[6] The Ethics Tribunal decision was not reached until after the 91st Legislative Assembly had finished its term and a new cohort of deputies was in office. Therefore, the Tribunal was not faced with the prospect of expelling so many deputies from the party as to sacrifice its partisan majority in the Assembly. Had such a crisis taken place earlier in the Legislative Assembly, however, the Tribunal would have had an even greater incentive not to impose serious sanctions on the maverick deputies.

Bank reform. In the 1980s, two laws that reformed the national banking system generated divisions within both major parties. The first was the Ley de moneda (Currency Law), originally submitted to the Legislative Assembly in 1983 by the Monge administration with personal requests to all PLN deputies for support. The law relaxes state regulation over international currency transactions, and also allows the deposit of public funds in private banks. The monopoly of state banks over public deposits had been established with the nationalization of banks under the Figueres Junta of 1948–1949 and remained an element of the PLN's platform.

When the bill reached the floor in 1984, a group of 13 PLN deputies opposed the reform on the basis that the prerogatives of the national banks could not be tampered with unless the PLN Congress formally eliminated this plank from the platform. Despite the objections of these 13, however, the PLN caucus decision was to support the reform. As in the Mayo Negro case a year earlier, much debate focused on the obligations of deputies to adhere to party lines, although in this case no one proposed that a party line could only be established by 2/3 majority. Instead, the dissidents relied on the PLN platform, their own consciences to defend their position. Notably, one deputy argued that the whole concept of party discipline had been attacked in the past by politicians and journalists who now championed the banking reforms on the basis that all PLN deputies were obligated to vote as a bloc. Miguel Guillén Elizondo asked:

What party have these politicians and editors attacked most strenuously for having demanded discipline? What party have they criticized for this? Haven't they always exalted any dissidents within the PLN on the ground that every deputy should be independent? Haven't we been hearing this for over 25 years? Why do they say nothing now, why are they frightened when some of us in the PLN think independently on one issue? (ALCR, 1983–1984, Exp.# 9736)

Guillén's statement underscores the point that the issue of whether Assembly parties should be able to impose voting discipline has been a point of constant dispute in Costa Rica, and his vote on the banking reform illustrates that the parties have not been able to enforce discipline effectively. Moreover, among PLN deputies, alliance building with the party's candidates for president in 1986 was likely more important than the decision of the caucus in motivating individual deputies to support or oppose the reform. The bill's ardent supporters among PLN deputies were openly linked to candidate Carlos Manuel Castillo, who was pushing for the legislation (Gutierrez Saxe and Vargas Cullell 1986). The vote on final passage of the currency bill – a rare roll call – found the PLN divided deeply, but it also demonstrates that the PUSC was not united in favor of the reforms. Although no PUSC deputies argued against the bill in floor debate, nearly half refused to support

Table 5.1. Partisan breakdown of vote on 1984 currency bill

Deputy's party	Favored	Opposed	Abstained
PLN	19	8	6
PUSC	10	0	8
Other	1	2	3
Total	30	10	17

*Table 5.2. Partisan breakdown of vote on 1988 financial
system modernization bill*

Deputy's party	Favored	Opposed	Abstained
PLN	18≤23	4	2≤7
PUSC	11≤16	3	6≤11
Other	0	3	0
Total	34	10	13

Note: Reconstructed from statements made in floor debate during plenary
session of the Assembly on October 20, 1988 (ALCR 1988), and from newspaper
accounts in *La Nación,* October 25, 1988, and *La República,* October 25, 1988.

the legislation, and abstained from the vote (Gutierrez Saxe and Vargas
Cullell 1986). Table 5.1 shows the breakdown of votes according to party.

In 1988, another banking reform bill divided the major parties. This
reform further facilitated the deposit of public funds in private banks,
granted greater discretion to the directors of the Central Bank in managing
state funds, ended preferential credit from state banks for the autonomous
institutions, and allowed the state to underwrite international loans to private banks. Again, a minority of PLN deputies opposed the reform on the
grounds that it violated the party platform, and they were joined in opposition by a handful of PUSC, as well as some minor party, deputies. The
October 1988 vote on the reform was not a roll call, so the partisan breakdown in Table 5.2 is reconstructed from floor speeches and newspaper
accounts, and is not complete. Nevertheless, it is clear that on this critical
piece of financial legislation, there was no semblance of party cohesiveness
by either major party.

Renter's Law. The month before the second banking reform law was passed,
a similar cross-party coalition was responsible for pushing through the Legislative Assembly a reform of the law regulating contracts between renters and
tenants, which relaxed rent controls that had been in place since the social

Table 5.3. Partisan breakdown of vote on 1988 renter's bill

Deputy's party	Favored	Opposed	Abstained
PLN	9	17	3
PUSC	17	4	4
Other	0	2	1
Total	26	23	8

reforms of President Calderón Guardia in the 1940s. This legislation had been favored by both the Monge and Arias administrations, but it relied primarily on PUSC support in the Legislative Assembly, as Table 5.3 demonstrates. In floor debate, members of both parties opposed to the bill defended their position primarily in the name of protecting tenants from eviction and general social democratic ideals. In many deputies' statements, the absence of clear party positions on the matter is striking. Oscar Saborio Vega (PUSC) declared:

My vote is "No." I vote against the Costa Rica envisioned by deputies Carvajal Herrera (PLN) and Chacón Jimenez (PUSC). I vote for the Costa Rica of deputies Corrales Bolaños (PLN) and Mendez Mata (PUSC). (ALCR, 1985–1988, Exp. 10,180: 110)

Corrales Bolanos himself, who had served as Assembly majority leader earlier in the term, was more self-conscious of his partisan stance, and in particular of the fact that President Arias supported the bill and wanted disciplined PLN support in the Legislative Assembly:

Needless to say, it has been said that I am undisciplined, and I have replied more than once that I would like to debate what my indisciplines consist of and who are the real undisciplined ones, but no one has accepted my challenge. This bill is an example of what I understand to be a case of discipline – of that discipline that I cannot ignore. If I could, I should not have been elected for the PLN, but for some other party, as was my colleague Brenes Castillo (UAC), and here I would be as free as the wind. But I am not as free as the wind, out of respect for the voters who believed that the PLN had political ideals, and that we had to defend them. (ALCR, 1985–1988, Exp. 10,180: 50)

Corrales Bolaños's argument was an effort to redefine the idea of party discipline on his own terms. The message that his statement sends most clearly is that party discipline in Costa Rica is an ambiguous concept, particularly in contrast with the Venezuelan case discussed earlier.

Other examples. These examples can be supplemented with other cases of internal party divisions on important issues. One of the past indisciplines that Corrales Bolaños is quoted as referring to transpired in 1986, when he refused to observe the PLN party line in supporting an international agreement between the United States, Panama, and Costa Rica regulating tuna fishing in the East Pacific (ALCR 1983–86). Corrales's intransigence initially cost the PLN its majority on the vote, which was opposed by all PUSC and minor party deputies. At the last minute, however, the PLN leadership succeeded in convincing the deputy from the UAC to change his vote to support the pact.[7]

As of 1992, the PUSC faced internal divisions over two treaties pending before the Legislative Assembly. The first, which would have committed Costa Rica to participation in a Central American Parliament, drew support as well as opposition from members of both the PUSC and PLN during the 1986–1990 Legislative Assembly, but had not been reported out of committee (ALCR, 1988–1989, Exp. 10,661). The second, an agreement with Colombia on rights to submarine resources, also drew support from deputies of both major parties (ALCR 1984–91). According to the assistant to the president's chief of staff, however, both treaties were stalled as of March 1992, due to divisions within the PUSC Assembly caucus (Madrigal 1992).

Summing up

The examples cited here are not meant to suggest that Costa Rican Assembly parties are ineffectual. On most important issues, the major party caucuses vote as blocs. Assembly partisan majorities certainly have been effective in monopolizing budgetary resources. But the fact remains that Costa Rican Assembly parties are far more likely to exhibit internal divisions and lack of cohesiveness on important issues than are their Venezuelan counterparts. And when Costa Rican deputies break party lines, they are far less likely to face formal sanctions from their parties.

Moreover, in explaining their independence from party lines, Costa Rican deputies do not acknowledge a single source of directives for partisan legislative action. Whereas the national party executive committees in Venezuela direct caucuses in Congress, Costa Rican deputies refer alternatively to their own internal caucus votes, to the incumbent president, to their party's presidential nominee, to their party's platform, or to their party's Ethics Tribunal, as the bases of party cohesiveness. Where so many potential bases exist, it is not surprising that cohesiveness suffers.

This section has established that Costa Rican legislative parties are less cohesive than Venezuela's. In the next, I argue that the primary cause of the difference is the presence of legislative term limits in Costa Rica.

---

[7] Recall that the UAC, which regularly elects one deputy from Cartago Province, is well known for its willingness to trade votes on national policy for a share of PEs.

Explaining levels of party cohesiveness

The central argument of this section is that the existence of legislative term limits in Costa Rica precludes the existence of a central principal with an interest in strong party cohesiveness who controls the political careers of all ambitious legislators, and therefore can impose sanctions on those who break party discipline. As usual, the contrast with Venezuela illustrates the case for Costa Rica most clearly, so the basis of strong party discipline in Venezuela is explained first.

Venezuela

The most important key to Venezuelan party cohesiveness is the control over nominations to congressional ballot lists by the national executive committees of the major parties. Recall that the section of Venezuela's electoral law entitled "Nominations" establishes no actual procedures that parties must follow in creating lists, so that party leaders are unconstrained by law in their control over ballot access (Congreso de la República de Venezuela, Ley de sufragio, 1992, Title IV, Chap. II, Arts. 102–111). Henry Wells describes the process as follows:

Every party's national executive committee reserves to itself the prerogative of making the final decision concerning the persons to be listed as legislative candidates and the position of each on the list . . . In the case of COPEI and AD . . . after receiving the regional committees' lists the national committee normally reviews and amends them as it sees fit. (Wells 1980: 43)

The domination of the nomination process by national party executive committees is confirmed in a number of other studies (Levine 1987; Myers 1973).

The characteristics of these national executive committees that are critical to ensuring cohesiveness in Congress are their stability and their ability to impose sanctions on legislators who buck party directives. Membership on party executive committees is relatively stable from one electoral cycle to the next. The only limitation on membership is that which prohibits Venezuela's president from simultaneously holding any administrative position in his party (Gil Yepes 1981). Executive committees tend to be composed largely of nonelected officials who dominate party decision making for extended periods, and whose positions are not subject to electoral control nor legal restrictions (Brewer-Carías 1989).

The stability of Venezuela's national party leadership, combined with its control over ballot access, means that all politically ambitious legislators respond to a similar set of political directives (Kelley 1977). Executive committees buttress the link between extraparliamentary and legislative leadership by naming the leadership of each party's caucus in Congress (Karl 1986). Party leaders in Congress are included as members of executive committees, and occupy the unique position as liaisons between the committees and rank-and-file legislators. This position can allow caucus leaders to play the role of brokers between legislators and their executive committees (Kelley 1977). But the relationship is stacked in favor of the executive committees, which can terminate the career of any legislator who breaks with the party line.

The first part of this chapter reviewed a couple of cases in which highly publicized breaches in party discipline were met with prompt expulsion from the AD by executive committees. Such cases are extremely rare, of course, precisely because swift and certain sanctions are effective deterrents against legislative indiscipline. Moreover, expulsion during a legislator's term is not the only, nor the most important, sanction imposed by executive committees. Public expulsion can be politically embarrassing and costly to parties, whereas control over ballot lists allows a more subtle means of control over political careers. As David Myers describes it:

Venezuelan political parties enforce strict internal discipline. All legislative positions are filled according to the vote received by the party list, and the ordering of candidates on party lists in each state must be approved by the party's national governing body. Independent senators and deputies are removed from the subsequent party list if they disobey the instructions from the national party leadership, and exclusion ends one's political career. (Myers 1977: 289)

Again, there is consensus among students of Venezuelan politics on the use of ballot control by national party leaders as a means of sanctioning maverick legislators (Brewer-Carías 1989; Levine 1987; Rachadell 1991). The result is nearly airtight party discipline among Venezuelan parties in Congress (Combellas 1986; Coppedge 1989; Gil Yepes 1981; Stambouli 1988).

Costa Rica

Party cohesiveness is looser in the Costa Rican Legislative Assembly than the Venezuelan Congress because there is no stable principal who can issue partisan political directives and who has the ability to sanction legislators for disobedience. The various sources claimed by deputies as the bases of party positions is evidence of this condition. The situation is also flatly described by Costa Rican politicians and activists. When I asked whether deputies regularly vote according to a party line, the Assembly minority leader told me:

It is not at all unusual for members of the party to vote differently on a given issue. But it is hard to say exactly what it means "Voting *with* the party" or "Voting *against* the party." There is such a difference of opinion within the country over *what is the*

PLN – whether it is defined by the presidential candidates (and *which* candidate), or defined by the secretary general of the party, or by the party leadership in the Legislative Assembly, or by the individual deputies – that it is difficult to say what the party is. Therefore, it's difficult to say what constitutes a vote *with* or *against* the party. (Interview Interview 93–12)

This opinion was shared by Carlos Arguedas, PLN counsel:

It is impossible to speak of the party as a whole imposing discipline on deputies . . . There are too many, often competing, power centers within the party that might command loyalty. And even these do not have at their disposal sufficient means to enforce discipline. (Arguedas 1992)

The sources of loose party cohesiveness in Costa Rica, then, are in the dissensus over how party lines are established and in the lack of enforcement through sanctions of party lines that are acknowledged. These topics are discussed in turn.

Among deputies of both parties interviewed, many stated that party line positions are generally established on issues that are important nationwide, but that deputies are left free to vote as they please on less salient and local issues (Interview 93–27; Interview 93–55). Discrepancies over how official partisan positions are determined, however, were also present in the accounts of deputies from both parties. Both the major party caucuses meet regularly on Monday mornings when the Legislative Assembly is in session. At these meetings, according to some deputies, each party's Assembly leadership clarifies party positions on issues on the Assembly agenda in the coming week, notifying deputies of required party line votes (Interview 93–15). One PLN deputy stated that such positions are originally determined at meetings of the party's executive committee which, as in Venezuela, is composed of nonlegislators (Interview 93–27). Others held that decisions were regularly taken by majority vote in caucus meetings (Villanueva Badilla 1992; Interview 93–49). Another claimed that caucus decisions were nonbinding, and that only if there is a vote of the national party assembly in plenary session are deputies obligated to vote as a bloc.

PUSC deputies, as well, varied in their versions of how party lines are established. Some simply indicated that deputies are notified of party positions by the Assembly leadership at weekly meetings (Interview 93–09). Another was firm that "in our system, the Majority leader does not make decisions that obligate the whole party. In general, he consults with the party before. Positions declared by the leadership are not binding. The leadership does not have the authority to establish a party position" (Interview 93–38). The majority leader himself concurred, explaining that a two-thirds majority vote in caucus is needed to impose a party-line vote. Nevertheless, "Even then, dissident deputies can plead to the leadership for permission to break discipline" (Interview 93–04). The variations in these

Table 5.4. Question: Do you ever vote against your party on a vote in the Assembly?

1990-1994 Assembly	All deputies	PUSC	PLN
Yes	5 (14)	2 (12)	3 (17)
No	27 (77)	13 (76)	14 (78)
Hedge[a]	3 (9)	2 (12)	1 (6)
Total asked	35 (100)	17 (100)	18 (100)

Note: Percentages are in parentheses.
[a] Deputies answered to the effect of "No, but I would if I saw reason," or "No, but I probably will on some upcoming votes."

accounts recall the fierce debate within the PLN during the Mayo Negro episode over what constitutes a partisan obligation for deputies. There is diversity of opinion on this issue, and it is not limited to the PLN.

In interviews, I also regularly asked deputies a series of questions regarding their own discipline on party-line votes. The first question was whether they ever voted against their own party when an official position was established. The results are shown in Table 5.4. The results are similar for each of the two major parties.[8] In each case, about one in six deputies claimed to have voted against a party line. Moreover, there is some reason to believe that this figure underestimates the proportion of deputies who are willing to break party ranks. In the first place, the interviews were conducted less than two years into the 1990–1994 Legislative Assembly. Over the four-year course of the Assembly, more deputies are bound to have voted independently. Second, deputies were always offered confidentiality on interview responses. Many immediately deferred, assuring me that whatever they said could be attributed to them directly; others accepted confidentiality. Nevertheless, on some questions, some deputies became cautious in their answers, regardless of whether the interview was open or confidential. Questions regarding party discipline frequently elicited such caution. And deputies who were hesitant to speak frankly about party discipline would be more likely to understate their conflicts with party leaders than to overstate them. Some of these cautious answers I have classified as "Hedges," rather than outright statements of discipline or indiscipline. Hedges did not confirm that they had broken party lines, but they suggested that they would, or will, if they disagreed with the party's position.

The next question, prompted by the evident attention that deputies devote

[8] The question was not asked of any of the minor party deputies, each of whom is his or her party's only representative in the 1990–1994 Legislative Assembly.

Table 5.5. Question: Would you vote against the party if its position conflicted with the interests of the communities you represent?

1990–1994 Assembly	All deputies	PUSC	PLN
Yes	16 (48)	11 (69)	5 (29)
No	6 (18)	4 (25)	2 (12)
Hedge[a]	3 (9)	0 (0)	3 (18)
Never a conflict	3 (9)	1 (6)	2 (12)
Principles[b]	5 (15)	0 (0)	5 (29)
Total asked	33 (100)	16 (100)	17 (100)

Note: Percentages are in parentheses.
[a] Answers to the effect that, "I'd ask permission of the leadership to break from the party line, and we would resolve the situation, so there would be no problem."
[b] Answers to the effect that, "Regardless of what the situation, one must always vote according to one's principles."

to local concerns, attempts to discern deputies' motivations for breaking party lines. Deputies were asked whether they would vote against their party if its position conflicted with the interests of their communities (bailiwicks). The results are in Table 5.5. In this case, the differences between deputies of the two major parties are notable. PUSC deputies were much more likely to answer the question head on, with a quarter saying no and more than two thirds saying yes. The stronger local ties among PUSC deputies, who held a majority in the 93rd Legislative Assembly, might explain their willingness to support community interests even in opposition to their party's line.[9] PLN deputies, like their PUSC counterparts, were more likely to answer yes than no, but a majority avoided answering the question directly altogether. Some 29% dismissed the potential for conflict between local and partisan positions by asserting that all votes must be based primarily on principles.[10] Another 12% dismissed the prospect that local interests could ever conflict with the party's position. And 18% avoided the dilemma by assuring me

---

[9] Unfortunately, analogous survey data are not available for previous Assemblies, in which the PLN held majorities. If it were, it would be possible to determine whether strong community ties are a characteristic of the PUSC, or simply of the party that controls most particularism.

[10] One deputy's account of breaking discipline for principles, however, suggests that more practical matters were also relevant: "I could not vote against my principles. I had to explain myself to the majority leader and to the president of the republic. My explanations were accepted. Of course, at the time we had a secure majority in the Legislative Assembly, so my vote was not critical" (Interview 93–47). It is not clear from this story whether principles would prevail, in the eyes of either the deputy or the party leaders, had the deputy's vote mattered.

Table 5.6. Question: If you were to vote regularly against the Assembly party, what kind of sanctions would you expect?

1990–1994 Assembly	All deputies	PUSC	PLN
Expulsion	10 (30)	4 (21)	6 (43)
Ethics Tribunal (nonspecific)	9 (27)	5 (26)	4 (29)
Informal sanctions	3 (9)	3 (16)	0 (0)
Reduce *partidas específicas*	2 (6)	2 (11)	0 (0)
No sanction	9 (27)	5 (26)	4 (29)
Total asked	33 (100)	19 (100)	14 (100)

Note: Percentages are in parentheses.

they could negotiate an independent position, and so avoid conflict with the party leadership.

Finally, I asked deputies to describe the sanctions they could expect if they broke party discipline regularly. The results are in Table 5.6.

About one-third of all deputies believe that regular breaches of discipline would prompt expulsion from their party by their Ethics Tribunal, but this belief is twice as common among PLN deputies as among PUSC deputies. In addition, nearly 30% of deputies in each party mentioned the possibility of being called before their party's Ethics Tribunal, although they failed to state explicitly what sanction the body might impose.[11] In addition, a couple of PUSC members mentioned the possible loss of PEs as punishment for independent voting – an issue obviously of no concern to PLN legislators in the 93rd Legislative Assembly. And three other PUSC members would expect informal sanctions. For instance, "There is political isolation. It's generally not a formal system, but it manifests itself in the attitudes of other deputies" (Interview 93–26).

Perhaps the heightened expectation of expulsion among PLN members is the product of the highly publicized expulsion of Guillermo Vargas Sanabria after the Mayo Negro, and the case pending before the Ethics Tribunal against those deputies who voted in favor of the 1988 banking reform, whereas no voting discipline case has ever reached the PUSC's Ethics Tribunal. On the other hand, even in the PLN, the Ethics Tribunal has been hesitant to follow through on expulsions. In the Mayo Negro, Vargas Sanabria was the only 1 of 16 renegades to be expelled, and no action had yet been taken against those who supported banking reform (Villanueva Badilla 1992). Overall, the PLN's Ethics Tribunal has proved a cumbersome and

[11] One PLN deputy explained that the Tribunal could "admonish, suspend, or expel deputies" (Interview 93–10).

reluctant organ for imposing sanctions on maverick legislators (Villalobos 1992). And as of 1992 the PUSC Tribunal has never imposed a sanction on a legislator for indiscipline (Madrigal 1992).

This record of inaction accounts for the fact that nearly 30% of deputies in each party would expect no sanctions from their parties, even for regular indiscipline. Assembly party leaders themselves were the most direct in explaining the constraints parties face in imposing sanctions. The majority leader explained: "No fixed penalty is specified for those who might break discipline . . . The leadership prefers to retain flexibility in dealing with such matters, because to expel a deputy means losing a vote for the party on many future issues" (Interview 93–04). The minority leader directly blamed term limits: "Because of term limits, as minority leader, I have no stick to beat anyone with" (Interview 93–27).

Overall, the interview responses indicate that a substantial minority of deputies had broken party lines within the first two years of the 93rd Legislative Assembly, or at least expected to do so. Majorities of deputies in both parties expressed a willingness to break party lines, either to support local interests, or on principle if necessary. A majority of all deputies expect persistent indiscipline to elicit some action from a party Ethics Tribunal, but more than a quarter expect no sanctions from their parties, even if they regularly break party lines. Moreover, the resignation of party leaders, along with the records of each party's Ethics Tribunal in imposing discipline, suggest that such brazenness among rank-and-file deputies is justified.

The picture presented here of Costa Rican Assembly parties is one of considerably looser cohesiveness than in Venezuela, where breaks with party lines are extraordinarily rare, and punishment is certain. The reasons for the difference are that Costa Rican parties lack a common central principal who issues party directives, and that even those party directives that are universally acknowledged by deputies are not backed up by dependable sanctions.

Conclusion

Costa Rican Assembly parties are less cohesive than their Venezuelan counterparts because of the existence of legislative term limits in Costa Rica. The logic is as follows. Term limits force incumbent deputies to be dependent on the country's next president for their post-Assembly careers, but the identity of the next president is uncertain. Even the identity of the next presidential nominee from the deputies' parties is uncertain for three of their four years in the Legislative Assembly.

There are two key differences between this and a system with unlimited legislative election. First, with term limits legislators have lower overall chances that party loyalty will be rewarded. Under unlimited reelection, loyal incumbents can expect high list positions, and thus reelection to the Assembly, even if their party loses the presidency or loses ground in the Assembly, provided that those who control ballot lists value party discipline. Under term limits, of course, ballot list positions are irrelevant to incumbent legislators. But even if those who control political careers value party loyalty and discipline, post-Assembly rewards will only be available to members of the party that wins the presidency; losers get nothing. In short, patronage is a riskier bet than reelection, and yields lower expected career benefits.

Second, intraparty competition for the presidential nomination forces legislators to choose among possible alliances with presidential hopefuls. Deputies, therefore, are tied to politicians whose primary goal is to distinguish themselves from other national party figures also competing for the nomination. The dependence of deputies on future presidents means that conflicts among presidential hopefuls infect Assembly parties. The result is the opposite of party cohesiveness; it is open party fragmentation.

The bottom line here is that the existence of a party leadership that values party cohesiveness, that controls legislators' careers, that is clearly and commonly known to legislators, and whose membership is stable across elections is the basis of legislative party cohesiveness in Venezuela. These qualities are missing in Costa Rican party leadership because of term limits.

I should note that this chapter is not meant to be an unconditional endorsement of airtight party discipline in legislatures. Evaluations of "more" versus "less" discipline do not translate directly to "better" and "worse." Indeed, a basic premise of this study is that party cohesiveness among legislators generally involves some trade-off with responsiveness to constituent demands (Carey and Shugart in press). The widespread dissatisfaction with the performance of the Venezuelan Congress has been largely based on the perception that the institution is a "partyocracy," and that highly disciplined legislators are insufficiently responsive to constituent demands. In contrast, Costa Rica's less cohesive parties, which also encourage deputies to promote local community interests, appear to be less objectionable to constituents. The comparison between Venezuela and Costa Rica suggests that resolving the cohesiveness versus responsiveness trade-off simply by sacrificing constituent responsiveness at the altar of party cohesiveness is not agreeable to voters. At any rate, this chapter does not attempt to offer normative evaluations of party cohesiveness, but rather to explain the effects of term limits on levels of party cohesiveness in Venezuela and Costa Rica.

This work also aims to develop conclusions about the effects of term limits on legislative representation that apply generally, beyond the cases discussed in detail here. The Costa Rican and Venezuelan electoral systems generate equal and strong incentives for party cohesiveness. The argument of this chapter is that the lower level of cohesiveness in Costa Rica than in Venezuela is a product of term limits. Where electoral systems provide strong career incentives for party cohesiveness, then, the model implies that term limits undermine these incentives. It does not necessarily hold, however, that term limits should damage party cohesiveness in any electoral system whatsoever. The effect of term limits on cohesiveness depends on what career patterns replace assembly careers for legislators. If those who control postassembly careers under term limits value party cohesiveness less than do those who control assembly careers, then term limits damage party cohesiveness. If those who control postassembly careers under term limits value party cohesiveness more than do those who control assembly careers, then term limits could increase cohesiveness. Thus, in electoral systems that do not generate strong incentives for cohesiveness to begin with, it is possible to imagine term limits strengthening cohesiveness. This possibility is especially relevant to the debate over term limits in the United States, where academics have persistently decried a lack of cohesiveness in congressional parties (Collie and Brady 1985; Shepsle 1978; Smith and Deering 1990), and where some have ventured that term limits would strengthen party discipline (Brady and Rivers 1991).

In Chapter 7, I discuss more thoroughly the degree to which the lessons about term limits and representation from Costa Rica apply to the United States. Before elaborating these conclusions, however, Chapter 6 presents a test that attempts to simulate the effects that term limits could have on the U.S. Congress. I examine how removing reelection constraints affects voting behavior in the House of Representatives.

Part III

Term limits and the United States

6

The last-term problem

The central argument of this chapter is familiar by now: legislators not bound to their current constituents through a reelection constraint will systematically alter their behavior to appeal to those who control their post-assembly prospects. The empirical focus of the analysis shifts in this chapter, however, away from the Costa Rican and Venezuelan cases that have been studied up to now, and toward the U.S. House of Representatives.

This book begins with an argument that the lack of U.S. experience with term limits mandates that any thorough empirical analysis of their effect on legislative representation should be comparative. Part II of the book engages this task. Of course, comparative analysis, too, has limitations. In the first place, the differences between the electoral systems of Costa Rica and Venezuela on the one hand, and the United States on the other, complicates the process of applying conclusions from the Latin American cases to the U.S. debate (Chapter 7). Second, difficult access to – or the outright nonexistence of – data on political careers, particularism, and legislative voting patterns presents a formidable barrier to any analysis of the Latin American cases. Preceding chapters attempt to scale or skirt this barrier and press on with the comparative project. This chapter attempts to complement the comparative work with analysis of the U.S. Congress, for which there is easy access to abundant data on political careers and legislative behavior, but which has never employed de jure term limits.[1] In lieu of actual term limits, this chapter presents a statistical test to evaluate the effects on legislative behavior of removing the electoral connection between U.S. legislators and their current constituencies. The conclusions drawn from this test are entirely consistent with those drawn with respect to the effects of term limits in Costa Rica.

The central question of the chapter is whether and how representatives

---

[1] In much of the 19th century, legislators from many states rotated from state offices, to Congress, and then back to state offices in a pattern similar to what might have existed under legal term limits. But the rotation system was never universal and was not enforced by law.

serving their last term, and so not subject to electoral control, will shirk the responsibility to serve their constituents.[2] I consider two general types of answers to the last-term question – one that relies on electoral markets as enforcers to prevent shirking, and one that relies on political parties – and I present some new data on the links between legislators and their parties. The chapter proceeds as follows. First, I examine how shirking has been defined and the methods used to detect it. I also address the question of whether such shirking necessarily implies a loss of voter control over politicians. Next, I consider the relation between shirking and a politician's last term, and describe the two principal methods by which last-term shirking can be controlled in theory: through sorting or through pensions. I review the evidence provided by the public choice literature as to whether and under what circumstances significant shirking exists. Then I conduct a series of tests that demonstrate that members of the U.S. Congress who aspire to statewide office do alter their voting behavior during their last term in the House of Representatives, and that political parties influence the voting of these aspirants, by controlling their opportunities to advance to higher office. Finally, I draw some conclusions about the effectiveness of such party-administered pension systems in providing for electoral control of politicians, particularly in conjunction with the prospect of constitutional term limitations for members of Congress (MCs).

Shirking

How to measure?

In recent years many studies have confronted the methodological problem of determining whether shirking takes place, presenting evidence of who shirks, how much, and when.[3] Much of this work has been devoted to detecting and measuring shirking detrimental to constituent interests; some has addressed the last-term problem as well. The fundamental question

[2] Note the difference from my approach in studying Costa Rica and Venezuela. In those cases, the electoral systems generated the hypothesis that any electoral connection would manifest itself primarily as loyalty to one's political party. Responsiveness to geographical constituencies became a puzzle needing extensive explanation (Chapter 4). In the U.S. case, the electoral connection generates primary loyalty to geographical constituencies. Moreover, patterns in voting behavior (including responsiveness to constituents, cohesiveness with copartisans, general ideological position, and changes in voting over time) can be measured quantitatively based on records of roll call votes. Thus, I am able to employ a concept such as "shirking" against constituency interests with some precision in studying the U.S. case.

[3] Kau and Rubin (1979), Peltzman (1984), Ferejohn (1986), Lott (1987), Davis and Porter (1989), Dougan and Munger (1989), Higgs (1989), Lott and Reed (1989), Lott (1990a, 1990b), VanBeek (1990), McArthur (1990), Kalt and Zupan (1990), Zupan (1990), Bender (1991), and Lott and Davis (1992) are the ones that will be considered here.

inevitably is, What is the responsibility that is or is not "shirked"?[4] Most analyses of shirking have sought to identify a battery of constituent interests based on economic and demographic data from a representative's district, and then to test how accurately the representative's votes reflect these interests (Bender 1991; Higgs 1989; Kau and Rubin 1979; Lott 1987; Peltzman 1984). The extent to which representatives' votes do not reflect constituent interests is sometimes taken to indicate the amount of personal ideology they are "consuming" on the job, and such consumption is considered shirking. Others have suggested that shirking can be nonideological and oriented toward maximizing the value of holding office or the probability of reelection. I agree with Bender (1991) that it is unimportant to constituents whether their interests are being ignored for ideological or other reasons. However, it is important to determine whether responsiveness to some other set of interests replaces responsiveness to constituent interests among last-term politicians.

In the standard methodology, representatives' votes on a given issue, or an index of their entire voting records, are taken to be a function of the interests of their constituencies and their proclivity to shirk. Voting as the dependent variable is regressed on a vector of demographic and economic variables representing constituent interests, as well as on a variable representing ideological consumption (or shirking). The more closely that voting corresponds to the values of the constituent interest variables, the lower the residual that is attributed to shirking. Higgs (1989) examined the voting of senators from the same state, assuming that when representatives from the same constituency vote differently, at least one must be shirking constituent interests.[5] However, Lott (1990b) and Lott and Davis (1992) counter that senators from the same state can represent different constituencies, and so vote differently without shirking. This fits with Fenno's (1978) well-known study of the ways in which representatives build personal support coalitions in their districts. McArthur (1990) and Lott (1990a) have measured attendance at roll call votes to determine whether some politicians shirk by consuming leisure, as opposed to shirking by voting against constituent interests.

One of the primary differences among the shirking studies is whether cross-sectional or time series data are used. Where data are cross-sectional,

---

[4] Public choice studies of shirking, including this one, embrace a delegate model of representation, as opposed to a trustee model (see Pitkin 1967; especially chaps. 6 and 9). MCs are assumed to be shirking when they fail to act on behalf of the interests of their constituents, as their constituents perceive them. Representatives are not supposed to act according to some alternative conception of constituent interests based on superior knowledge or long-term strategy.

[5] Dougan and Munger (1989) also use the relative voting records of senators from the same state to detect shirking.

absolute levels of shirking can be measured for each representative, and relative levels can be measured among representatives for that one cohort at that time. For example, one could determine whether representatives in their last term shirk more than others. Only by using time series data, however, can one determine whether specific representatives shirk more in their last term than they had previously. The use of time series data, then, is essential to testing whether the behavior of a given representative is likely to change in the last term. And this question must be at the center of any study of the effects of term limits.

Does shirking imply a loss of electoral control?

A normative question that this literature has raised is whether shirking necessarily constitutes a loss of control over politicians by the electorate. Lott (1990b) has suggested that individual shirking will not necessarily matter to policy output if political markets are self-correcting. Voters may elect candidates who balance perceived discrepancies between voter preferences and the policy outputs of the government as a whole. Thus, if policy is too liberal for voters, they compensate by electing a representative more conservative than their policy ideal. If political markets were entirely self-correcting, however, voters would act without regard to their attitudes toward specific candidates, and only with regard to their attitude toward overall policy outputs. But we know that representatives consider the implications of their own specific votes on prospects for reelection, and that voting records are often used effectively by challengers to office. Self-correcting markets, then, cannot render irrelevant the issue of shirking for constituent–representative relationships.

Other work suggests that representatives' votes may not correspond with the interests of their districts for a number of reasons. Kau and Rubin (1979) find evidence of stable coalitions in the Senate that logroll in order to pass packages of particularistic legislation, each element of which may be in the interests of only a few coalition members. Standard methods of detecting shirking do not allow for vote trading, and so would interpret logrolling as shirking. Both Peltzman (1984) and Fenno (1978) argue that representatives do not respond to their entire district, but rather to the coalition of voters that support them and the monied interests that finance their campaigns. Again, the argument is that a vector of variables reflecting the interests of an entire district will not accurately show a politician's responsiveness to those who elected him or her. Moreover, it is possible that representatives maintain ideological consistency across all votes, even at the occasional expense of district interests, in order to send clear signals to the electorate about what pattern of representation can be expected. Such clear signaling can be an investment in electoral capital if voters value predictability as well as interest voting (Dougan and Munger 1989; Lott 1987; Peltzman 1984).

All these explanations – logrolling, coalition building, and signaling – explain patterns of legislative behavior observationally equivalent to shirking as efforts to garner electoral support. Yet if the last-term problem generates shirking, it is precisely because representatives are no longer concerned with garnering electoral support. None of these explanations, then, can account for any shirking that takes place due to the last-term problem, nor do any of them imply that last-term shirking is not relevant.

The problem of a legislator's last term

The last-term problem can be described as the destabilization of a cooperative equilibrium between representative and constituency.[6] Cooperation for representatives entails acting as good agents of constituency interests; and for voters it entails rewarding good agents with reelection. As long as both sides view the relationship as indefinite – or at least without an identifiable last period – cooperation is possible, and electoral control can function. Once the relationship is viewed as finite by either party, however, rational players will defect, and the game will unravel. The two principal solutions to the last-term problem are (1) to create some sort of pension system for representatives who have performed adequately all the way through the last period, or (2) to rely on the electoral market to sort potential shirkers out of office.

Pensions

The logic of pensions developed by Becker and Stigler (1974) is generalizable to all principal–agent relationships, including that between constituents and their elected representatives. Employees[7] who approach their final pay period will be increasingly tempted to shirk, since the benefits will increasingly outweigh the wages forgone if shirking is detected. The solution is a compensation system in which employees who might gain by shirking are rewarded for good behavior with a bonus that is positively related to the potential gains from malfeasance, and inversely proportional to the risk of detection. Thus, as the potential gains from shirking increase, so does the

---

[6] The logic here is a variant of that of the chain store paradox, described by Ordeshook (1986: 451–462). See also Barro (1973), Becker and Stigler (1974), and Kreps and Wilson (1982).

[7] Becker and Stigler (1974) developed this argument to explain how law enforcement officers might be discouraged from engaging in corruption.

bonus needed to prevent shirking. But as the odds of detecting malfeasance grow, the size of the bonus can be reduced. The bonus is, of course, paid only on satisfactory completion of the last pay period, and is forfeited otherwise. Thus, the prospect of losing the pension is increasingly frightening as one approaches retirement.

Arguing along essentially the same lines, Barro (1973) suggested that political parties might serve as enforcers of good behavior among last-term representatives by administering pension systems. Later, I shall examine whether there is evidence that political parties play this role, insofar as they can deliver or withhold the "pension" of nominations and electoral support for House members seeking higher office.[8]

Sorting

Lott and Reed (1989) argue that the last-term problem is already solved, not by an enforcer, but prior to the vaunted last term itself, by market forces. The logic is that representatives who are ideologically compatible with their constituencies naturally perform so as to maximize the probability of reelection. The opportunity costs of good agency are lower for such representatives than for those who are ideologically incompatible with their constituents. Competition in producing good performance, and credible signals that good performance will continue, yield too low a return to the incompatibles, so they shirk more. Thus, potential shirkers are sorted out of office by the electoral market before voluntary retirement is an option. Surviving representatives are exceptionally compatible with their constituents, and so there is little agency loss even in the last term (Lott and Reed 1989).

Two additional points should be made regarding the sorting argument. First, sorting need not be immediately thorough to overcome the last-term problem. Where representatives generally serve multiple terms, sorting can diminish last-term shirking as long as it removes from office potential shirkers over a series of reelection bids. To check shirking in the context of compulsory term limits, however, sorting must work quickly. Second, even if sorting works, those representatives who make it to retirement will not necessarily be naturally perfect agents. They will merely be those for whom the opportunity costs of good agency were lowest. Their last-term incentive will still be to shirk. So we can imagine a combination of the sorting and shirking effects, in which retiring politicians shirk more than they did in previous terms, but less than do the cross section of their peers.

[8] Of course, MCs receive federal pensions as well. But in order to disqualify themselves for these pension payments, MCs have to go some distance beyond merely shirking on their constituents. Thus, I shall only concern myself here with party pensions.

The existing evidence

While studies of the last-term problem have yielded differing results, the work as a whole suggests two broad conclusions. First, the sorting argument is borne out by cross-sectional analyses of MCs showing that those who retire tend not to shirk in their last term any more than do nonretirers (Dougan and Munger 1989; Lott 1987; Lott and Reed 1989).[9] Second, Zupan's (1990) time series analysis indicates that retiring MCs shirk more as they approach retirement than they did previously.[10]

There are a number of studies that offer various evidence that last-term shirking should cause negligible slack in the electorate's control over politicians. Lott (1987) and Lott and Reed (1989) provide evidence demonstrating that retiring MCs as a group are better agents of their districts than are nonretirers, shirking less in their last term than do cross sections of their peers. Dougan and Munger (1989) present time series evidence that senators do not shirk more when more years remain until their next reelection bid. This suggests that shirking is unrelated to electoral maneuvering, provided we assume that politicians discount the future somewhat. VanBeek (1990) detects no increase in shirking in the months between MCs' decisions to retire and the end of their terms. Moreover, Lott and Davis (1992) provide a time series test of shirking among senators to determine whether shirking increases with tenure, with years until the next election, or in the last term. They find no consistent correlation between shirking and any variable except whether a senator is subsequently defeated at the polls. Their evidence suggests that electoral markets are quite effective in sorting shirkers out of office.

Contending against these arguments are a number of studies suggesting for various reasons that last-term shirking does cause slack in the constituent–representative relationship. Kau and Rubin (1979) find that MCs consume ideology (shirk) against both vectors of constituent interests and logrolling coalitions. Bender's (1991) study of voting on campaign finance reform laws shows that MCs first and foremost maximize the value of holding office, and honor ideological obligations only when the opportunity

---

[9] See Davis and Porter (1989) and Kalt and Zupan (1990) for cross-sectional analyses that reach the opposite conclusion – that shirking increases as retirement approaches. This remains a point of serious contention. Lott and Davis (1992) challenge Kalt and Zupan's (1990) methodology on a number of counts. Zupan (1990), however, provides a more focused and compelling argument that voting behavior changes among MCs in their last term than does Kalt and Zupan.

[10] VanBeek's (1990) results contradict Zupan's. The last word in this debate surely has not been written.

costs are not prohibitive.[11] Davis and Porter (1989) find that shirking against their states' interests increases with age once senators pass a threshold age of 53 years. These results suggest that the last-term temptation to shirk applies more generally as the probability that politicians are in their last term increases. Kalt and Zupan (1990) find that senators shirk more the more political capital (committee chairmanships, large margins of past electoral victories) they possess, the longer until they face reelection, and in their last terms before retirement. However, the Kalt and Zupan methodology is subject to a simultaneity bias, as it is not clear that causality runs in only one direction between their dependent and independent variables – shirking and levels of political capital.

In an effort to correct for this problem, Zupan (1990) examines changes in the voting behavior of House members between the sessions of the same Congress. He distinguishes among those members who run for reelection, those who decide to retire before the last term, those who decide to retire during the last term, and those who leave the House to run for other offices. Zupan finds that retiring members shirk significantly more in the second session than the first, and this pattern is particularly pronounced for late deciders and aspirants to other offices. Despite this pattern, however, Zupan finds that absolute levels of shirking are no greater among retirers and aspirants than among the entire cross section of members. This supports the argument that the sorting effect removes rampant shirkers before retirement. Third, aspirants as a group exhibit low absolute levels of shirking despite the fact that they shirk more in the second session than in the first. Thus, it seems that exceptionally good agents are rewarded with the opportunity to run for higher office.

Much more attention has focused on determining whether shirking exists than on whether political pensions do. Nevertheless, two studies have included limited tests of Barro's (1973) suggestion that parties might prevent shirking by controlling the future careers of officeholders. Peltzman (1984) holds that the key determinants of voting are the nature of senators' support coalitions and their interest group contributors. He tests whether national party organizations might affect voting behavior as any other interest group does – according to the proportion of campaign funding a senator receives from the party. Peltzman's results are negative and suggest that parties may actually fund shirkers at a greater rate than nonshirkers. His test, however, compares funding from national party organization with the level of shirking against state constituencies. There is no reason to believe that the interests of these two entities coincide.

---

[11] In this case, the obligation was to what Bender (1991) characterizes as the "liberal agenda," rather than to indicators of district interests. The critical test that Bender constructs to detect shirking, nevertheless, is impressive.

Lott (1990a) and McArthur (1990) have shown that regardless of how they vote, retiring MCs shirk by consuming leisure on the job, with levels of absenteeism almost twice as high as for nonretirers. Lott goes on to determine, however, that among members who have children running for elective office, the increase in absenteeism is only half as great. And for members pursuing postcongressional careers in lobbying or other government work, who also have children in politics, there is no increase in absenteeism. Lott's results suggest that some sort of pension system based on future career opportunities exists to deter at least one type of shirking among certain retirers.

To this point, it is evident that the logic of sorting does not preclude a rise in shirking in the last term among heretofore good agents. Zupan's (1990) results support this interpretation, particularly for aspirants. The combined evidence from all the studies reviewed tells the story that sorting removes potentially big shirkers, and that the last-term effect remains for retirers. But the question of pensions remains open. If aspirants increase the level of shirking against their districts in their last year, how could a pension system be working? The answer, of course, is that if pensions are administered by parties, then to examine patterns of shirking against the old district will tell us nothing about the quality of enforcement. We need to know whether aspirants shirk against their party, and ultimately against their state. If political parties do administer pension systems, then the last-term effect of shirking against current constituents should be accompanied by increased responsiveness to the interests of state parties. While Barro (1973) and Becker and Stigler (1974) suggested 20 years ago that parties may act as enforcers through control over postretirement career opportunities, none of the studies of last-term behavior tests for such a phenomenon.

A test for state and party pensions

The test conducted here determines whether aspirants move systematically toward either their state or their state party interests at the expense of their current constituencies during the second session of their last House term. Such movement indicates a trade-off for responsiveness to those who control access to higher office against responsiveness to current district interests (Schlesinger 1966). The first step is to demonstrate that aspirants alter their voting behavior more between the two sessions of their last Congress than do nonaspirants. I also offer evidence that the shift in voting behavior among aspirants is greater the more ideologically extreme is the MC. The next step is to demonstrate that this increased movement between sessions can be accounted for as movement toward the aspirant's respective delegations (the state delegation and the state party delegation). Again, the effect is greater as the aspirant's ideological extremism increases. Finally, I present evidence that it is movement toward the state party delegation that distinguishes aspirants' voting behavior from that of nonaspirants.

I use NOMINATE scores as indicators of individual voting patterns, and mean NOMINATE scores of state and state party delegations as indicators of state and party interests.[12] NOMINATE (NOMINAl Three-step Estimations, developed by Poole and Rosenthal 1985) scores are derived from all nonunanimous roll call votes taken during a session of Congress and register each MC's location on a single liberal–conservative dimension. The scores are normally distributed and centered on zero. Those used here have a standard deviation of 0.59, and at the extremes range from -2.23 on the liberal end to 1.96 on the conservative end.

The first test determines that aspirants do in fact alter their voting behavior more between the first and second session of their last House term than do nonaspirants. The average magnitude of the difference between first- and second-session NOMINATE scores for nonaspirants is 0.096. But among aspirants the average magnitude of the difference is 0.023 points higher, this difference being discernible at conventional levels of significance.[13]

Another way of demonstrating this point is to show that the first-session NOMINATE score predicts the second-session NOMINATE score less effectively for aspirants than for nonaspirants. The relevant OLS regression is:

$$(6.1) \quad NOMINATE_2 = a(CONSTANT) + b_1(ASPIRANT)$$
$$+ b_2(NOMINATE1) + b_3(NOMINATE1 \times ASPIRANT),$$

where $NOMINATE_2$ is the second-session NOMINATE score, CONSTANT is set equal to 1, ASPIRANT is a dummy variable scored 1 if an MC leaves the House after that term to run for statewide office, and 0 otherwise, $NOMINATE_1$ is the first-session NOMINATE score, and $NOMINATE_1 \times ASPIRANT$ is an interactive term designed to pick up the difference between the effectiveness of $NOMINATE_1$ as a predictor of $NOMINATE_2$ for aspirants as opposed to nonaspirants, (see Table 6.1).

The constant term determines whether there is any systematic difference between NOMINATE scores between sessions for nonaspirants – that is,

---

[12] The methodology used in compiling the data is discussed in detail in Appendix A to this chapter. The statistical qualities of NOMINATE scores are discussed at greater length in Appendix B.

[13] The relevant OLS regression is as follows:

DIFFERENCE = 0.096(CONSTANT) + 0.023(ASPIRANT)
                      (70.5)   (3.08)

Adjusted $R2 = .002$,

where DIFFERENCE is the absolute value of the difference between an MC's NOMINATE scores for the two sessions of the Congress, CONSTANT is set equal to 1, and ASPIRANT is a dummy variable scored 1 if an MC leaves the House after that term to run for a statewide office, and 0 otherwise.

Table 6.1. The effect of aspirant status on variance between first–session and second–session NOMINATE scores

Dependent variable: Second–session NOMINATE score	
Independent variables	Coefficient (t-score)
Constant	-0.001 (-0.276)
ASPIRANT	0.004 (-0.382)
NOMINATE1	0.980 (286)
NOMINATE1 × ASPIRANT	-0.053 (-3.01)
Adjusted R^2	0.952
N	4,247

whether such MCs are consistently more liberal or conservative in one session rather than the other. The ASPIRANT dummy determines the same thing for aspirants only. The negligible and nonsignificant coefficients of these terms indicate that there is no such systematic movement for either set of MCs. The coefficient of $NOMINATE_1$ and the t-score show that second-session voting behavior tends to follow first-session voting closely. And the coefficient and t-score for the $NOMINATE_1 \times$ ASPIRANT variable show that second-session voting follows first-session voting significantly less closely for aspirants than for nonaspirants. The 0.980 slope coefficient for aspirants falls to 0.927 among nonaspirants, and the groups are statistically discernible at conventional significance levels.[14] This confirms the result of equation 6.1, that aspirants alter their voting behavior more than nonaspirants between the sessions of their last Congress. Second, the equation suggests that the more NOMINATE scores differ from zero, the more voting behavior changes between sessions. The interactive variable is constructed such that its absolute value grows as the NOMINATE score increases in magnitude – that is, as the MC becomes more ideologically extreme. And as the value of the interactive term grows, the same coefficient predicts a greater change in voting behavior for the aspiring MC.

At first glance, this may appear puzzling. Why should changes in voting behavior among aspirants grow as the magnitude of the NOMINATE score grows? There are two possible reasons for this – one of which applies to all MCs, and the other only to aspirants. First, the estimation of ideological position with NOMINATE is more difficult for more ideologically extreme, or pure, legislators than for moderates (Poole and Rosenthal 1985: 364–365). Given the estimation problems, we might expect more variance in scores between sessions among more extreme MCs, whether they are aspirants or not. This is in fact the case. Nevertheless, it is also reasonable to

---

[14] The coefficient for aspirants is determined by simply adding the negative coefficient for the interactive term to the coefficient for $NOMINATE_1$.

Table 6.2. The effect of ideological extremism on variance between first–session and second–session NOMINATE scores

Dependent variable: Absolute value of the difference between first–session and second–session NOMINATE scores	
Independent variables	Coefficient (*t*-score)
Constant	0.074 (30.2)
ASPIRANT	-0.042 (-3.13)
MAGNITUDE NOMINATE1	0.044 (10.8)
MAGNITUDE NOMINATE1 × ASPIRANT	0.118 (5.71)
Adjusted R^2	0.042
N	4,247

expect that extremists who are also aspirants will shift their voting even more dramatically than nonaspiring extremists, if they are attempting to court a new, statewide constituency; and more than moderate aspirants, given that statewide constituencies are likely to be more heterogeneous, and so less ideologically pure, than House districts.

The following equation tests these hypotheses:

$$(6.2) \quad \text{DIFFERENCE} = a(\text{CONSTANT}) + b_1(\text{ASPIRANT})$$
$$+ b_2(\text{MAGNITUDE NOMINATE1})$$
$$+ b_3(\text{MAGNITUDE NOMINATE}_1 \times \text{ASPIRANT}),$$

where DIFFERENCE is the absolute value of the difference between first- and second-session NOMINATE scores for an MC, CONSTANT is set equal to 1, ASPIRANT is the dummy variable used earlier, MAGNITUDE NOMINATE$_1$ is the absolute value of the first-session NOMINATE score, and MAGNITUDE NOMINATE$_1$ × ASPIRANT is an interactive term designed to pick up any difference between the effect of ideological extremism on DIFFERENCE for aspirants versus for nonaspirants (see Table 6.2).

These results refine our picture of aspirant voting patterns considerably. In the first place, the positive coefficient for MAGNITUDE NOMINATE$_1$ demonstrates that, among nonaspirants, those who are more ideologically extreme also show greater differences between their scores from session to session. This could be a result of the estimation difficulties among extreme legislators. But the coefficient for the interactive variable indicates that this effect is four times greater among aspirants than among nonaspirants, and the *t*-score shows that the difference between the groups is strongly significant.[15]

---

[15] The total effect for aspirants is the value of the coefficient for nonaspirants (.044) plus the value of the coefficient for the interactive term, which indicates only the additional effect for aspirants (.118). The total effect for aspirants, then, is .162.

Moreover, the slope coefficients and the intercept values together tell a more precise story. The negative coefficient on the ASPIRANT dummy indicates that, among ideologically moderate MCs, aspirants actually vary less between sessions than do nonaspirants. Among MCs for whom the absolute value of $NOMINATE_1$ is less than 0.36, aspirants show less volatility than nonaspirants.[16] As MCs become more ideologically extreme, however, aspirants move more between sessions. The dramatic movement among more extreme aspirants is sufficient to generate the initial results that, overall, aspirants are more erratic in their voting patterns than nonaspirants.

The results so far indicate:

1. Overall, aspirants to statewide office change their voting behavior between sessions of their last term in the House more than do nonaspirants; but
2. The voting patterns of moderate aspirants are more stable than those of nonaspirants. Those who change the most between sessions are those aspirants who are originally the most ideologically extreme.

These points suggest a scenario similar to that proposed by James Madison (1961), in Federalist #10, wherein larger and more heterogeneous constituencies demand more moderation on the part of their representatives than do smaller ones. If this "heterogeneity breeds moderation" hypothesis is apt, then statewide constituencies should be more moderate on the whole than House districts; and it follows that moderate aspirants should not have to change their voting behavior as much as extremists in order to appeal to the statewide constituency.

This generates the question of whether the changes in voting behavior among aspirants detected earlier can be explained as movement toward the new statewide constituencies the aspirants seek to attract. If so, then the dramatic changes in voting behavior among extreme aspirants detected in equation 6.2 should translate into movement toward the state delegation. The following equation tests this hypothesis:

$$(6.3) \quad \text{MOVEMENT TOWARD STATE} = a(\text{CONSTANT}) + b_1(\text{ASPIRANT}) + b_2(\text{MAGNITUDE NOMINATE1}) + b_3(\text{MAGNITUDE NOMINATE1} \times \text{ASPIRANT}),$$

---

[16] Running equation 6.2 separately for aspirant and nonaspirants, the results are:

(6.2a) Aspirants DIFFERENCE = 0.032 + 0.162(MAGNITUDE $NOMINATE_1$),
(6.2b) Nonaspirants DIFFERENCE = 0.074 + 0.044 (MAGNITUDE $NOMINATE_1$),

The expected DIFFERENCE is equal for aspirants and nonaspirants alike when MAGNITUDE $NOMINATE_1$ = 0.36. Below that score, aspirants' expected difference is less than that for nonaspirants. Above 0.36, aspirants' expected difference is substantially greater.

Table 6.3. Effects of ideological extremism and aspirant status on shifts toward statewide delegations from first to second session

Dependent variable: House members' movement, from first–session to second–session, toward mean NOMINATE score of the rest of their state delegation	
Independent variables	Coefficient (*t*-scores)
Constant	-0.047 (-6.58)
ASPIRANT	-0.081 (2.06)
MAGNITUDE NOMINATE1	0.082 (6.80)
MAGNITUDE NOMINATE1 × ASPIRANT	0.19 (3.08)
Adjusted R^2	0.016
N	4,247

where MOVEMENT TOWARD STATE is the magnitude of the difference between an MC and the purified mean of his or her state party delegation in first session, minus the same measure in the second session.[17] In short, if MOVEMENT TOWARD STATE is positive, the MC moved closer to her state party delegation between sessions; if it is negative, the MC moved further from his or her state party delegation; and if it is zero, the MC's relative distance from the state party delegation remained the same; CONSTANT is set equal to 1; ASPIRANT is the familiar dummy; MAGNITUDE NOMINATE$_1$ is the absolute value of the MC's first-session NOMINATE score; and MAGNITUDE NOMINATE$_1$ × ASPIRANT is an interactive term designed to pick up any difference in the effect of MAGNITUDE NOMINATE$_1$ between aspirants and nonaspirants (see Table 6.3).

The results strongly support the hypothesis. One slight surprise is the negative coefficient on the ASPIRANT variable, indicating that aspirants near the center of the ideological spectrum tend to move slightly further from their state delegations between sessions – even more than do nonaspirants. But the slope coefficients for the MAGNITUDE variables tell the expected story. Even among nonaspirants, the more extreme tend to move toward their state delegation between sessions. But among aspirants, this effect is more than three times as great. And the *t*-score for MAGNITUDE NOMINATE$_1$ × ASPIRANT shows that the effect on aspirants versus nonaspirants is statistically discernible at conventional significance levels. In short, the more extreme the aspirants, the more they tend to move toward the rest of their state delegations between the two sessions of their last House term.

[17] For a explanation of "purified means," and a general discussion of the voting and career data on MCs used here, see Appendix A.

Of course, access to statewide office is controlled first by the party, in providing the nomination, and then by the state electorate as a whole. The same logic that suggests that aspirants should move toward their state delegations suggests that they should move toward their state party delegations.[18] When equation 6.3 is run to test for movement relative to state party delegations, rather than state delegations as a whole, the results are strikingly similar.[19] Again, the more extreme the aspirants, the more they tend to move toward their state party delegations between sessions. And this effect is more than twice as great among aspirants than among nonaspirants.

The similarity of results in the tests for movement relative to state delegation and state party delegation are not surprising, largely because the state delegation by definition subsumes the party delegation. For this reason, the tests run so far cannot distinguish whether movement among aspirants represents an effort to court the state constituency for the general election, or the state party constituency for the primary. A test that simultaneously examines the effects of the relevant (state and state party) delegations on aspirant voting behavior is necessary to untangle these effects.

Equation 6.4 offers this simultaneous analysis. The OLS regression model used to test this hypothesis is an extension of equation 6.1, which determined the extent to which second-session NOMINATE scores followed first-session scores for aspirants versus nonaspirants. Here, that basic logic is expanded to test for the additional explanatory power of state party, and statewide, delegation scores. To the extent that aspirants to statewide office move closer to the state party delegation's mean NOMINATE score, they demonstrate an effort to court the state party to secure the nomination. To the extent that they move toward the mean NOMINATE score of the state delegation as a whole, they demonstrate an effort to court the state electorate. Movement on either front would account in a rational manner for the increased shirking against their districts that Zupan (1990) finds by aspiring House members. Movement on the first front would support Barro's (1973) speculation that parties control pensions for last-term MCs – at least for

---

[18] It should not matter whether control over the nomination is administered by the party as an organization or, more likely, by the rank-and-file party members through primary voting. Either scenario implies that aspirants to statewide office must court the general interests to which the entire state party delegation is responsive.

[19] (6.3a)   MOVEMENT TOWARD PARTY =
$-$ 0.095(CONSTANT) $-$ 0.049(ASPIRANT)
   (-8.31)   (-0.78)
$+$ 0.14(MAGNITUDE NOMINATE1) $+$ 0.18(MAG NOM1 × ASPIRANT)
         (7.10)   (1.90)
Adjusted R^2 = .015
N = 4,247.

*Table 6.4. Movement toward average state party delegation
NOMINATE scores between sessions by aspirants to statewide office*

Dependent variable: Second session NOMINATE score	
Independent variables	Coefficient (*t*-score)
Constant	-0.001 (0.615)
ASPIRANT	-0.017 (-1.40)
NOMINATE1	0.978 (209)
NOMINATE1 × ASPIRANT	-0.108 (-4.15)
STATE DELEGATION AVG2	0.041 (6.27)
STATE DELEGATION AVG2 × ASPIRANT	-0.010 (-0.270)
PARTY DELEGATION AVG2	-0.007 (-1.37)
PARTY DELEGATION AVG2 × ASPIRANT	0.071 (2.32)
Adjusted R^2	0.953
N	4,108

those who plan to run subsequently for an office in their state. The equation is as follows:

$$(6.4) \quad \text{NOMINATE}_2 = a(\text{CONSTANT}) + b_1(\text{ASPIRANT})$$
$$+ b_2(\text{NOMINATE}_1)$$
$$+ b_3(\text{NOMINATE}_1 \times \text{ASPIRANT})$$
$$+ b_4(\text{STATE DELEGATION AVG}_2)$$
$$+ b_5(\text{STATE DELEGATION AVG}_2 \times \text{ASPIRANT})$$
$$+ b_6(\text{PARTY DELEGATION AVG}_2)$$
$$+ b_7(\text{PARTY DELEGATION AVG}_2 \times \text{ASPIRANT}).$$

Here, the use of NOMINATE_1 and NOMINATE_2 as indicators of the extent to which second-session voting follows first-session voting is the same as in equation 6.1, as is the use of the term interacting NOMINATE_1 with ASPIRANT. The terms STATE DELEGATION AVG_2 and PARTY DELEGATION AVG_2 are the purified means of the NOMINATE scores for the legislators from an MC's state, and state party, respectively. These terms measure the extent to which the ideological locations of an MC's respective delegations can explain variance in NOMINATE_2 that is not explained by NOMINATE_1. Finally, the interactive terms corresponding to each delegation average pick up the extent to which the influence of state and state party delegations on NOMINATE_2 is different for aspirants and nonaspirants.

The results tell a more complex story than do the previous regressions (Table 6.4). The constant term and the ASPIRANT dummy demonstrate that second-session scores are not significantly different from first-session scores, and that aspirants are not significantly more liberal or conservative than are nonaspirants. As in equation 6.1, the coefficients to $NOMINATE_1$ and to the interactive term $NOMINATE_1 \times ASPIRANT$ demonstrate clearly that $NOMINATE_2$ follows $NOMINATE_1$ less closely for aspirants than for nonaspirants. This reflects the degree to which aspirants alter their voting behavior more than do nonaspirants between sessions. The .041 coefficient to the STATE DELEGATION AVG_2 variable indicates that, among nonaspirants, the state delegation's voting in the second session exerts some pull on individual MCs; that is, some of the change in an MC's scores between sessions can be attributed to movement toward the state delegation mean. But the small value for the corresponding interactive term is not significantly different from zero, suggesting that this pull is no stronger for aspirants than for nonaspirants. The effects for state party delegation, however, are exactly the reverse. The small and nonsignificant coefficient to PARTY DELEGATION AVG_2 suggests that, among nonaspirants, the voting pattern of the state party delegation does not exercise an independent influence on individual voting. But the relatively large (.071) and significant coefficient to the interactive term PARTY DELEGATION $AVG_2 \times ASPIRANT$ demonstrates that changes in voting behavior between sessions among aspirants to statewide office are systematically related to the positions of their state party delegations.

The results of this regression confirm and clarify those of the earlier tests. The story that this evidence tells is one in which aspirants alter their voting behavior more during their last Congress than do nonaspirants; and more extreme aspirants alter their voting more than moderates. Equation 6.4 demonstrates that the relative position of MCs to their state delegations can explain a part of the variance in members' voting between sessions, but that the effect of the state delegation per se is no greater for aspirants than for nonaspirants. Finally, it shows that the relative position of MCs' state party delegations explains a larger part of this variance for aspirants only.

Conclusion

This chapter contrasts two schools of thought on how last-term shirking by members of the U.S. House of Representatives is controlled: the first focuses on electoral market forces, and the second on pensions. Those who make the strongest case for the efficiency of electoral markets argue that shirking among last-term MCs against their constituencies is not significant. This implies that voting patterns among last-term MCs should be stable and consistent with prior voting. The tests conducted here indicate, however, that for MCs who aspire to statewide office – particularly those who are ideologically extreme – this conclusion is not valid. Although I have not tested for whether changes in voting patterns among last-term MCs represent systematic violations of district interests, it is clear that aspirants change their voting behavior more than do nonaspirants.

Those who are less sanguine about the efficiency of electoral markets have suggested that political parties might control postcongressional career opportunities. If such a pension system is effective, then one should expect some last-term representatives to show increased sensitivity to party interests. The tests conducted here demonstrate that among MCs who aspire to statewide office, this is the case.[20] And the more extreme the aspirants, the more dramatic the movement toward their state and state party delegations. This evidence supports the Madisonian hypothesis that larger electoral units should be more politically moderate than smaller ones. And it supports in a straightforward manner the proposition that ambitious politicians are responsible to future principals, perhaps even at the expense of current principals.

Thus, there are reasons to be cautious about the electoral control of politicians under term limits. Although electoral sorting limits the absolute level of shirking by last-term politicians, these representatives evidently still shirk more than they did prior to their last term. Moreover, if sorting is not perfect now, term limits would likely further undermine its effectiveness for two reasons. First, term limits would curtail the period over which sorting could work. Voters would have fewer opportunities to identify and defeat shirkers while rewarding naturally good agents with reelection. Second, term limits would impose an end point to the game between representatives and constituents that would be recognized by all parties before the game even begins. Thus, the pattern of mutual defection – of preemptive shirking and of throwing the bums out – would be encouraged.

If all of this could be mitigated by a party-administered pension system, then term limits would imply a shift, but not necessarily a loss, of electoral control. Responsiveness among legislators might gradually shift, as their term limits approached, from their district constituency to the party constituency that controlled access to their next intended office. As long as individual legislators remained responsive to parties, which in turn are subject to electoral competition, then a collective electoral connection might remain. Arguably, this may have been the case during the 19th century in the United States, at least among those legislators whose state parties systematically rotated politicians through Congress and then back to more desirable posts

---

[20] It is important to reiterate that I am not claiming that parties *as organizations* systematically wield sanctions over aspiring MCs. Rather, aspirants' movement toward their state party delegations is consistent with the idea that they are altering their behavior to court a new primary election constituency. Thus, I am using the word "pension" in the sense of a reward administered by the party in the *electorate* to politicians who shift their responsiveness to the statewide set of party voters, even at the expense of their current constituency.

in state politics. Preceding chapters have demonstrated that a similar system operates currently in Costa Rica, with the difference that pensions are administered exclusively by presidents. This decreases incentives for legislators to remain loyal to their parties, and creates a need to rely on personal alliances with presidential candidates for post-Assembly career prospects.

This chapter suggests an important point of comparison between Costa Rican and U.S. term limits, on the issue of bicameralism versus unicameralism. Almost every term limits proposal in the United States, at the state as well as federal level, allows legislators who have served the maximum allowable time in one chamber to run immediately for the other legislative chamber. By contrast, in Costa Rica the Legislative Assembly is the only legislature with any significant lawmaking power, so that at the end of one's Assembly term, there is only one attractive electoral office to consider: the presidency. One might expect, then, that bicameralism would fundamentally alter the impact of term limits in the United States from what is seen in Costa Rica. Indeed, this chapter provides some evidence that, under bicameralism, term limits could shift the electoral connection, rather than severing it, for legislators who aspire to election in another chamber. Moreover, U.S. federalism dramatically increases the possibilities for shifting electoral connections. Politicians proscribed from running for reelection to state legislatures can run immediately for Congress; and it is not inconceivable that some term-limited MCs and senators might run for state legislative seats once their time in Washington has expired. Indeed, increasing the circulation of legislators among offices is one of the most frequently expressed goals of term limit advocates.

On this possibility, two qualifications are in order. First, if term limits have the intended effect of encouraging legislators to leave their current seats to run for other offices, then we should expect this progressive (or, in the case of federal legislators running for state legislatures, retrogressive) ambition to diminish their responsiveness to current constituencies. Second, although federalism and bicameralism will allow for different political career trajectories in the United States than in Costa Rica, one should be careful not to overstate the differences. As in Costa Rica, most U.S. legislators will not be able to move on to another desirable elected office once their limits are up. Only a handful of U.S. House members displaced by term limits would have realistic prospects of winning one of the 33 Senate seats contested every two years.[21] The outlook for the 7,500 state legislators to move up to the U.S. Congress would be even more bleak. Some would no doubt run for state government posts, but as in Costa Rica the vast majority of

[21] Remember that at least half these seats would be occupied by incumbents eligible to run for another term.

ambitious legislators displaced by term limits in the United States would need to look outside electoral politics for postlegislative employment. I examine postcongressional career paths of U.S. legislators, and their implications under term limits, briefly in the next chapter. For now, the important point is that U.S. bicameralism and federalism expand electoral opportunities, but will still leave most term-limited legislators on the job market as their terms end. Finally, consistent with evidence from the Latin American cases, this chapter's broadest conclusion is that legislators whose electoral connection has been severed will systematically shift responsiveness from those responsible for putting them in office to those who control their next career step.

Appendix A: Career and voting data on members of the U.S. House of Representatives

I combined biographical profile data provided by the Inter-University Consortium for Political and Social Research (ICPSR 1987) with NOMINATE scores (see Appendix B) for members, matching the data by ICPSR identification numbers. NOMINATE scores broken down by congressional sessions were available for the 89th through 98th congresses, so my analysis is limited to this time span.

Coding

Identifying aspirants to state office proved somewhat troublesome using the ICPSR biographical data, because the best variable to distinguish whether a given member aspired to another office during a given Congress does not establish unequivocally whether he or she actually ran for a statewide office. "Why Member Left Congress of Record" is coded such that a value of 5 means "Sought or accepted other office," and a value of 7 means "Went to Senate" (Codebook for ICPSR, dataset 7803). A value of 5, then, is not exclusive to aspirants to statewide office; and a value of 7 is not exhaustive. Those scored at 5 could include aspirants to the presidency or other offices. On the other hand, those who ran for the Senate and lost, and those who ran for governor, would not be scored at 7.

Nevertheless, the best solution is to include as an aspirant any MC who scored a 5 or 7 on this variable, for the following reasons. Those who were appointed to any federal office would be scored a 6, and so would not be included among those who "accepted other office." Thus, those who could be scored a 5, but who did not aspire to statewide elected office, would include those members who left Congress to run for the presidency, or those who accepted appointments below the federal level, or those who actually left Congress to run for an office with less than a statewide constituency. I am confident that those fitting into this last category are few in number during the period being studied, if any exist at all. In addition, for MCs to be appointed at the state level, it seems straightforward that their performance in the House would have to be acceptable to politicians in their home states. Since we are testing here for whether aspirants curry favor in their home state, and with their state party, at the expense of their district, such appointees would seem to fit the bill as aspirants well.

The coding ambiguity in the ICPSR data, then, seems problematic only for cases of presidential aspirants. However, it is important to keep in mind that only those who left the House to campaign for higher office are classified as aspirants. MCs who consider running for the presidency, and may even compete in presidential primaries, need not give up their House seats. Indeed only those who gain their party's nomination for another office need leave Congress. But over the period studied, no incumbent House member gained the presidential nomination of either party. Thus, by including as aspirants those who scored either a 5 or a 7 on "Why Member Left Congress of Record," we are including all those aspirants to statewide office who succeeded in gaining nominations, and no MCs who do not face the incentives to court state and state party delegations.

Delegation averages

Mean NOMINATE scores for state delegations and for state party delegations are used as indicators of state and party interests, respectively. The regressions test whether mean delegation scores act as better predictors of voting patterns among aspirants than among nonaspirants. Two adjustments had to be made to the data, however, before mean delegation scores could be used. First, delegations with only one member were eliminated. Thus, in the regressions that test for movement relative to state delegations, those states with just one MC are removed. This left me with 4,247 observations (MCs) over the 10 congresses I studied, including 137 aspirants. Likewise, in the regressions that test for movement relative to state party delegations, any state party delegation with only one MC is not included. This left me with 4,108 observations over the 10 congresses, with 127 aspirants.

Second, the impact of the individual MC being tested had to be "purified" from the mean for each delegation, to eliminate autoregressive effects. If a given MC's NOMINATE score is included in calculating a mean for his or her delegation, and then that mean is subsequently used as a predictor of the MC's NOMINATE score, one should expect the measured impact of the mean to be biased upwards. To eliminate this effect, the NOMINATE scores of each of the MCs were eliminated from the calculation of the mean scores for their corresponding delegations. The "purified" delegation means were then used as predictors of second-session NOMINATE scores.

Appendix B: Characteristics of NOMINATE scores

NOMINATE scores are estimates of MCs' locations on a unidimensional, liberal–conservative scale. They are derived from each MC's votes on all nonunanimous roll calls taken in each session of Congress, by the dynamic nominal three-step estimation procedure described by Poole and Rosenthal (1985, 1988). Nonunanimous roll calls, for the purposes of NOMINATE, are all those in which at least 2.5% of MCs voted against the majority. The scores used here are scaled on a normal distribution, centered at 0, with standard deviation of 0.59. The minimum score is -2.23 (the most liberal), and the maximum is 1.92 (most conservative). The vast majority of scores, however, fall between -1.0 and 1.0.

As measures of ideology, NOMINATE scores are superior to interest group rating scores used in other analyses for a number of reasons. First, NOMINATE scores are derived from all contested roll calls, not from smaller – and potentially biased – selections of votes chosen by interest groups. In addition, because interest group ratings are constructed to identify ideological friends and enemies, they often display an exaggerated, skewed distribution of MCs across the scale. (For a discussion of the relative strengths of NOMINATE scores vs. interest group ratings, see Kiewiet and McCubbins 1991.)

A related point is that in calculating NOMINATE scores, absences are treated as missing data, rather than being given some value determined by political interests implicit in the estimator. In calculating Americans for Democratic Action (ADA) scores, for example, absences on the relatively small number of key votes included in the estimation are regarded as conservative votes. Thus, estimates are distorted for those MCs with unusually high levels of absenteeism. MCs in their last House term – such as aspirants to statewide office – are just such a group (Lott 1990a). Using NOMINATE, on the other hand, eliminates this problem because NOMINATE regards nonvoting as noninformation. And because NOMINATE scores are derived from a far larger, and nonbiased, group of roll calls, they can be estimated with good precision even for MCs with higher than average rates of absenteeism.

In the end, NOMINATE scores have correlations above .9 with ADA scores, and with the coordinates derived from a set of interest group ratings compiled by Poole and Rosenthal (1985: 360). So clearly, using NOMINATE scores does not imply the use of a radically different metric of ideology from studies that use interest group scores. But NOMINATE does offer some distinct advantages in terms of completeness and precision.

Another feature of the NOMINATE scores used here is that they are constrained at the extremes according to a function determined by the position of each of the legislators relative to all those who overlap with their service periods. Some constraint is necessary, given the problems in estimation for those MCs who are the most ideologically pure, or extreme (Poole and Rosenthal 1985). But the constraining ellipse employed by NOMINATE does not invite end point problems in estimation by truncating the scores at arbitrary boundaries. Rather, scores for extreme MCs are constrained by the relative positions of their contemporaries. Ultimately, the constraining mechanism has to be employed for only 4.2% of all legislators (Poole and Rosenthal 1988).

NOMINATE scores have the additional feature of representing actual scalings of ideological positions rather than only relative scalings. This means that NOMINATE scores calculated jointly across more than one session of Congress can detect and measure aggregate shifts in ideology across all members, and that any such shifts can be distinguished from the effects of ideological shifts in legislative agenda. Because I am interested in the ideological movement of aspiring MCs relative to their state and state party delegations, I do not want to pick up statistical noise from whatever aggregate ideological shifts may take place among groups of MCs, such as delegations.

There are two straightforward ways of doing this. One would be to convert NOMINATE scores to percentile rankings that would reflect the relative ideological positions of legislators. This is done, however, only at the expense of forcing the normal distribution of scores into a uniform distribution of rankings. The uniform distribution necessarily sacrifices information about the relative ideological distances among MCs. In fact, when I run my regressions on percentile rankings, the results are consistent with those derived using raw scores, but the statistical significance of the coefficients is weaker, as would be expected. The other solution is to use NOMINATE scores calculated session by session, rather than jointly across sessions. Thus, for each session all individual scores, as well as the average scores of state and state party delegations, are in a metric unique to that session. Such a method ignores the issue of aggregate ideological shifts across congresses, but is particularly sensitive to the positions of MCs relative to their delegations. NOMINATE scores used here are calculated session by session.

The fact that such scores are each scaled in unique metrics, of course, poses a problem when scores from one session are used to predict scores in subsequent sessions. To the extent that there are shifts in ideology between sessions, we might expect predictive powers to be limited. In fact, however, Poole and Rosenthal find such shifts to be minimal, at both the individual and aggregate levels. Based on jointly calculated scores, individual MCs in the modern era tend to vary at 1–2% across congresses. And session-by-session scores correlate with jointly calculated scores at better than .98 (personal communication with Poole). So we should expect NOMINATE scores calculated by session to predict subsequent session scores with slightly less than .98 accuracy. This is precisely what the regressions run here find, across all MCs. Predictions based on prior session scores for MCs aspiring to statewide office, however, are significantly less accurate. The magnitude of the difference, and its uniqueness to aspirants, preclude the possibility that the existence of unique metrics could be causing the predictive inaccuracy. The inaccuracy can be explained, however, as significant shifts in voting patterns among aspirants.

7

Applying lessons about term limits

The broadest conclusion drawn from the empirical evidence in this study is that legislators are responsive to those who control their future careers. There are a number of other conclusions, more specifically pertaining to term limits, that can be drawn as well. First, term limits do not necessarily eliminate political careerism among legislators, even where they preclude parliamentary careers. Chapter 3 shows that most Costa Rican deputies have substantial political experience prior to their service as legislators, and that they overwhelmingly seek to continue their political careers after their Assembly service. A second conclusion is that term limits do not necessarily eliminate behavior normally associated with pure personal electioneering among legislators. Chapter 4 shows that Costa Rican legislators, despite their absolute lack of personal electoral connection with constituents, still devote tremendous amounts of energy to providing favors for constituents and pork-barrel spending projects for specific communities. A third conclusion is that term limits are likely to affect the cohesiveness of parties within legislatures. The comparison between Costa Rica and Venezuela in Chapter 5 demonstrates that where term limits reduce the control party leaders have over legislators' future careers, they also reduce the voting discipline of legislative parties. It stands to reason, of course, that the converse should hold as well: if imposing term limits on an electoral system were to increase the control of party leaders over postassembly careers, then term limits should increase the voting discipline of legislative parties (Weldon 1994). This possibility, and the conditions under which it might hold, are discussed later in this chapter.

The issues surrounding these conclusions – careerism, particularism, party cohesiveness, and legislator responsiveness in general – are all central to the debate over the adoption of term limits in the United States. Advocates and opponents of term limits alike have made various arguments about the specific effects that prohibiting reelection could have on legislative representation. However, because the United States has not experienced legislative term limits, and because there have been no thorough comparative analyses of term limits, neither side has been able to base its claims on empirical evidence. As is evident from the brief literature review presented in Chapter 1, the arguments made so far in the term limits debate have been highly speculative (American Enterprise Institute 1979; Cain 1991; Kessler 1990; Klein 1989; Montgomery 1990; Will 1992). It is a goal of this concluding chapter to examine the extent to which the conclusions drawn in the preceding chapters are applicable to the current U.S. debate.

The chapter proceeds as follows. The first section provides some historical perspective on the idea of term limits and rotation in office in the United States, and reviews the central themes in the current debate over how term limits would affect representation in the U.S. Congress. The point is to assess how well the claims made by participants in the U.S. debate jibe with the empirical evidence provided earlier. The next section of the chapter generalizes some of the preceding conclusions even more broadly, focusing on the impact of term limits on whether legislators provide their constituents with cohesive partisan, or independent, personal representation. The argument is that the effects on legislator behavior of imposing term limits will depend on the incentives for party cohesiveness and personal reputation building generated by other elements of the electoral system. In closing, I review the conclusions generated by this study and consider the prospects for further research on term limits.

The term limit debate in the United States

Legacy of the founding era

The only effort to limit the reelection of U.S. legislators predates the current Constitution. Under the Articles of Confederation, members of the Congress were ostensibly prohibited from serving for more than three years in any six-year period (Sec. V). By 1784, the Articles were three years old, and five delegates to Congress were technically ineligible to continue serving. Two of these refused to retire, prompting a fierce debate over the enforcement of Section V. Congress was unable to resolve the debate, and ultimately simply dropped the issue without removing the delegates (Petracca 1992). The effort so far to enforce legislative term limits in this country, then, ended in failure.

Despite the failure of term limits under the Articles of Confederation, the idea of rotation in office was hotly contested again during the constitutional debate. A number of Antifederalists based their opposition to the Constitution in part on its failure to include limitations on reelection for legislators. Among the rationales these Antifederalists offered, some are echoed in today's discourse on term limits, whereas others are less than central to the current debate. Among the less salient themes, for example, were Antifederalist preoccupations that a legislature with stable membership would attempt to usurp the powers of state governments, and would encourage the formation of political parties (Smith, June 25, 1788, in Storing 1985). Also, it should be noted that much of this debate between Federalists and Antifederalists focused on whether terms should be limited for senators, without any mention of the House of Representatives (Hamilton [301], and Lansing [293]; Robert Livingston [291], in Elliot 1966).[1] Because of senators' longer terms, and their appointment by state legislatures, some Antifederalists worried that they would be unresponsive to popular sentiment (Brutus, April 10, 1788, and Smith, June 25, 1788, in Storing 1985). These concerns were not prevalent, however, with respect to House members, who are subject to biannual direct elections.

Not all the historical legacy of enthusiasm for term limits, then, is relevant to the current debate. Nevertheless, many of the themes central to the constitutional debate over term limits are at the heart of today's debate as well. Advocates of limits then and now, for example, have argued that legislators who must rotate out of public office are likely to be more familiar with the needs of their constituents than are careerists (Brutus, April 10, 1788, in Storing 1985; Mitchell 1991). Likewise, term limit proponents have consistently held that lengthy congressional careers inevitably breed arrogance and a sense of privilege among legislators. The following passages, from 1788 and 1993, respectively, indicate that this perception, and the level of rhetoric it inspires, has changed little in over 200 years. Gilbert Livingston wrote:

What will be [senators'] situation in a federal town? Hallowed ground! . . . In this Eden they will reside with their families, distant from the observation of the people. In such a situation, men are apt to forget their dependence, lose their sympathy, and contract selfish habits. (in Elliot 1966: 287–288)

More recently, George Will wrote:

If the political class fought the nation's problems as tenaciously as it fights term limits, America would be paradise by next Tuesday. The Arkansas politicians trying to overturn what their voters did [by passing a term limits initiative] in November include Democratic Sen. Dale Bumpers, who is using the services of the Senate's counsel. That means Arkansans are suffering the indignity of seeing their decision contested by their (and our) tax dollars. (1993: A19)

Opponents of limits, like proponents, have staked similar claims in both eras, among them that the voters should be allowed to choose their representative without the restriction implied by term limits (Livingston [291] and

---

[1] The numbers in square brackets refer to pages in Jonathan Elliot (1966).

Lansing [293], in Elliot 1966). Likewise, opponents of term limits, both at the founding and today, have also argued that the reform would damage congressional performance by eliminating from office the most experienced legislators (Hamilton [301], in Elliot 1966; Hibbing 1991).[2]

These themes were common to the term limits debate both at the founding and currently. But the normative nature of the claims – regarding perceptions of constituents' proper needs, arrogance among politicians, and claims about who ought to select representatives – make them difficult to evaluate and test. Some other themes from the historical debate, however, lend themselves more readily to evaluation in light of this study's results. For example, some opponents of term limits at the founding supported their position by arguing that removing the possibility of reelection eliminates institutional incentives for legislators to be responsive to constituent demands (Livingston [292] and Harrison [298], in Elliot 1966). Similarly, Alexander Hamilton argued explicitly that legislators denied the prospect of reelection would spend their time in office providing for their own interests in anticipation of the inevitable day when they would be turned out of office:

When a man knows he must quit his station, let his merit be what it may, he will turn his attention chiefly to his emolument: nay, he will feel temptations, which few other situations furnish, to perpetuate his power by constitutional usurpations. Men will pursue their interests. It is as easy to change human nature as to oppose the strong current of the selfish passions. (in Elliot 1966: 320)

These arguments – with regard to legislators' responsiveness and their behavior in anticipation of leaving office – were the subjects of Chapters 4–6. The results of this study, moreover, support the claims of the Federalists who held that legislators will alter their behavior to be responsive to whomever controls their postcongressional career prospects. In the Costa Rican case, of course, that control is exercised by subsequent presidents who control patronage appointments. In this way, the Costa Rican system under term limits resembles the 19th-century U.S. system, in which legislators regularly rotated among public offices even in lieu of any legal term limits.

Rotation in the 19th-century United States

The practice of rotation of officeholders in the 19th-century United States applied most widely to appointed posts. Rotation was a manifestation of political parties' use of appointed offices as patronage. Nevertheless, during this period, congressional careers were consistently far shorter than they

---

[2] It is noteworthy that the explicit argument in favor of legislative amateurism was largely absent from the original constitutional debate. The Antifederalists' rationales for term limits did not include a claim that novices were naturally suited to the job of legislating. This claim did not gain wide currency until the Jacksonian era.

have been throughout the 20th century, and lifetime politicians rarely spent their entire careers in Congress (H. Price 1975).

A number of factors, besides just party-enforced rotation, discouraged long congressional careers throughout much of the 19th-century. Early in the century in particular, Washington, D.C., itself was a singularly unpleasant place to live – remote, humid, and dull (Young 1966). Moreover, throughout most of the century, the scope of federal government activities and authority was limited relative to those of the state governments. Correspondingly, compensation for members of Congress was meager (Fish 1963: 58). Not surprisingly, then, most national legislators who sought political careers preferred to return to positions in their home states, either to elective or appointed office. In short, throughout the 19th century, congressional careers were far less attractive relative to alternative political career paths than is the case today.

This said, it is also the case that an explicit policy of rotation was applied by many state parties to legislators, and that rotation contributed to the pattern of short congressional careers. Andrew Jackson made rotation a central part of his program of government, hailing it as a guarantee against the use of public office for personal gain. In his 1829 inauguration speech, Jackson stated directly that "the more secure an office holder, the more his interests would diverge from those of his constituents" (Petracca 1992: 37). It was Jackson who popularized the ideal of the amateur politician. Jackson developed and exploited distrust of Washington insiders and professional politicians as vigorously as do current candidates and reformers. His motivation, however, and that of his mid-century Democratic partisans, was at least as much political ambition as zeal to purify government (White 1963). Carl Russell Fish, a critic of the patronage system established under Jackson, writes:

It is evident that the end to be obtained was exactly opposite to that which made rotation popular . . . offices came to be regarded simply as prizes; and the phrase "rotation in office" served to give a pleasing and respected form to the doctrine that they should be shared as widely and as rapidly as possible. (Fish 1963: 86)

Even historians who are more charitable toward the spoils system, as having afforded expanded access to public office, concede that its base motive was ambition, rather than the expressed desire to remove personal ambition from politics (A. Schlesinger 1946).

Some advocates of term limits have pointed to the 19th-century practice of rotation among offices as the manifestation of the ideal of the citizen-legislator, the amateur who brings to office the perspective of those being represented, and the expectation of returning to private station immediately after serving in Congress. Petracca, for example, writes, "In Jacksonian democracy, rotation reduced the chances of corruption borne of familiarity with government and reinstated service on behalf of the public interest as the norm for public officials" (1992c: 37). To interpret rotation in the United States in this way, however, is to ignore altogether that rotation was driven by the demand of party machines for patronage offices. In the case of appointed public servants, rotation generally entailed dismissal from their posts by each new administration (White 1963). In the case of MCs, rotation resulted either from the failure of the local party to provide its nomination for reelection or from the efforts of legislators themselves to secure more desirable, and lucrative, appointed positions. Fish relates the situation as follows:

The pay of congressmen continued small until 1856, when it was raised from the eight dollars a day and mileage, that had held for so long, to three thousand dollars per annum, also with mileage. It is not surprising that before 1856 members made many applications for office. The Herald said in 1853: "The Louisiana applicants are in a melancholy way. Their members are so busy . . . grinding their own axes, that their constituents are little better than orphans." (1963: 178)

White portrays a similar picture, in quoting a letter from Congressman John Bell in 1841:

In truth, I begin to fear that we are, chiefly swayed by the thirst for power and plunder. Would you think that Senator Talmadge is willing to descend from the Senate to the New York customs house? This is yet a secret, but it is true! God help us all and keep us, I pray. I fear to speak of the list of congressional applicants. (1963: p. 326)

In short, rotation in the 19th-century U.S. Congress was voluntary only insofar as it involved politicians seeking to further their careers by securing better positions. Access to these more desirable positions – indeed the entire rotation system for elected and appointed posts alike – was administered by party machines as a means of distributing patronage to win votes. And those who served in Congress, albeit for short spans, were ambitious office seekers for whom securing a postlegislative position was a priority. Proponents of term limits who portray the U.S. rotation system as evidence that the ideal of the citizen-legislator once prevailed in the United States (Petracca 1992; Will 1992) are either ignoring facts that undermine their arguments or are simply historically misinformed.

At any rate, the 19th-century U.S. experience with informal rotation for legislators is reminiscent of the current Costa Rican experience with constitutional term limits. In both cases, career paths for legislators are built around postassembly appointments, and access to desirable posts are controlled by party leaders. In both cases, control over access to patronage is a critical component of party leaders' ability to command responsiveness among legislators to party directives. These similarities suggest that the

19th-century U.S. system, as well as the current Costa Rican system, could be instructive as to the effects that term limits would have on legislative representation in the present-day United States.

Of course, it is worth noting as well a number of factors that distinguish the United States today either from itself in the 19th century or from Costa Rica. In the first place, civil service reforms have dramatically reduced the ability of politicians to remove appointed public officials and replace them with political cronies. If the supply of desirable appointed public posts cannot satisfy the demand among ex-legislators, then it is likely that ex-legislators will be responsive to private groups that offer attractive postcongressional job opportunities, and that are willing to provide access to those jobs in exchange for responsiveness among incumbent legislators. Second, unlike in Costa Rica, control over access to the most desirable appointed positions in the United States is shared between the president and the Senate, through the confirmation process. Thus, the responsiveness of U.S. legislators seeking postcongressional appointments would be split between future presidents, who control nominations, and the Senate, which controls confirmations. A third difference from Costa Rica is that U.S. presidents would inevitably control nominations to appointments for at least some of the legislators serving concurrently with the president, both because some legislators would be ejected from office at the presidential midterm election, and because U.S. presidents can be reelected once. Thus, whereas incumbent U.S. presidents early in their terms might have more influence with legislators based on the ability to dispense nominations, this influence would inevitably dissipate throughout the presidential term, as the proportion of legislators who could benefit from the incumbent president's patronage shrinks.

Current claims made about term limits

Many of the claims currently made about how term limits would affect legislative representation in the United States are echoes of historical comments and criticisms of the reform. Present-day reformers revile professional politicians and extol amateurism with Jacksonian enthusiasm. Skeptics continue to point out, as Hamilton did, that legislators subject to term limit will be tempted to feather their nests as quickly as possible. Within the various arguments launched in this debate, there are four central themes – two associated with advocates of term limits, and two with opponents.[3] In gen-

[3] The one common belief that binds all term limit supporters is that congressional elections in the United States are not sufficiently competitive, and that incumbents are blessed with unfair advantages over challengers. I shall not review this argument for a couple of reasons. First, there is an exhaustive literature on incumbency advantage, and a number of well-developed

eral, the results of this study support the arguments of the term limits opponents and cast doubts on some of the claims made by reformers.

Pro–term limits: Amateurs and civic virtue. The two central themes of authors favoring term limits are the romanticization of the amateur legislator, and the idea that term limit will encourage legislators to act virtuously rather than selfishly. In the first case, term limit proponents generally prefer the term "citizen-legislator" to describe representatives for whom reelection is proscribed. The term has gained such wide currency in the term limits debate that in popular fora like newspaper op-ed pages, it is frequently not even made explicit how citizen-legislators are expected to differ from our current legislators in perspective and demeanor (Novak 1993). Petracca (1991) offers an argument that professionalization implies a separation between professionals (politicians) and clients (citizens) based on expertise. The effect of professionalization is to distance and disconnect politicians from the needs of those they represent; and conversely, the effect of term limits would be to close that gap.

The bottom line for many term limit advocates is that citizen-legislators are uncorrupted by career interests and cognizant of the problems facing most Americans. This position is stated most unreservedly by Cleta Deatherage Mitchell, former president of Americans to Limit Congressional Terms, as follows:

Amateurs are the very people envisioned by this system of government as belonging [in Congress]. The battle over the divine right to be in charge was fought over two hundred years ago. The American people rightly understand that it is the amateur, the man from the log cabin, the "anyone can be president" belief system that is the centerpiece of our democracy. (1991: 3)

And later: "Term limits would inject more amateurs into the process, citizens who would not be bound by the years of mutually beneficial relationships and scratched backs which paralyze the current Congress" (1991: 5). Mitchell's rhetorical exuberance aside, she states most clearly the expected advantage of amateurism. Amateurs are putatively unconstrained by obligations to those who have helped them reach office. Term limit advocates argue that current congressional candidates are more responsive to the demands of organized interest groups that finance campaigns, than to the proper needs of their constituents. Without congressional careers, the argument goes, so goes the need to cater to selfish special interests, so that legislators will make law in the interest of the country as a whole.

---

explanations for declining rates of turnover in the 20th century (see Fiorina 1977 and Jacobson 1990 for reviews). Second, and more important, the case that incumbents enjoy unfair advantages in congressional elections is not an argument about term limits and how term limits would affect legislative representation.

The argument romanticizing amateurism involves a couple of logical steps. First, term limits must generate a legislature of amateur, or citizen-, politicians. Second, amateurs must in fact act without obligation to the interests that currently fund and support professional legislators. This study does not address the second step of the argument, because it does not examine the behavior of amateur politicians. This study does, however, demonstrate that term limits do not necessarily eliminate political careers. Despite the fact that Costa Rican term limits have virtually eliminated Assembly careers, most Costa Rican legislators have held elected office and/ or office within their political party prior to serving in the legislature, and the vast majority seek political appointments after their Assembly terms (Chapter 3). Moreover, in Costa Rica, the dependence of deputies on party leaders for their political career prospects is manifest in legislative behavior (Chapters 4 and 5). Thus, the Costa Rican experience suggests that the reform should not be expected to produce a legislature of politically unconstrained citizen-legislators.

The second broad theme among reform advocates is that term limits promote civic virtue among legislators (American Enterprise Institute 1979; Klein 1989; Petracca 1992). This position has been most clearly forwarded by George Will, for whom "virtue is a tendency to prefer the public good to personal interests; it is a readiness to define the public good as more than an aggregation of private interests" (1992: 165). Will separates himself from other term limit proponents by explicitly rejecting arguments that the measure would strengthen the connection between legislators and constituents. According to Will, professionalization obliterates the proper distance between the representative and the represented. It prohibits deliberation and creates legislators who are too effective at being perfectly responsive to constituents' demands, even when the aggregate of all those demands describes policies that are not in the country's best interests. The advantage of term limits, for Will, is that they would shift the U.S. Congress from a delegate to a trustee model of representation. In his words, this "would strengthen the authority of representatives to deliberate at a constitutional distance from those they represent" (1992: 141–142).

Will's defense of term limits is interesting in part because it is the only argument that the measure would generate better representation by giving constituents less of what they demand from their representatives. But it is interesting as well in the context of the historical debate in which Will self-consciously places himself. Will explicitly embraces the Federalist idea that representatives ought to act as filters of popular demands, not responding immediately to public sentiment, but rather deliberating on the proper needs of the polity. Yet to achieve this antipopulist, Federalist goal, he is advocating what was, during the founding, a populist, Antifederalist measure (Wilentz 1992: 42). At any rate, it is not within the scope of this study to assess such arguments as Will's because the deliberative democracy he seeks, and the civic virtue it requires, presume the existence of certain proper needs of the polity that are different from the expressed needs of its members. Without presuming to know what those proper needs are, it would be impossible to determine whether legislators under term limits are more or less effective at satisfying them than are current MCs.

Anti–term limits: Novices and opportunists. Opponents of term limits likewise offer arguments about their expected effects on legislative representation that fall within two broad themes. The first is that amateur legislators are ineffective, the second that lame duck legislators are dangerous to their constituents.

The argument against novices cuts in two directions. It has been used to convince voters not to support term limit initiatives for their own representatives, irrespective of whether term limits in general are a good idea. The logic is that for any one state to commit itself to short-term legislators is to forfeit the legislative influence implied by committee and party leadership positions that are dominated by senior members of Congress. This argument was used effectively by House Speaker Thomas Foley in narrowly derailing a term limits initiative in his home state of Washington in 1991 (Olson 1992).[4]

The argument against novice legislators is made more generally by John Hibbing (1991), who uses longitudinal, as opposed to cross-sectional (see Chapter 6), data on congressional careers to identify changes in various elements of congressional work and productivity throughout House members' careers. Hibbing's study provides elaborate detail on changes in electoral safety, committee and party offices, ideological positions, and constituency service work, both within congressional cohorts and among various cohorts over time. Among the clearest of Hibbing's discoveries is that House members are more active in sponsoring legislation, and far more efficient at securing its passage, as their tenure increases. Moreover, this increased legislative effectiveness is not a product of senior members' having better access to committee chairmanships and party offices. Even when such formal positions are controlled for, the relationship between tenure and effectiveness is strong. Hibbing reads his data as conclusive evidence that experience is critical to good legislation, and that term limits, conversely, "would likely result in a devastating loss of legislative acumen, expertise, and activity . . . For these reasons, my conclusion is that mandatory term limits for members of Congress is a bad idea" (1991: 180). Hibbing's conclusion is supported,

---

[4] Washington voters, however, passed a term limits measure the next year, which, unlike the failed measure, is not retroactive, and kicks in only after 10 other states adopt similar measures.

albeit less systematically, by complaints by Costa Rican deputies that that country's term limits eliminate nearly all legislative experience automatically every four years, meaning that the first year of every Assembly is nearly lost to inexperience (Chapter 3).

Finally, another set of objections to term limits is based on the suspicion that legislators for whom the electoral connection is legally severed will abandon their constituents' interests in favor of the interests of those who might provide postcongressional rewards (Kesler 1990; Montgomery 1990).[5] Clearly, this position is more skeptical than Will's (1992) that politicians without electoral accountability will act virtuously, or even be able to determine precisely what policies virtue requires, in the absence of reliable directions from constituents. This study consistently supports this skepticism – the expectation is that legislators are systematically responsive to those who control their political futures. The behavior of Costa Rican deputies is explained as effort to secure post-Assembly appointments (Chapters 4 and 5), and the changing voting patterns of aspirant U.S. House members is explained as responsiveness to new constituencies (Chapter 6).

Of course, in the cases examined here, the responsiveness of lame duck legislators has been to political parties that control access to postlegislative office. The suspicion of term limit opponents in the United States, however, is that the primary providers of employment for ex-legislators will not be political parties, which maintain some electoral connections to voters, but rather private corporations and lobbying groups, which can absorb the large numbers of ex-legislators seeking jobs. It is again beyond the scope of this study to predict who would be the main employers of ex-legislators in the United States under term limits.[6] However, this study does support unambiguously the premise that legislators under term limits will be responsive to interests of prospective future employers, even at the expense of the interests of their current electoral constituency.

In sum, with regard to the current U.S. debate over term limits, the empirical findings of this study suggest that there is no reason to expect term

---

[5] Although it is not written in the context of the current term limits debate, the most thorough statement of this theory is by Joseph Schlesinger (1966).

[6] In California, where term limits have been imposed – but have not yet taken effect – on state legislators, anecdotal evidence is materializing that politicians are considering rotating from state office back to municipal office. Mark Gladstone writes, "Instead of term limits shattering their political futures, the restrictions have prompted some lawmakers to consider rerouting their careers through Los Angeles City Hall." Gladstone then cites a host of local Los Angeles issues on which State Assembly members had suddenly begun trumpeting positions, and legislative proposals in the State Assembly that focus exclusively on local city interests. According to Assemblywoman Lucille Roybal-Allard, "Everyone is looking for an opening where they can move to." And with regard to the Los Angeles City Council, Assemblyman Richard E. Floyd notes, "It's an excellent job. [You] don't have to maintain two residences" (Gladstone 1992: A17).

limits to produce either the fabled citizen-legislator or any notion of civic virtue that requires legislators to ignore their own career interests. Term limits in Costa Rica have not produced an amateur legislature. And the behavior of legislators in Costa Rica, Venezuela, and the United States can consistently be explained in terms of personal ambition and careerism.

Term limits and electoral incentives

This study began with the question of how term limits affect legislative representation. The preceding section suggests that, on some specific counts, the effects of term limits in the United States would be different from what their proponents expect. But to suggest conclusions on the effects of term limits that are generalizable across the range of electoral systems presumes some expectations about representation where reelection is possible. Without such expectations, no effect of term limits could be detected. Much of this work has focused on two elements of legislative behavior: personal reputation building among constituents and loyalty to party positions in the legislature.[7] In other work, Carey and Shugart (in press) generate expectations about the relative value to politicians of personal versus partisan reputations in systems that allow reelection.[8] In that model, the relationship is explained as a dependent variable, driven by electoral rules. Once these expectations are established, however, they can serve as a basis from which the impact of term limits can be studied.

The model rests on two assumptions: first, that legislators want to be reelected; and second, that there sometimes are conflicts between behavior that would maximize legislators' personal popularity among voters and behavior that would maximize the popularity of their party. This tension between personal and party reputation generates the potential for conflict between individual politicians and party leaders, especially when politicians are dependent on both their personal and party reputation for reelection.

---

[7] Other authors have offered general models of other elements of legislative behavior, such as proclivity to take moderate vs. extreme ideological positions on policy issues (Cox 1987) and preferences in dividing public resources among constituents (Myerson 1993).

[8] The concept of personal reputation needs little explanation. Simply, if a politician's electoral prospects improve as a result of being personally well known and liked by voters, then personal reputation matters. The more this matters, the more valuable personal reputation is. Party reputation refers to the information that party label conveys to voters in a given electoral district. Maintaining a reputation requires that politicians refrain from taking positions or actions that conflict with the party's platform. If the quality of their party's reputation is all that matters to politicians' electoral prospects, then there is no problem – there is no incentive to weaken party reputation by staking out independent positions. But if electoral prospects depend on winning votes cast for the individual politician instead of, or in addition to, votes cast for the party, then politicians need to evaluate the trade-off between the value of personal and party reputations. Some electoral systems create greater incentives than others for politicians to cultivate personal reputations.

The severity of the problem is determined by electoral rules governing the control of party leaders over access by candidates to the party label, the method of aggregating votes among candidates, and the number of seats available in each electoral district.

This model of electoral incentives makes clear that the effects of term limits on the values of personal reputations and party cohesiveness depends on two critical factors. The first factor is the electoral system on which term limits are imposed. For example, some systems generate weak electoral incentives for legislators to cultivate personal reputations, and strong incentives to maintain party reputations. Costa Rica and Venezuela are two such cases.[9] Imposing term limits effectively severs direct electoral incentives, so term limits on such systems might be expected to weaken party cohesiveness. This is, in fact, the case in Costa Rica (Chapter 5). On the other hand, some electoral systems generate strong incentives to cultivate personal reputations, even at the expense of party reputations. The United States is an example of this type of system, although by no means the most extreme type (Ames 1992; McCubbins and Rosenbluth 1995). Where electoral incentives to maintain party discipline are weak to begin with, as in the United States, term limits may or may not further weaken parties. The impact of term limits will be different depending in part on the original electoral incentive structure they displace.

The second factor determining the impact of term limits is the shape of postassembly careers in the absence of reelection. Consider a scenario in which parties control access to the most attractive postassembly careers. In this case, legislators have strong incentives to obey the directives of party leaders, even in the absence of reelection. Costa Rica displays a variant of this phenomenon. The potentially dilatory effect of term limits on party cohesiveness is mitigated by the common desire among legislators for appointed posts, which are available only if their party wins the subsequent presidential election. But uncertainty over which party leaders might control access to appointments simultaneously undermines party cohesiveness. The result is significant party discipline, but not as strong as would be expected under the same electoral system without term limits – as in Venezuela (Chapter 5).

Now consider a second scenario in which the most attractive career options open to legislators prohibited from reelection are not controlled by parties. Knowing only this much about postassembly career paths, it is impossible to say much specifically about the responsiveness of legislators. But the absence of reelection and the absence of careers within parties

---

[9] Recall that the efforts of Costa Rican legislators to provide constituent service and pork-barrel projects for their bailiwicks are driven by the demands of their parties, rather than by any personal electoral connection.

suggests that legislators should be responsive to other principals besides their constituents or party leaders. These principals could include any individuals or groups who have an interest in lobbying assemblies and the resources to provide postassembly employment – or at least compensation – to legislators subject to term limits. The possibility that such legislators would systematically cater to the demands of prospective future employers, rather than to those of their constituents, is a persistent theme among current opponents of the reform in the United States.

Recent research on postcongressional career paths of U.S. House members supports this story. Relying on survey data from 67% of all surviving former House members who left Congress between 1971 and 1992, Herrick and Nixon (1994) examine subsequent career patterns. They distinguish ex-legislators who were forced out of office, as many would be under term limits, from those who left voluntarily.[10] They also distinguish those who took "revolving door" jobs in government-related work immediately after leaving the House from those who retired or worked in the private sector, remaining politically active only as volunteers, if at all. Herrick and Nixon find that, overall, only 27% of ex–House members immediately passed through the revolving door into lobbying or the bureaucracy. More significantly, however, those who were forced out of office were *more likely than not* to have taken paid positions in lobbying or the bureaucracy. They conclude:

Perhaps the most important implication of [this] finding is that reforms intended to increase turnover are likely to have dramatic effects outside Congress. Members who were forced out of office remained interested in politics and furthered their political careers in pressure politics or the bureaucracy. Thus, reforms intended to increase congressional turnover are unlikely to alter the motives of professional politicians. (Herrick and Nixon 1994: 13–14)

This result is entirely consistent, of course, with the general conclusions reached throughout this book. It extends beyond the results reported in previous chapters, however, insofar as it suggests specifically how career ambitions are likely to manifest themselves among U.S. legislators forced out of office by term limits. With party-administered patronage scarce relative to Costa Rica, U.S. ex-legislators who hold career ambitions find ample opportunities in lobbying firms and in the bureaucracy. The next obvious question, of course, is whether ambitious legislators who knew they were to be forced out of office, and knew precisely when, would alter their behavior while in office so as to improve their prospects of securing a good job on the

---

[10] Those forced out either lost reelection bids (or did not run because they were redistricted out of seats) or expected to lose; but they expressed a desire to have remained in office. Those who left voluntarily did so either for age or health reasons, because Congress was "not fun anymore," because of better opportunities elsewhere, for family reasons, or to seek higher office.

other side of the revolving door. Herrick and Nixon clearly expect this to be the case, and the evidence from Costa Rica and from U.S. House roll call voting presented earlier certainly suggests that legislators are sensitive to the wishes of their future employers. In sum, term limits will certainly weaken the electoral link between legislators and constituents. Under some conditions, this may strengthen politicians' dependence on their parties for post-legislative careers and increase incentives for party cohesion. But where some other actors control the best postlegislative job opportunities, term limits will likely simply undermine the strength of both constituent and partisan attachments, leaving legislators to act as individual entrepreneurs in lining up their next jobs.

Speaking generally, then, the effects of term limits on legislators' incentives to cultivate personal versus party reputations will vary according to two factors: the electoral system on which term limits are imposed, and the prospective career paths open to ex-legislators. Where electoral rules would otherwise generate strong party discipline, term limits will likely weaken that discipline. Where electoral rules would otherwise generate strong incentives to cultivate personal reputations, term limits may mitigate that tendency. Whether these patterns hold is determined, in turn, by the types of career paths that replace parliamentary careers under term limits. Where parties control postlegislative careers, legislators will be responsive to the directives of party leaders. Where parties do not control careers, it is an open question to whom legislators will be responsive, but we can expect it will not be to either their constituents or their party leaders. It is possible to imagine a situation in which parties maintain some control over postlegislative careers, but not as much as they would have without term limits. This describes Costa Rica. It is also possible to imagine a situation in which parties maintain more control over postlegislative careers – perhaps through appointments – under term limits than they would have under an electoral system where personal reputation is highly valuable to legislators seeking reelection. Term limits have contributed to this effect in Mexico (Weldon 1994). For this situation to hold in the United States under term limits would require the development of a party patronage system for ex-legislators that currently does not exist. Instead, it seems more likely that term limits would weaken the electoral connection with constituents without replacing that connection to any institutions that, like parties, are subject to electoral competition.

Conclusions

Term limits do not eliminate political careerism, much less produce legislators who are motivated exclusively by civic virtue rather than by personal ambition. It is curious that advocates of term limits, like Will and Petracca, who lay claim simultaneously to both the Federalist and Antifederalist intellectual traditions, so enthusiastically embrace the promise of virtuous legislators that they fail altogether to acknowledge the most fundamental insight of the founders: that institutional design can harness, but not transform, human nature. Political institutions, including electoral systems, channel personal ambition in different directions. But no electoral system, including that which denies its winners the opportunity to win again, can eliminate personal ambition from the forces that motivate politicians.

Term limits redirect the ambition of politicians by legally severing their direct dependence on voters for career advancement. In the absence of an electoral connection, political parties' ability to control careers is critical in determining the nature of legislative representation. Depending on the electoral rules, and on the resources controlled by party leaders, term limits can conceivably either strengthen or weaken party control over political careers, but they will more likely weaken it. Because parties remain subject to electoral review by voters, even when individual politicians do not, an indirect and collective electoral connection can remain under term limits – as long as politicians are dependent on parties for career advancement. Where term limits weaken both party and constituent control over politicians, they simply undermine electoral accountability.

In summing up, a couple of points are critical. Most straightforward is that if parties do not control access to postlegislative careers, then term limits do eliminate the electoral connection, and with it any instrument by which voters can reward or punish politicians for their performance. Second, even where parties exercise significant control over careers, politicians' responsiveness to parties can manifest itself in various ways. Parties may demand strict voting discipline among members, to ensure the maintenance of clear collective reputations, and ignore activities that would enhance the personal reputations of individual politicians. But parties may also require politicians with no personal incentive to do so to engage in pork-barreling and constituent service work, as in Costa Rica. In short, prohibiting reelection will not necessarily eliminate the kinds of particularistic activities that political science has traditionally attributed to personal electioneering by legislators.

The conclusions regarding legislative term limits drawn in this study are broad. I have contended that term limits will not generate all the results suggested by their proponents in the United States. I have also argued that the specific effects of term limits will depend on the electoral system on which they are imposed, and I have discussed the factors intrinsic to electoral systems and political parties that determine the impact of term limits across various systems. The conclusions here are supported by evidence from Costa Rica, Venezuela, and the United States. Of these cases, however, only in Costa Rica was it possible to observe directly the effects of term limits on legislative representation. The most pressing need in the further study of term limits, then, is for more empirical evidence, to compare with that analyzed here. After 1996, as term limits begin to kick in at the state level in the United States, the shortage of empirical evidence should cease to be an obstacle.

Beyond the general call for more data, however, a number of specific issues remain puzzling in light of this study, and all merit further attention. First, there is the question of why legislators would ever impose term limits on themselves. The historical record from Costa Rica does not provide a satisfying answer to this riddle (Chapter 2). In the U.S. context, the question has yet to present itself, because the term limits have been overwhelmingly the product of direct democracy. Pressure on Congress has grown, however, to act on a constitutional amendment. The outcome of that internal struggle will provide rich fodder for students of institutional reform. Studies of other countries that have adopted term limits without direct democracy would be relevant as well. The Filipino case is as yet unstudied. Weldon's (1994) work on the adoption of term limits by the Mexican Congress is a fascinating examination of the importance of electoral reform, even in nondemocratic systems.

This study also questions the conditions under which political parties will require their legislators to engage in particularistic activities, even when legislators have no personal incentive to do so. Differences in the behavior of Costa Rican and Venezuelan legislators in this area are not accounted for by the existence of term limits in Costa Rica. One conclusion that can be drawn here is that term limits do not preclude particularism (Chapter 4). Beyond that, the specific questions remain as to whether and how particularism helps parties electorally, and how parties force legislators to engage in particularistic activities.

Also with regard to legislative parties, the straightforward conclusion of Chapter 5 is that term limits undermine cohesiveness in Costa Rica, relative to Venezuela. But the absence of roll call voting data in each country makes precise conclusions about the extent of the effect difficult to assess. Once term limits are implemented in the United States, more extensive data on party cohesiveness will become available quickly. Nevertheless, the ability to compare such data across a broad array of electoral systems depends on the availability of recorded roll call votes in legislatures where such records are frequently not kept.

Finally, this study underscores the important question of how term limits affect legislative representation when parties do not control access to postlegislative careers. Given the current lack of any extensive party-administered system of patronage in the United States, it appears that term limits in this country would leave legislators dependent on other sources for future employment. Herrick and Nixon (1994) provide a first cut on what these sources might look like, but how this situation would affect legislative behavior under term limits remains to be addressed directly.

Legislative term limits are uncommon, existing in only a few countries and now in a substantial minority of U.S. states. They are, however, the most important electoral reform currently on the agenda in the United States. Their implications are profound, both for the quality of representation and for the study of politics. Term limits inevitably change the incentives and the responsiveness of legislators. They also force political scientists to reevaluate a set of familiar expectations about legislative behavior that is based on the assumption of unrestricted reelection. This study demonstrates that the effects of term limits could be quite different from what reformers in this country propound, and it establishes a method to assess the impact of term limits on legislative behavior across a range of electoral systems.

References

Aguilar Bulgarelli, Oscar (1981). *Democracia y partidos políticos en Costa Rica.* San José: Editorial Universidad Estatal a Distancia.

Aguilar Bulgarelli, Oscar (1986). *La Constitución de 1949: Antecedentes y proyecciones.* San José: Editorial Costa Rica.

Ahuja, Sunil, and Michael K. Moore (1992). "Tenure in the Senate: Implications for the Term Limits Debate." Presented at the Annual Meeting of the American Political Science Association.

[ALCR], Asamblea Legislativa de Costa Rica. Constitutional and Electoral Reform Proposals: Expediente A-15-E-2154 (July 28, 1960); Exp. A-18-E-4131 (October 19, 1964); Exp. A-29-E-6304 (May 1966); Exp. A-25-E-5803 (October 28, 1971); Exp. A-30-E-6566 (October 22, 1974); Exp. 8484 (May 5, 1980); Exp. 10,541 (October 14, 1987); Exp. 11,407 (November 26, 1991). San José: Archivo de la Asamblea Legislativa.

[ALCR], Asamblea Legislativa de Costa Rica (1983–1984). Ley de la moneda. (Decreto 6965, Exp. 9736). San José: Archivo de la Asamblea Legislativa.

[ALCR], Asamblea Legislativa de Costa Rica (1983–1986). "Convenio para la pesca de atun" (Expediente 9884). San José: Archivo de la Asamblea Legislativa.

[ALCR], Asamblea Legislativa de Costa Rica (1984–1991). "Tratado sobre delimitación de areas marinas y submarinas y cooperacion maritima con Colombia." San José: Archivo de la Asamblea Legislativa.

[ALCR], Asamblea Legislativa de Costa Rica (1985a). "Actas de las Sesiones Plenarias," No. 1, Asamblea Legislative No. 18, May 1985, Tomo 405: 1–41. San José: Archivo de la Asamblea Legislativa.

[ALCR], Asamblea Legislativa de Costa Rica (1985b). *Mayo Negro: Historia de una conjura.* San José: Documentos de la Asamblea Legislativa.

[ALCR], Asamblea Legislativa de Costa Rica (1985–1988). "Ley de inquilinato" (Dec. 7101, Exp. 10,180). San José: Archivo de la Asamblea Legislativa.

[ALCR], Asamblea Legislativa de Costa Rica (1988). "Modernización del sistema financiero de la República" (Dec. 7107, Exp. 10,523). San José: Archivo de la Asamblea Legislativa.

[ALCR], Asamblea Legislativa de Costa Rica (1988–1989). "Tratado constitutivo del Parlamento Centroamericano y otras instancias políticas" (Exp. 10,661). San José: Archivo de la Asamblea Legislativa.

[ALCR], Asamblea Legislativa de Costa Rica (1992). Interviews with Deputies from the 1990–1994 Cohort. Coded as 93–1 through 93–57. The number 93 signifies that deputies serve in the 93rd Costa Rican Assembly. The 57 members are identified by number in order to maintain confidentiality.

American Enterprise Institute (1979). *Legislative Analysis Series,* "Limiting Presidential and Congressional Terms." Washington, DC: AEI.

Ames, Barry (1987). *Political Survival in Latin America.* Berkeley: University of California Press.

Ames, Barry (1992). "Disparately Seeking Politicians: Strategies and Outcomes in Brazilian Legislative Elections." Latin American Studies Association conference paper.

Anagnoson, J. Theodore (1983). "Home Style in New Zealand." *Legislative Studies Quarterly* 8:157–175.

Arguedas, Carlos (1992). Staff counsel for the National Assembly Committee on Electoral Subjects. Interview, January 24.

Arias Sanchez, Oscar (1979). *¿ Quién gobierna en Costa Rica?* San José: Editorial Costa Rica.

Arias Sanchez, Oscar (1987). *Grupos de presión en Costa Rica.* San José: Editorial Costa Rica.

Arroyo Talavera, Eduardo (1986). *Elections and Negotiation: The Limits of Democracy in Venezuela: 1958–1981.* Ph.D. Thesis: London School of Economics and Political Science.

"Asamblea Nacional Constituyente de 1949." San José: Asamblea Legislativa, 1951.

Baker, Christopher E. (1971). "The Costa Rican Legislative Assembly: A Preliminary Evaluation of the Decisional Function," in Weston H. Agor, ed., *Latin American Legislatures: Their Role and Influence.* New York: Praeger.

Barro, Robert J. (1973). "The Control of Politicians: An Economic Model." *Public Choice* 14 (Spring): 19–42.

Becker, Gary S., and George J. Stigler (1974). "Law Enforcement, Malfeasance, and Compensation of Enforcers." *Journal of Legal Studies* 3(1) (January): 1–18.

Bender, Brian (1991). "The Influence of Ideology on Congressional Voting." *Economic Inquiry* 29: 416–428.

Benjamin, Gerald, and Michael J. Malbin (1992). "Term Limits for Lawmakers: How to Start Thinking About a Proposal in Process." In Gerald Benjamin and Michael J. Malbin, eds., *Limiting Legislative Terms.* Washington, DC: Congressional Quarterly Press.

Benjamin, Gerald, and Michael J. Malbin (1992). "Legislatures After Term Limits." In Benjamin and Malbin, eds., *Limiting Legislative Terms.* Washington, DC: Congressional Quarterly Press.

Blank, David (1980). "The Regional Dimension of Venezuelan Politics." In Howard R. Penniman, ed., *Venezuela at the Polls: The National Elections of 1978.* Washington, DC: American Enterprise Institute.

Brady, David, Joseph Cooper, and Patricia A. Hurley (1979). "The Decline of Party in the U.S. House of Representatives, 1887–1968." *Legislative Studies Quarterly* 4(3): 341–408.

Brady, David, and Douglas Rivers (1991) "Term Limits Make Sense." *New York Times.* October 5: 21.

Brewer-Carías, Allan R. (1989). "Evolución Institucional de Venezuela (1974–1989)." In *Venezuela contemporanea, 1974–1989.* Caracas: Fundación Eugenio Mendoza.

Caiden, Gerald E. (1983). *International Handbook of the Ombudsman: Country Surveys.* Westport, CN: Greenwood.

Cain, Bruce E. (1984). *The Reapportionment Puzzle.* Berkeley: University of California Press.

Cain, Bruce E. (1991). "Term Limits: Predictions About the Impact upon California." Working Paper delivered at the Conference on Term Limits, University of California, Irvine, June.

Cain, Bruce E., John Ferejohn, and Morris Fiorina (1987). *The Personal Vote: Constituency Service and Electoral Independence.* Cambridge, MA: Harvard University Press.

Carey, John M., and Matthew Soberg Shugart (in press). "Incentives to Cultivate a Personal Reputation: A Rank Ordering of Electoral Systems." *Electoral Studies* 14.

Carey, John M., and Matthew Soberg Shugart (1995). "Presidential Decree Authority: A Theoretical Framework." Unpublished.

Caro, Robert A. (1974). *The Power Broker: Robert Moses and the Fall of New York*. New York: Knopf.

Casas Zamora, Kevin, and Olman Briceno Fallas (1991). *Democracia representativa en Costa Rica? Analisis del sistema de elección de diputados en Costa Rica y sus perspectivas de cambio*. Law School Thesis. San José: University of Costa Rica.

Clarke, Harold D. (1978). "Determinants of Provincial Constituency Service: A Multivariate Analysis." *Legislative Studies Quarterly* 4: 501–523.

Cohen, Linda, and Matthew Spitzer (1991). "Term Limits." Working paper delivered at the Conference on Term Limits, University of California, Irvine, June.

Collie, Melissa, and David Brady (1985). "The Decline of Partisan Voting Coalitions in the House of Representatives." In Lawrence Dodd and Bruce Oppenheimer, eds., *Con gress Reconsidered* (3rd Edition). Washington, DC: Congressional Quarterly Press, 272–289.

Combellas, Ricardo (1986). "Reflexiones sobre los partidos políticos venezolanos." In Manuel Vicente Magallanes, ed., *Reformas electorales y partidos políticos*. Caracas: Consejo Supremo Electoral.

Conaghan, Catherine (1994). "Loose Parties, 'Floating' Politicians, and Institutional Stress: Presidentialism in Ecuador, 1979–88." In Juan J. Linz and Arturo Valenzuela, eds., *The Failure of Presidential Democracy*. Baltimore: Johns Hopkins University Press.

Congreso de la Republica de Venezuela (1989). "Ley de reforma parcial de la ley organica del Sufragio." September 14. Caracas.

Congreso de la Republica de Venezuela (1992). "Reforma Parcial de la Ley Organica del Sufragio." May 7. Caracas.

Copeland, Gary W. (1991). "The End of Professionalism: The Dynamics of Legislative Term Limitations." In *Extensions*. Norman, OK: Carl Albert Research Center.

Copeland, Gary W. (1992). "Term Limitations and Political Careers in Oklahoma: In, Out, Up, or Down." In Gerald Benjamin and Michael J. Malbin, eds., *Limiting Legislative Terms*. Washington, DC: Congressional Quarterly Press.

Coppedge, Michael (1989). "Venezuela: Democratic Despite Presidentialism." Paper delivered to the research symposium, "Presidential or Parliamentary Democracy: Does It Make a Difference?" Georgetown University, Washington, DC, May 14–16.

Coppedge, Michael (1992). "(De)Institutionalization of Latin American Party Systems." Latin American Studies Association conference paper.

Coppedge, Michael (1994). *Strong Parties and Lame Ducks: Presidential Partyarchy and Factionalism in Venezuela*. Stanford, CA: Stanford University Press.

[COPRE], Comisión Presidencial para la Reforma del Estado (1988). *La Reforma del Estado: Proyecto de reforma integral del estado*. Caracas: Editorial Arte.

[COPRE], Comisión Presidencial para la Reforma del Estado (1990a). "Folletos para la discusión, no. 14." Caracas.

[COPRE], Comisión Presidencial para la Reforma del Estado (1990b). *Estado y Reforma, Segunda Etapa, No. 3*. Caracas.

Corrales, Jose Miguel (1992). "Reconstruiremos el P.L.N." *La República*. San Jose. March 14.

Cox, Gary (1987). *The Efficient Secret*. Cambridge University Press.

Cox, Gary, and Mathew McCubbins (1993). *The Legislative Leviathan*. Berkeley: University of California Press.

Craig, Ann, and Wayne Cornelius (1995). "Houses Divided: Parties and Political Reform in Mexico." In Scott Mainwaring and Tim Scully, eds., *Building Democratic Institutions: Parties and Party Systems in Latin America*. Stanford, CA: Stanford University Press.

Crisp, Brian F. (1995). "Presidential Decree Authority in Venezuela." Unpublished.

Dahl, Robert (1971). *Polyarchy.* New Haven, CT: Yale University Press.

Davis, M. L., and P. K. Porter (1989). "A Test for Pure or Apparent Ideology in Congressional Voting." *Public Choice* 60(2): 101–111.

Dougan, W. R., and M. C. Munger (1989). "The Rationality of Ideology." *Journal of Law and Economics* 32: 119–142.

Downs, Anthony (1957). *An Economic Theory of Democracy.* New York: Harper.

Dunkerley, James (1988). *Power in the Isthmus: Political History of Modern Central America.* New York: Verso.

Ehrenhalt, Alan (1991). *The United States of Ambition: Politicians, Power, and the Pursuit of Office.* New York: Times Books.

Elder, Neil, Alastair H. Thomas, and David Arter (1988). *The Consensual Democracies? The Government and Politics of the Scandinavian States.* New York: Basil Blackwell.

Elliot, Jonathan, ed. (1966). *The Debates in the Several State Conventions on the Adoption of the Federal Constitution,* vol. 2. New York: Burt Franklin.

Epstein, Leon D. (1967). *Political Parties in Western Democracies.* New York: Praeger.

Fenno, Richard F. (1973). *Congressmen in Committees.* Boston: Little, Brown.

Fenno, Richard F. (1978). *Home Style: House Members in Their Districts.* Boston: Little, Brown.

Ferejohn, John (1986). "Incumbent Performance and Electoral Control." *Public Choice* 50: 5–25.

Ferry, Jonathan (1994). "Coming to Terms with Term Limits: A Summary of State Term Limit Laws." Term Limits Outlook Series, III(4). Washington, DC: U.S. Term Limits Foundation.

Fett, Patrick J., and Daniel E. Ponder (1993). "Congressional Term Limits, State Legislative Term Limits and Congressional Turnover: A Theory of Change." *PS: Political Science and Politics,* Vol.26(2): 211–216.

Fiorina, Morris P. (1989). *Congress: Keystone of the Washington Establishment.* New Haven, CN: Yale University Press.

Fish, Carl Russell (1963). *The Civil Service and the Patronage.* New York: Russell and Russell.

Freed, Kenneth (1992). "Trouble in Paradise? Venezuelans Sense It." *Los Angeles Times,* World Report, October 13.

Gabaldón, Arnoldo José, and Luis Enrique Oberto (1985). *La reforma parlamentaria: Necesidad y alternativas de modernización de la acción legislativa,* vols. 1 and 2. Caracas: Congreso de la República.

Geddes, Barbara (1990a). "How the Cases You Choose Affect the Answers You Get: Selection Bias in Comparative Research." In James A. Stimson, ed., *Political Analysis,* vol. 2: 131–150. Ann Arbor: University of Michigan Press.

Geddes, Barbara (1990b). "Democratic Institutions as a Bargain Among Self-Interested Politicians." American Political Science Association conference paper.

Geddes, Barbara, and Arturo Ribeiro Neto (1992). "Institutional Sources of Corruption in Brazil." *Third World Quarterly* 13(4): 641–661.

Geertz, Clifford (1973). *The Interpretation of Cultures.* New York: Basic.

Gil Yepes, Jose Antonio (1981). *The Challenge of Venezuelan Democracy.* New Brunswick, NJ. Transaction Books.

Gladstone, Mark (1992). "Legislators Look Homeward for Future in Politics." *Los Angeles Times.* June 4: A17.

Glazer, Amihai, and Martin P. Wattenberg (1991). "Promoting Legislative Work: A Case for Term Limits." Working paper delivered at the Conference On Term Limits, University of California, Irvine, June.

Gutierrez Gutierrez, Carlos Jose (1984). "Sistema Presidencialista y Sistema Parlamentario." *In El modelo político costarricense.* San José: Asociación Nacional de Fomento Económico.

Gutierrez Saxe, Manuel, and Jorge Vargos Cullell (1986). *Costa Rica er el nombre del /uego.* Heredia, Costa Rica: Institute Costarricense de Estudias Sociales.

Hamilton, Alexander, John Jay, and James Madison (1961). *The Federalist Papers.* New York: Mentor.

Hartz, Louis (1955). *The Liberal Tradition in America: An Interpretation of American Political Thought Since the Revolution.* New York: Harcourt, Brace.

Hernandez Poveda, Rubén (1991). *Desde la barra.* San José: Editorial Costa Rica.

Hernandez Valle, Rubén (1991). *Derecho parlamentario costarricense.* San José: Investigaciones Jurídicas.

Herrick, Rebekah, Michael K. Moore, and John R. Hibbing (1994). "Unfastening the Electoral Connection: The Behavior of U.S. Representatives when Reelection Is No Longer a Factor." *Journal of Politics* 56(1): 214–227.

Herrick, Rebekah, and David L. Nixon (1994). "Is There Life After Congress?: Patterns and Determinants of Post-Congressional Careers." Paper delivered at the Conference of the American Political Science Association.

Hibbing, John R. (1991). *Congressional Careers: Contours of Life in the U.S. House of Representatives.* Chapel Hill: University of North Carolina Press.

Higgs, R. (1989). "Do Legislators' Votes Reflect Constituency Preference? A Simple Way to Evaluate the Senate." *Public Choice* 63(2): 175–181.

Hughes, Steven W., and Kenneth J. Mijeski (1973). *Legislative–Executive Policy-Making: The Cases of Chile and Costa Rica.* Beverly Hills, CA: Sage.

Inter-University Consortium for Political and Social Research (Fall 1987): Roster of U.S. congressional officeholders and biographical characteristics of members of the U.S. Congress, 1789–1987 (ICPSR 7803).

Jacobson, Gary C. (1990). *The Electoral Origins of Divided Government: Competition in U.S. House Elections, 1946–1988.* Boulder, CO: Westview.

Kalt, J. P., and M. A. Zupan (1990). "The Apparent Ideological Behavior of Legislators: Testing for Principal–Agent Slack in Political Institutions." *Journal of Law and Economics* 33(1): 103–131.

Karl, Terry Lynn (1986). Petroleum and Political Facts: The Transition to Democracy in Venezuela." Guilleruo O'Donnell, Phillippe C. Schmitter, and Laurence Whitehead, eds., *Transitions from Authoritarian Rule: Latin America.* Baltimore: Johns Hopkins University Press.

Kau, J. B., and P. H. Rubin (1979). "Self-Interest, Ideology, and Logrolling in Congressional Voting." *Journal of Law and Economics* 22: 365–384.

Kelley, R. Lynn (1971). "The Role of the Venezuelan Senate." In Weston H. Agor, ed., *Latin American Legislatures: Their Role and Influence.* New York: Praeger.

Kelley, R. Lynn (1973). "Venezuelan Constitutional Forms and Realities." In John D. Martz and David J. Myers, eds. *Venezuela: The Democratic Experience.* New York: Praeger.

Kelley, R. Lynn (1977). "Venezuelan Constitutional Forms and Realities." In John D. Martz and David J. Myer, eds., *Venezuela: The Democratic Experience.* New York: Praeger Publishers.

Kelley, R. Lynn (1986). "Venezuelan Constitutional Forms and Realities." In John D. Martz and David J. Myers, eds., *Venezuela: The Democratic Experience (Revised Edition).* New York: Praeger Publishers.

Kesler, Charles R. (1990). "Bad Housekeeping: The Case Against Congressional Term Limitations." *Policy Review* (53): 20–25.

Kiewiet, D. R., and M. D. McCubbins (1991). *The Logic of Delegation: Congressional Parties and the Appropriations Process*. Chicago: University of Chicago Press.

Klein, Michael H. (1989). "Limiting Congressional Terms: An Historical Perspective." Washington, DC: Americans to Limit Congressional Terms.

Krehbiel, Keith (1992). *Information and Legislative Organization*. Ann Arbor: University of Michigan Press.

Kreps, D. M., and R. Wilson (1982). "Sequential Equilibria." *Econometrica* 50: 863–894.

Laakso, Markku, and Rein Taagepera (1979). "Effective Number of Parties: A Measure with Application to Western Europe." *Comparative Political Studies* 12:3–27.

La Gaceta Oficial de la Asamblea Legislativa de la República de Costa Rica (*The Gazette* of the Legislative Assembly of the Republic of Costa Rica). San José: Asamblea Legislativa.

Lehoucq, Fabrice Edouard (1991a). "Class Conflict, Political Crisis and the Breakdown of Democratic Practices in Costa Rica: Reassessing the Origins of the 1948 Civil War." *Journal of Latin American Studies* 24(1): 37–60.

Lehoucq, Fabrice Edouard (1991b). "Institutional Reform, Electoral Laws and Political Conflict: The Origins of Costa Rica's Modern Electoral Code." Unpublished.

Lehoucq, Fabrice Edouard (1993). "Presidentialism, Electoral Laws and the Development of Political Stability in Costa Rica, 1882–1990." Latin American Studies Association conference paper.

Levine, Daniel (1973). *Conflict and Political Change in Venezuela*. Princeton, NJ: Princeton University Press.

Levine, Daniel (1978). "Venezuela Since 1958: The Consolidation of Democratic Politics." In Juan J. Linz and Alfred Stepan, eds., *The Breakdown of Democratic Regimes: Latin America* Baltimore: Johns Hopkins University Press.

Levine, Daniel (1987). "Venezuela." In Myron Weiner and Ergun Ozbudin, eds., *Competitive Elections in Developing Countries*. Durham, NC: Duke University Press.

Ley Orgánica del Tribunal Supremo de Elecciones y del Registro Civil y Código Electoral y otras disposiciones cinexons. San José Costa Rica: Imprenta Nacional.

Lijphart, Arend (1971). "Comparative Politics and the Comparative Method." *American Political Science Review* 65(3): 682–693.

Lijphart, Arend (1986). *Democracies*. New Haven, CT: Yale University Press.

Linz, Juan J. (1994). "Presidential or Parliamentary Democracy: Does It Make a Difference?" In Juan J. Linz and Arturo Valenzuela, eds., *The Failure of Presidential Democracy*. Baltimore: Johns Hopkins University Press.

Lott, J. R., Jr. (1987). "Political Cheating." *Public Choice* 52(2): 169–186.

Lott, J. R., Jr. (1990a). "Attendance Rates, Political Shirking, and the Effect of Post-Elective Office Employment." *Economic Inquiry* 28 (January): 133–150.

Lott, J. R., Jr. (1990b). Why Opportunistic Behavior in Political Markets Tends to Be Self-Correcting: An Explanation for Why Senators from the Same State Vote So Differently. Business Economics Working Paper no. 90–15 (July).

Lott, J. R., Jr., and M. L. Davis (1992). "A Critical Review and Extension of the Political Shirking Literature." *Public Choice* 74(4): 461–484.

Lott, J. R., Jr. and W. R. Reed (1989). "Shirking and Sorting in a Political Market with Finite-Lived Politicians." *Public Choice* 61(1) (April): 75–96.

Lowenthal, Daniel Hays (1993). "Are Congressional Term Limits Constitutional?" Paper presented at the American Political Science Association annual conference.

Madison, James (1961). *"Federalist No. 10."* In A. Hamilton, J. Madison, and J. Jay, The Federalist. New York: Signet.

Madrigal, Alvaro (1992). Assistant to the Minister of the Presidency, 1992. Interview, March 11. San José.

Maheshwari, Shiram (1976). "Constituency Linkage of National Legislatures in India." *Legislative Studies Quarterly* 1: 331–354.

Mainwaring, Scott (1994). "Presidentialism, Multiparty Systems, and Democracy: The Difficult Equation." *Comparative Political Studies* 26(4): 198–228.

Mainwaring, Scott, and Timothy Scully (1992). "Party Systems in Latin America." Latin American Studies Association conference paper.

Malbin, Michael J. (1992). "Federalists v. Antifederalists: The Term Limits Debate at the Founding." In Gerald Benjamin and Michael J. Malbin, eds., *Limiting Legislative Terms*. Washington, DC: Congressional Quarterly Press.

Malbin, Michael J., and Gerald Benjamin (1992). "Legislatures after Term Limits." Benjamin & Malbin, eds., *Limiting Legislative Terms*. Washington, DC: Congressional Quarterly Press.

Marshall, Tyler (1993). "A Shoulder To Cry On: In Poland, an Ombudsman Takes Pity on Citizens Buffeted by the Winds of Change." *Los Angeles Times*, Tuesday, May 4: H3.

Martz, John D. (1980). "The Evolution of Democratic Politics in Venezuela." In Howard R. Penniman, ed., *Venezuela at the Polls: The National Elections of 1978*. Washington, DC: American Enterprise Institute.

Mayhew, David (1974). *Congress: The Electoral Connection*. New Haven, CT: Yale University Press.

McArthur, J. (1990). "Congressional Attendance and Political Shirking in Lame Duck Sessions." Unpublished draft (May).

McCubbins, Mathew D., Roger Noll, and Barry Weingast (1989). "Structure and Process, Politics and Policy: Administrative Arrangements and the Political Control of Agencies." *Virginia Law Review* 75: 431–82.

McCubbins, Mathew D., and Frances McCall Rosenbluth (1995). "Party Provision for Personal Politics: Dividing the Vote in Japan." In Peter Cowhey and Mathew D. McCubbins, eds., *Structure and Policy in Japan and the United States: An Institutionalist Approach*. Cambridge University Press.

McCubbins, Mathew D., and Thomas Schwartz (1984). "Congressional Oversight Overlooked: Police Patrols Versus Fire Alarms." *American Journal of Political Science* 28: 165–179.

Mijeski, Kenneth (1977). "Costa Rica: The Shrinking of the Presidency?" In Thomas DiBacco, ed., *Presidential Power in Latin American Politics*. New York: Praeger.

Miller, Alan C. (1992). "Other States Join Term Limit Movement." *Los Angeles Times*, Sunday, October 25: A8-A9.

Mitchell, Cleta Deatherage (1991). "Limit Terms? Yes!" In *Extensions*. Norman, OK: Carl Albert Research Center. Spring.

Molinar, Juan, and Jeffrey Weldon (1993). "Electoral Determinants and Consequences of National Solidarity." In Wayne Cornelius, Ann Craig, and Johnathan Fox, eds., *Transforming State–Society Relations in Mexico: The National Solidarity Strategy*. La Jolla, CA: Center for U.S.–Mexican Studies, University of California, San Diego.

Moncrief, Gary F., Joel A Thompson, Michael Haddon, and Robert Hoyer (1992). "For Whom the Bell Tolls: Term Limits and State Legislatures." *Legislative Studies Quarterly* 17(1): 37–47.

Montgomery, Peter (1990). "Should Congressional Terms Be Limited?" *Common Cause* (July/ August): 31–33.

Muñoz Quesada, Hugo Alfonso (1981). *La Asamblea Legislativa en Costa Rica*. San José: Editorial Costa Rica.

Myers, David J. (1973). *Democratic Campaigning in Venezuela: Caldera's Victory*. Caracas: Editorial Sucre.

Myers, David J. (1977). "Policy Making and Capital City Resource Allocation: The Case of Caracas." In John D. Martz and David J. Myers, eds., *Venezuela: The Democratic Experience*. New York: Praeger.

Myers, David J. (1986). "The Venezuelan Party System: Regime Maintenance Under Stress." John D. Martz and David J. Myers, ed., *Venezuela: The Democratic Experience (Revised Edition)*. New York: Praeger Publishers.

Myerson, Roger B. (1993). "Incentives to Cultivate Favored Minorities Under Alternative Electoral Systems." *American Political Science Review* 87(4): 856–869.

Novak, Robert D. (1993). "Term Limits, In Trenton . . ." *Washington Post*, Thursday, June 24: A19.

Obregón Loria, Rafael (1966). *El poder legislativo en Costa Rica*. San José: Universidad de Costa Rica.

O'Donnell, Guillermo, Philippe C. Schmitter, and Laurence Whitehead (1986). *Transitions from Authoritarian Rule: Comparative Perspectives*. Baltimore: Johns Hopkins University Press.

Olson, David J. (1992). "Term Limits Fail in Washington: The 1991 Battleground." Gerald Benjamin and Michael J. Malbin, eds., *Limiting Legislative Terms*. Washington, DC: Congressional Quarterly Press.

Opheim, Cynthia (1994). "The Effect of U.S. State Legislative Term Limits Revisited." *Legislative Studies Quarterly* 19(1): 49–59.

Ordeshook, Peter C. (1986). *Game Theory and Political Theory: An Introduction*. Cambridge University Press.

Paredes Pisani, Edgar (1991). "Los partidos frente al reto de la decentralización." In Comisión Presidencial para la Reforma del Estado, ed., *Venezuela, democracia y futuro: Los partidos políticos en la decada de los 90*. Caracas: Grafisistem.

[PLN], Partido Liberación Nacional (1992). *Estatutos del Partido Liberación Nacional* (Statutes of the National Liberation Party). San José, Costa Rica: Partido Liberaciáu Nacional.

Peltzman, S. (1984). "Constituent Interest and Congressional Voting." *Journal of Law and Economics* 27: 181–210.

Petracca, Mark P. (1991). "The Professionalization of American Politics: Representational Consequences and a Principled Response." Working paper delivered at the Conference on Term Limits, University of California, Irvine.

Petracca, Mark P. (1992). "Rotation in Office: The History of an Idea." In Gerald Benjamin and Michael J. Malbin, eds., *Limiting Legislative Terms*. Washington, DC: Congressional Quarterly Press.

Pitkin, H. F. (1967). *The Concept of Representation*. Berkeley: University of California Press.

Polsby, Nelson (1968). "The Institutionalization of the U.S. House of Representatives." *American Political Science Review* 62(2): 144–168.

Poole, K.T., and H. Rosenthal (1985). "A Spatial Model for Legislative Roll Call Analysis." *American Journal of Political Science* 29(2): 357–384.

Poole, K.T., and H. Rosenthal (1988). "Patterns of Congressional Voting." GSIA Working Paper no. 88–89–07.

Powell, G. Bingham (1989). "Constitutional Design and Citizen Electoral Control." *Journal of Theoretical Politics* 1: 107–30.

Power, Timothy J. (1995). "The Pen Is Mightier than the Congress: Presidential Decree Authority in Brazil." Unpublished.

Price, H. Douglas (1975). "Congress and the Evolution of 'Legislative Professionalism.'" In Norman J. Ornstein, ed., *Congress in Change*. New York: Praeger.

Rachadell, Manuel (1991). "El sistema electoral y la reforma de los partidos." In Comisión

Presidencial para la Reforma del Estado, ed., *Venezuela, democracia y futuro: Los partidos políticos en la década de los 90*. Caracas: Grafisistem.

Rae, Douglas W. (1971). *The Political Consequences of Electoral Laws*. New Haven, CT: Yale University Press.

Ragin, Charles (1987). *The Comparative Method: Moving Beyond Qualitative and Quantitative Strategies*. Berkeley: University of California Press.

Rangel, Domingo Alberto (1978). *Los mercaderos del voto*. Valencia: Vadell Hermanos.

Reuters News Service (1992). "Venezuela's Perez Averts Leadership Challenge" (March 23); "Venezuela to Vote on Fate of Economic Ministers" (March 25); "Venezuela Congress Votes to Keep Economic Cabinet" (March 26); "Venezuela's Perez Won't Quit or Dump Reforms" (March 26); ""Venezuelan Ruling Party Expels Renegade Deputies" (March 30).

Riordan, William C. (1963). *Plunkitt of Tammany Hall*. New York: Dutton.

Robinson, Donald L., ed. (1985). *Reforming American Government*. Boulder: Westview.

Rohde, David (1991). *Parties and Leaders in the Post-Reform House*. Chicago: University of Chicago Press.

Rojas Bolaños Manuel(1979). *Lucha social y guerra civil en Costa Rica, 1940–1948*. San José: Juricentro.

Roverssi, Carlos (1992a). "Distritales de PLN a Sala IV." *La República*. San José: 6A.

Roverssi, Carlos (1992b). "Figuerismo hizo su fiesta." *La República*. San José: 2A.

Salazar, Jorge Mario (1981). *Política y reforma en Costa Rica: 1914–1958*. San José: Editorial Porvenir.

Sartori, Giovanni (1976). *Parties and Party Systems: A Framework for Analysis*. Cambridge University Press.

Schlesinger, Arthur M. (1946). *The Age of Jackson*. Boston: Little, Brown.

Schlesinger, Joseph. A. (1966). *Ambition and Politics: Political Careers in the United States*. Chicago: Rand McNally.

Seligson, Mitchell (1987). "Costa Rica and Jamaica." In Myron Weiner and Ergun Ozbudin, eds., *Competitive Elections in Developing Countries*. Durham, NC: Duke University Press.

Shepsle, Kenneth (1978). *The Giant Jigsaw Puzzle*. Chicago: University of Chicago Press.

Shepsle, Kenneth (1979). "Institutional Arrangements and Equilibrium in Multidimensional Voting Models." *American Journal of Political Science* 23(1): 27–59.

Shugart, Matthew Soberg (1988a). *Duverger's Rule, District Magnitude, and Presidentialism* Ph.D. dissertation, University of California, Irvine.

Shugart, Matthew Soberg, and John M. Carey (1992). *Presidents and Assemblies: Constitutional Design and Electoral Dynamics*. Cambridge University Press.

Shugart, Matthew Soberg, and Daniel Nielson (1993). "Liberalization Through Institutional Reform: Economic Adjustment and Constitutional Change in Colombia." Unpublished.

Sinclair, Barbara (1989). "House Majority Party Leadership in the Late 1980s." In Lawrence Dodd and Bruce Oppenheimer, eds., *Congress Reconsidered* (4th edition). Washington, DC: Congressional Quarterly Press.

Smith, Steven S., and Christopher J. Deering (1990). *Committees in Congress*. Washington, DC: Congressional Quarterly Press.

Sojo Obando, Carlos (1992). Researcher for the Facultad Latinoamericano de Ciencias Sociales (FLACSO). Interview, January 9. San José.

Stambouli, Andres (1988). "Innovación y continuidad en la democracia venezolana." In Manuel Vicente Magallanes, ed., *Innovación democratica, mitos políticos, y organización electoral*. Caracas: Consejo Supremo Electoral.

Stanley, Harold, and Richard Niemi (1995). *Vital Statistics on American Politics.* Washington, DC: Congressional Quarterly Press.

Stepan, Alfred (1978). *The State and Society: Peru in Comparative Perspective.* Princeton, NJ: Princeton University Press.

Storing, Herbert J., ed. (1985). *The Anti-Federalist.* Chicago: University of Chicago Press.

Taagepera, Rein, and Matthew S. Shugart (1989). *Seats and Votes.* New Haven, CT: Yale University Press.

Taylor, Michelle M. (1992). "Formal Versus Informal Incentive Structures and Legislative Behavior: Evidence from Costa Rica." *Journal of Politics* 54(4): 1055–1073.

Tribunal Supremo de Elecciones (1989). *Codigo Electoral y otras disposiciones conexas.* San José: Imprenta Nacional.

Uslaner, Eric M. (1985). "Casework and Institutional Design: Redeeming Promises in the Promised Land." *Legislative Studies Quarterly* 10: 35–52.

Valenzuela, Arturo (1994). "Party Politics and the Crisis of Presidentialism in Chile: A Proposal for a Parliamentary Form of Government." In Juan J. Linz and Arturo Valenzuela, eds., *The Failure of Presidential Government.* Baltimore: Johns Hopkins University Press.

Valenzuela, Arturo, and Alexander Wilde (1979). "Presidential Politics and the Decline of the Chilean Congress." In Joel Smith and Lloyd Musolf, eds., *Legislatures in Development: Dynamics of Change in New and Old States.* Durham, NC: Duke University Press.

VanBeek, J. R. (1990). Does the Decision to Retire Increase the Amount of Political Shirking? Unpublished (August 18).

Vanderdijs, Miguel G., and Felix Eloy Torres (1981). "Algunos problemas del sistema política venezolano." *Revista de Estudios Políticos* (10): 89–107. Caracas: Editorial Jurídica Venezelana.

Ventura Robles, Manuel E. (1984). *La representación política.* San José: Editorial Juricentro.

Villanueva Badilla, Jorge Luis (1992). Costa Rican deputy for the PLN, 1966–1970, 1982–1986; president of the Legislative Assembly, 1983–1984. Interview, March 17. Cartago.

Villalobos, José Miguel (1992). Secretary of the Costa Rican PLN Tribunal de Ética, 1986–1987; Assistant to PLN Assembly Caucus, 1982–1989; Assistant to José Miguel Corrales Bolanos, PLN presidential candidate, 1991–1992. Interview, February 28. San José.

Villegas Antillón, Rafael (1992). Magistrate of the Costa Rican Tribunal Supremo de Elecciones. Interview January 6. San José.

Volio Guevara, Julieta (1988). *La organización del poder legislativo en Costa Rica.* Law School Thesis. San José: Ciudad Universidad Rodrigo Facio.

Volio Jimenez, Fernando (1992). PLN deputy, 1966–1970, 1986–1990; president of Costa Rican National Assembly, 1987–1988. Interview, February 3.

Warren, Jenifer, and Alan C. Miller (1992). "Wins in 14 States Fuel U.S. Term Limit Drive." *Los Angeles Times,* Thursday, November 5: A13, A26.

Weingast, Barry R., and William Marshall (1988). "The Industrial Organization of Congress." *Journal of Political Economy* 96: 132–163.

Weldon, Jeffrey (1994). *No Reelection and the Mexican Congress.* Doctoral dissertation, University of California, San Diego.

Wells, Henry (1980). "The Conduct of Venezuelan Elections: Rules and Practice." In Howard R. Penniman, ed., *Venezuela at the Polls: The National Elections of 1978.* Washington, DC: American Enterprise Institute.

White, Leonard D. (1963). *The Jacksonians: A Study in Administrative History: 1829–1861.* New York: Macmillan.

Wilentz, Sean (1992). "Over the Hill." *New Republic* (October 12): 40–43.

Wilke, James W., and Carlos Alberto Contreras, eds. (1992). *Statistical Abstract of Latin America,* Vol. 29, Parts 1 and 2. Los Angeles: University of California Press.

Will, George F. (1992). *Restoration: Congress, Term Limits, and the Recovery of Deliberative Democracy.* New York: Free Press.

Will, George (1993). "And Across the Nation." *Washington Post,* Thursday, June 24: A19.

Young, James Sterling (1966). *The Washington Community, 1800–1828.* New York: Harcourt, Brace, and World.

Zupan, M. A. (1990). "The Last Period Problem in Politics: Do Congressional Representatives Not Subject to a Reelection Constraint Alter Their Voting Behavior?" *Public Choice* 65(2): 167–180.

Index

Acción Democrática (AD)
  Costa Rica, 33
  Venezuela, 55–58, 73–75, 138–139
Americans to Limit Congressional
  Terms, 190
Ames, Barry, 105
Antifederalists, 25, 184–186, 191–192,
  198
appointments, to postassembly posts,
  22, 72, 88–93, 186, 191
  rates in Costa Rica, 23, 85, 94–102,
  127–133, 142
Aquino, Corazon, 17
Arguedas, Carlos, 39–40, 149
Arias Sanchez, Oscar, 123, 132–133,
  141–142, 145
Articles of Confederation, 184
aspirants to statewide office, 167–
  175
assemblies, party nominating, 88–93,
  131–133

bailiwicks, 23, 105–115, 126–130, 134,
  151
ballot access restrictions, 14
Barro, Robert, 164, 166, 173
Becker, Gary, 163–164
Bell, Hon. John, 188
break in service requirements, 14–15
Betancourt, Rómulo, 53, 56
Brenes Castillo, Juan Guillermo, 50–51

Caldera, Rafael, 53, 56–57, 138
Calderón Fournier, Rafael Angel, 123
Calderón Guardia, Rafael Angel, 31–35,
  81, 145

California, 193n
candidates, for president in Costa Rica,
  86, 88–102, 131–133, 141–142,
  153–155
careerism, 5, 8, 183, 197
Castillo, Carlos Manuel, 123, 143
Catholic Church, 19, 112
Center for the Study of National Problems (CEPN), 33, 40
Central American Parliament, 146
Chajud Calvo, Carlos María, 141
citizen-legislator ideal, 7, 25, 41, 46, 66,
  82–86, 187–188, 190–194
Civil War of 1948, 18, 22, 26, 29, 33
Comisión para la Reforma del Estado
  (COPRE), 58, 117
Comité de Organización Politíca Electoral Independiente (COPEI), 56–
  58, 73–75, 138
committees in legislatures, 7,
  Costa Rica, 28–29, 47–51, 112
  United States, 59–64, 192
  Venezuela, 55–56
comparative analysis and methodology,
  8, 18, 22, 60, 159
competition within parties, 104, 109,
  118, 131–135, 145, 154
competitiveness of elections, 7
constituencies, 71–72, 154–155, 160,
  193
  service to, 23, 105–106, 111–115,
  116–117, 125, 198
  shirking against, 160–167, 175–176
  statewide versus district, 170–175
Constituent Assembly of 1949, 35–37,
  40–41, 65, 81

213

constitutions
  1871 of Costa Rica, 34–37
  1949 of Costa Rica, 18, 22, 26, 29, 31,
    42
  1961 of Venezuela, 52
Contract With America, 66
Coppedge, Michael, 53, 55, 138–139
Corrales Bolaños, José Miguel, 91, 145
Cortes, Leon, 31, 33–34

data, availability, 8
  Costa Rica, 18, 39, 94–98, 107–109,
    120–121, 128–130
  United States, 159, 161–162
deliberation, 191–192
Democratic Party, Costa Rica, 32
deputies, national versus local, 106–
  107
development, economic and social, 19–
  20
direct democracy, 9, 199

Echeverría Brealey, Juan José, 85
Ecuador, 3–4, 17
electoral connection, 24, 58, 63, 98–101,
  103–104, 177–178, 183, 193, 198
electoral incentives, 4–5, 21, 23–24, 63,
  104, 118–119, 127–128, 134–135,
  195
electoral systems, 18, 21, 159, 197–198
Ethics Tribunals, 141–142, 152–153
Esquivel, Ricardo, 37
experience in legislatures
  Costa Rica, 43–45, 82–86
  United States, 186, 192–193

Facio Brenes, Rodrigo, 38
Federalist Paper #10, 171
Federalists, 25, 184–186, 191–192,
  198
Fenno, Richard, 114, 161, 162
Figueres, José María, 131–132
Figueres Ferrer, José, 29, 34–35,
  143
Fish, Carl Russell, 187, 188
Foley, Hon. Thomas, 192

Gamboa Rodriguez, Celso, 38
grandfather clauses, 48–51
Guillén Elizondo, Miguel, 143

Hamilton, Alexander, 186, 189
Herfindahl–Hirschman Concentration
  Index, 110–111
Herrick, Rebekah, 196–197, 200
Hernandez Poveda, Rubén, 37–38
Hibbing, John, 192–193

Inter-University Consortium for Political and Social Research (ICPSR),
  178–179

Jackson, Andrew 187–189

Lacle Castro, Ricardo, 49–50
Lehoucq, Fabrice Edouard, 32–33
Leoni, Raúl, 56
lists, party candidates for legislative elections
  closed, 18, 24, 46, 50, 54, 59, 63, 85–
    86, 104
  control over, 55, 88–93, 147
  open, 58
Livingston, Gilbert, 185
lobbying, 7, 196
Lott, John, 162, 164, 165, 167
Luscinchi, Jaime, 53, 58

Madison, James, 45, 171, 176
magnitude of electoral districts (*M*), 18,
  29, 43, 50, 54, 104
Marcos, Ferdinand, 17
Marin Chinchilla, Matilde, 141–142
Matos Azócar, Luis, 139
Mayo Negro, 132–133, 140–142
Mexico, 3–4, 16, 37–38, 126, 197
midterm elections, 38–39, 43
Mitchell, Cleta Deatherage, 190
Monge, Carlos, 123, 145
Mora, Manuel, 31
Morales, Fernando, 49
Movimiento al Socialismo (MAS), 74
Muñoz, Edwin, 49
Muñoz Retaña, Benjamin, 142
Myers, David, 52, 148

Nixon, David, 196–197, 200
NOMINATE (Nominal Three-Step Estimation) scores, 168, 179–182
nominations, legislative
  Costa Rica, 88–93

United States, 173, 179
Venezuela, 53–54, 86–88
nominations, presidential in Costa Rica, 92, 131–133

Ortiz, Eduardo, 89

Pacto del Caribe, 34
parliamentarism, 59–60
partidas específicas (PEs), 105–115
    distribution across counties, 109–111, 122–125
    electoral impact of, 120–127
Partido, Comunista (PC), 31–35, 38
Partido Liberación Nacional (PLN), 29, 31, 47, 51, 77, 96, 108, 131–132
    divisions within, 140–146, 148–151
Partido Republicano (PR), 29, 31–35, 47
Partido Social Democrático (PSD), 33–35, 38–40
Partido Unificación (PUNIF), 47
Partido Unión Generaleña (PUGEN), 108
Partido Unión National (PUN), 29, 31, 37–39, 47, 77
Partido Unión Social Cristiano (PUSC), 29, 47, 77, 108, 131
    divisions within, 143–146, 149–151
party leaders, 71–72, 197
    Costa Rica, 88–93, 148–155
    Venezuela, 53–56, 58, 86–88, 136, 147–148
party machines, 188
Peltzman, Sam, 162–163, 166
pensions, 160, 163–164, 167–175, 176
Perez, Carlos Andrés, 53, 58, 138–139
Perez Jimenez, Marcos, 56
Petracca, Mark, 187, 190, 197
Picado Michalski, Teodoro, 31–33, 35
Philippines, 3–4, 16–17
Poole, Keith, 180–182
pork barrel, 105–115, 116, 125, 183, 198; see also *partidas específicas*
presidentialism, 19, 21, 27, 60
presidents
    strength in Costa Rica, 27–28
    strength in Venezuela, 52–53
    term limits for, 17, 37, 93–94, 136

productivity of legislatures
    Costa Rica, 43–45
    United States, 186, 192–193
professionalism of legislatures, 66, 75, 77, 82–86, 190–191
proportional representation, 18, 29–30, 53, 59, 86, 105

Qualifications Clauses, U.S. Constitution, 14

reelection rates, 22
    Costa Rica, 76–81
    Venezuela, 73–76
reform of electoral systems
    Costa Rica, 26, 43–51
    United States, 9–15, 64–65, 199
    Venezuela, 51, 58
reform, social, Costa Rica, 31–36, 145
reputation, personal versus partisan, 5, 7, 21, 23, 50, 58–59, 63, 103–104, 111, 115, 118, 194–195, 197
Rodriguez Echeverría, Miguel Angel, 46, 92
Rosenthal, Howard, 180
rotation in office, 25, 79, 176, 184–189

Saborio Vega, Oscar, 145
Sanabria, Bishop Monseñor Victor Manuel, 31, 34
sanctions against legislators
    Costa Rica, 140–146
    Venezuela, 137–140, 147–148
sectoral delegates, 91–93
seniority in legislatures, 9, 62, 192
Shugart, Matthew, 30, 59
single-member districts (SMDs), 46, 50–51, 58–59, 86–88, 106, 117
sorting, 160, 176–177
spoils system, 187–189
staff, legislative, 6, 55–56
state legislatures, U.S., 3, 6, 9–15, 64–65
Stigler, George, 163–64
Supreme Court
    Costa Rica, 93
    United States, 14, 64
Supreme Electoral Council (CSE), 54

Taylor, Michelle, 119–120
Tribunal Nacional Electoral (TNE), 32, 34
Tribunal Supremo Electoral (TSE), 38, 89–92
trigger mechanisms, 9, 14–15
two-party systems, 20, 29–30, 56

Ulate, Otilio, 29, 33–35, 37, 77
Unión Agrícola Cartaginés (UAC), 47, 50, 108, 146

Vargas Fernandez, Fernando, 39
Vargas Sanabria, Guillermo, 141–142
Ventura Robles, Manuel, 88–89

Villegas Antillón, Rafael, 92
veto power, 28, 52, 60
virtue, 190–192, 193, 197–198
voting in legislatures
    attendance, 6, 167
    indiscipline, 137
    roll calls, 6, 24, 47, 137–138, 142, 168, 197, 199

Weldon, Jeffrey, 199
Will, George, 185, 191, 193, 197
women's suffrage, 34–35

Zupan, Mark, 165, 166, 173

John M. Carey is Assistant Professor of Political Science at the University of Rochester. He is coauthor of *Presidents and Assemblies: Constitutional Design and Electoral Dynamics* (with Matthew S. Shugart, Cambridge University Press, 1992) and author of numerous articles that have appeared in scholarly journals, including *Electoral Studies, Public Choice,* and *Estudios Publicos,* and newspapers, including the *Los Angeles Times* and the *Christian Science Monitor.*